YOUNG CHILDREN

AND

THEIR DRAWINGS

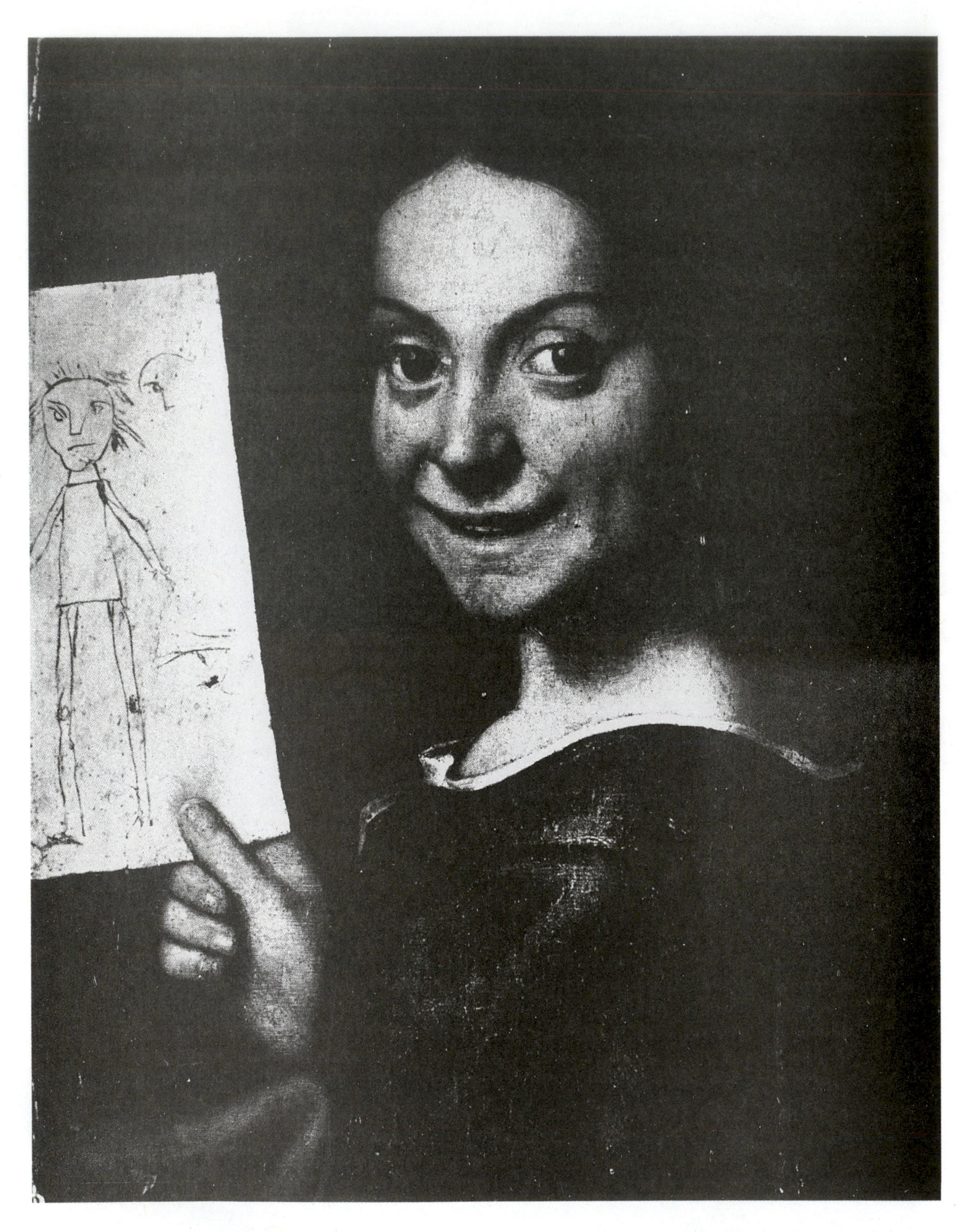

FRONTISPIECE Caroto, G.F: *Fanciullo con pupazzetto. Museo di Castelvecchio, Verona. (1480-1546)*

YOUNG CHILDREN AND THEIR DRAWINGS

Joseph H. Di Leo, M.D.

BRUNNER/MAZEL, *Publishers* • NEW YORK

PLATES AND ACKNOWLEDGMENTS

The Author's acknowledgments are gratefully made to the directors and curators of the museums, gallery, and library listed above for permission to reproduce works of art in their collections.

Special thanks are due the Casa Editrice Nicola Zanichelli of Bologna for the generous authorization to reproduce freely from Corrado Ricci's 1887 volume *L'Arte dei Bambini.*

to Judith, Daniel, and Paul

Published by
BRUNNER/MAZEL, Inc.
19 Union Square West
New York, New York 10003

Library of Congress Catalog Card No. 69-20312
ISBN 87630-018-2
Paperback edition 1996 ISBN 0-87630-833-7

Printed in the United States of America

10 9 8 7 6 5 4 3 2 1

CONTENTS

FOREWORD

The author of this book on children's drawings is a man of varied interests and talents. He developed an early and abiding interest in the visual arts and, for a time, considered art history and art appreciation as a career. Fortunately he directed his energies to the field of child development and in the area of children's art productions found a fruitful outlet.

Children's drawings have attracted the attention of art lovers, psychologists and psychiatrists for many years. Lovers of art find in them a pleasing freshness and naivete which is quickly lost as sophistication and conformity take over and creativity is stifled. Psychiatrists sometimes read into them meanings which are of questionable validity. Pediatricians are increasingly using children's drawings as a quick method of assaying intellectual functioning.

The material is presented in two parts. The major portion of the book is devoted to the representations of the normal child. The author begins with the random scrawls of the 13-month-old and traces the progression of drawings up to the beginning of elementary school. The author has limited his studies to the productions of young children because their drawings are fresh, direct and individual. The second part treats of the drawings of children with various deviations—deafness, cerebral palsy, emotional disturbances, and others.

Interpretations of the drawings are made sparingly and with restraint. The author avoids sweeping generalizations, but certain interpretations are cautiously made. The Goodenough Draw-a-Man score is accepted as a measure of the child's intellectual status except in cerebral dysfunction and certain emotional disorders. A considerable amount of attention is paid to the child's representation of his family as a way of gaining insight into his emotional life. Dr. Di Leo regards the family drawings as projections of the child's inner feelings.

Another section of the book is devoted to the early detection of perceptuo-motor defects as a means of predicting reading difficulty later on. Here the reproduction of geometric forms rather than figure drawings is used. By early detection of perceptuo-motor impairment it is hoped that training in perception and in understanding symbols will help to prevent the intense feelings of frustration and defeat which often accompany dyslexia.

In this delightful book the author has combined the systematic approach of the investigator and the intuitive insight of the artist to produce a book which is at once revealing and esthetic.

HARRY BAKWIN, M.D.
Professor of Clinical Pediatrics
New York University
School of Medicine

PREFACE

Though drawings form the material of this book, it is really about young children. That is why they have been given precedence in the title. Of course, that is assuming that the drawings can tell us something about the children. It has been said that the drawings of young children are mere meaningless scribbles. If so, then this book, too, is meaningless. One may have to recognize, however, that the drawings do evoke curiosity, amusement, interest; that they have been the object of serious study by an impressive array of educators, psychologists, and artists; that they have given rise to a voluminous literature.

The response of the eighteen-month infant of today to a crayon and a blank sheet of paper repeats the archaic, universal, abiding, and uniquely human response to a blank wall in cave or palace: the urge to cover it with marks, symbols, graffiti, slogans, designs, pictures. The response is so specifically human, that the mere discovery of such graphic activity is prima facie evidence that Man was there—thirty thousand years ago and yesterday. And recapitulating, as it were, the history of the species, the infant of today will take up scribbling with vigor and gusto, eventually leaving behind him—in the manner of his paleolithic ancestors—a record of his interests, pleasures, and fears. But all this assumes that the drawings are significant. Better to let the reader decide for himself whether the material presented deserves to be taken seriously.

I have had a life-long interest in the graphic arts. But children's drawings first came to my attention when, as a student at the University of Bologna, I discovered a little volume by Corrado Ricci *"L'Arte dei Bambini"* published in that city in 1887. This was the first published collection of children's drawings. The author was an eminent art critic. It made fascinating reading; the reproductions were delightful, their meaning obscure, provocative. I put it aside, little realizing that I would return to it with heightened interest for its relevancy to my life's work.

Science and Art mingled during years in Bologna and Rome, as I pursued post-graduate studies with excursions into various fields of medicine and even surgery. It finally became evident that disposition, inclination, and fate were leading me into pediatrics, where I was to achieve homeostasis. After residency in pediatrics at St. Vincent's Hospital in New York, I entered the New York Foundling Hospital. From there the road led to New Haven and Yale, where I was to learn about developmental diagnosis from Arnold Gesell and Catherine Amatruda. These past twenty-five years have been devoted to the study of child development and to the practical application of available knowledge in the interest of infants and young children. During these years, I have gone back to Corrado Ricci and to the many who followed: psychologists and psychiatrists, educators, anthropologists, art critics, and to the great artists who have detected and appreciated the value of children's drawings as statements about the child and his world.

During twenty odd years, I have been fascinated by the drawings of young, untutored children and have accumulated a vast and varied assortment of productions by young artists from a variety of environments, and bearing a variety of assets and liabilities. What they had in common was the ancient, universal, human urge to draw. They have left an extensive and valuable heritage that is the substance whence the present study has emerged. Care has been taken to let the drawings speak for themselves, to have the text serve the material and not the other way round.

A closer look at the drawings will reveal differences as well as similarities in comparing the graphic activity of children with that of primitive man and his civilized descendants of the ancient, medieval, and modern world. The same scrutiny will be applied when comparing the drawings of the normally immature with those of the mentally subnormal or disordered.

This volume is in two parts. In the first, I try to remind the reader that the drawings of normal young children are essentially those of most other young children of today and of the past, for they are expressions of the mind of the universal child. Striking similarities will be noted between the childhood of the individual and that of the race. Ontogeny and history touch at various points but similarity is not sameness. The analogy must not be carried too far.

The second section treats of the unusual and the deviant. What does it mean? How can the drawings aid the clinician in arriving at a diagnosis? At detecting a trend towards recovery or deterioration?

My gratitude is due to the hundreds of young children who cooperated enthusiastically leaving me something of themselves: a graphic record of their movements, feelings, and thoughts.

Acknowledgment is gratefully made to the directors of museums and collections both here and abroad for permission to reproduce works that I considered essential to the comparisons rendered inevitable by the striking similarities between the fresh vision of the young child and the mature artist's perception and insight into the essence of beings and things. Specific acknowledgments will be found elsewhere in this volume.

To the administrators of the New York Foundling Hospital I owe a debt of gratitude for the opportunity to serve and learn from the many thousands of children cared for and placed into foster and adoptive homes.

At Saint Joseph's School for the Deaf, I have learned to understand children with communication disorders better through their drawings. The administrators and staff have been most helpful in discussion and in providing many of the drawings by their students.

I must add specific mention of Miss Elizabeth Lynam for her kind assistance in providing me with drawings by hearing-impaired children.

My deepest gratitude goes to my wife, Joan, who has assisted me in more ways than she realizes.

Part One

THE USUAL AND NORMATIVE

1

INTRODUCTION

The drawings that enrich and enliven this volume are for the most part the work and play of children between the ages of thirteen months and six years. Drawings by older children have been included to add perspective, and to illustrate changes that occur as the child matures beyond the preschool years and is increasingly influenced by the culture.

The "artists" came from a wide range of social, racial, ethnic, and educational backgrounds.

The infants, that is, those under two, were either in adopting homes, foster homes, or in residence at New York Foundling Hospital.

The preschoolers, unless otherwise indicated, were living with their own families, and were applicants for admission to nursery schools. Others were in adopting or foster homes.

As consultant to St. Joseph's School for the Deaf, the writer has been able to familiarize himself with the drawing behavior of hundreds of children with communication disorders.

Over a long period of time, a formidable collection of drawings has been acquired. Much of this material has been of value in the differential diagnosis of mental subnormality, emotional, organic, and perceptuo-motor disorders. In his own practice, the writer has found the drawings to be indispensable for an understanding of the child and his difficulties.

The first section of this book deals with the usual or normative. It traces the progression that can be expected as the scribbling infant becomes a preschooler, whose graphic activity has matured from movement for its own sake to movement for representation. The peculiarities in these drawings and their significance are discussed at some length, for herein lies a key to the secret of childhood. The child is ever changing and yet ever himself. As he changes, his drawings will reflect the change. Only those who know how the child expresses himself graphically can aspire to detect and interpret the deviant and the unusual. It is difficult but generously rewarding.

PROCEDURE

All drawings were made by children in individual sessions, not in a group.

Present were the parent or parent surrogate, the examiner (the writer presented the situation in each instance).

A sheet of green-tinted letter-sized paper was placed on the table top directly before the child. The examiner then placed the red lumber crayon in the center of the paper, pointing away from the child.

In most cases it was not necessary to say anything but if the child hesitated, he was asked to "make something." Scribbling was demonstrated to all infants under 18 months, when most will scribble spontaneously.

A pencil was given to those able to control it adequately, generally to children over four.

The following sequence was adhered to:

13 to 18 months:
demonstration of scribbling by examiner
18 to 24 months:
spontaneous drawing
demonstration of vertical stroke, of circle.
24 to 36 months: spontaneous drawing
demonstration of vertical
copy of circle—if unsuccessful, demonstration of circle
demonstration of horizontal
demonstration of cross
36 to 48 months:
spontaneous drawing
draw a man
copy of cross
copy of circle—if unsuccessful,
demonstration of cross and circle
48 to 60 months:
spontaneous drawing
draw a man
draw a lady
draw your family
copy of triangle,
copy of square
copy of circle—if unsuccessful,
the figures were demonstrated.

over 60 months:
same procedure as for 48 to 60 months,
with addition of copy diamond.

Note that all drawing situations in children from 18 months begin with spontaneous drawing. This is a completely unstructured situation in which the child is free from any model or suggestion. Where the child is old enough (over three) the examiner then asks that he draw a man. The less said the better. When the child responds "I can't" the examiner encourages him, using the instructions given by F. Goodenough but adapting them to an individual child, viz., "I want to see if you can make one as well as the boy (or girl) who was here this morning". This or similar gentle prodding is usually sufficient. Most children who say "I can't" will prove themselves quite capable and will respond to encouragement.

The examiner refrains from any comment or suggestions even when the child draws just a big head instead of a whole man. When the child indicates that he has finished, the examiner takes the drawing and presents the child with another sheet of paper, saying "now make a whole man". If the child again makes just a head, the examiner accepts the drawing of a person as represented by the head alone and considers the situation terminated.

It will be noted that geometric forms to be copied or imitated are not presented prior to the spontaneous drawing and draw-a-man, -lady, and -family situations. This order is aimed at avoiding any suggestion whatsoever, that might arise from the copying or imitation.

It should also be noted that the present writer is opposed to having children copy or imitate drawings and that the exception is made only for purposes of diagnosis.

3

DEVELOPMENTAL SEQUENCES

The term "development" will be used in its generally accepted sense, to indicate differentiation and increase in complexity of function, thereby distinguishing it from "growth", a term used to express increase in size and weight. In reality, these two aspects of maturation are intimately related and begin inseparably, with life. At conception, when the 23 chromosomes from each parent interact with their mates, the sequence of bases in the DNA lays the ground plan for growth and development. There is a general ground plan for the species and within it variations for individual differences resulting from familial inheritance. Millions of years of evolutionary differentiation are summed up and telescoped into the brief time that covers the child's ontogenetic development. From its very onset, development is a continuous, orderly process teleologically directed towards maturity. Structure and function become increasingly complex and differentiated, according to a biological time-table. Expressed in chronological time, variations may be noted between individuals, yet the order in which the changes occur—the sequence—is remarkably uniform until variations in the environment are great enough to deviate the organism from its predetermined course. Accordingly, uniformity is most striking during prenatal development, for it is during that time that the environment is basically the same for all uncomplicated pregnancies: "for no king had any other first beginning..." Everyman began as a zygote, passed through stages of ovum, embryo, and fetus, and appeared at birth with the same behavior repertory that had been maturing in the womb. From remote and proximate forebears he inherited his cry, rooting and sucking reflexes, hand and toe grasp, the Moro reflex and other behavior patterns, some transient, some permanent, all related either to his survival or to his future development. And like the rest of mankind, he would achieve encephalic control over his action system, in cephalo-caudad sequence. Sequences are most clearly manifest in those fields of behavior that are more closely interwoven with neuro-muscular maturation, as in the development of prehension. Though rate may vary, the sequences appear in an orderly, predictable way, as expressions of a phylogenetic inheritance common to all members of a species. The order is invariably from generalized response to specific, from egocentricity to objectivity, from concrete to abstract thinking, from precausality to causality. Even the organization of personality passes through identifiable stages of maturation, so that here, too, one may properly speak of arrest of development. Can the same principle of development be detected in the development of graphic activity? Are there, as in other activities, features common to all and only secondarily influenced from the outside? Upon the answers to these questions will depend the importance that shall be attached to the drawings of children. For if they are simply imitation, they are basically influenced from without and may not be interpreted as expressions of the child's individuality. But, if they are they reveal universal, qualitative changes occurring in time and in sequence, and with direction, then the drawings may be considered expressive of changes in the child himself.

Let us begin by examining the first of these basic propositions:

Are There Stages and Sequences in Drawing Behavior?

A review of the vast literature devoted to children's drawings, American as well as European, strongly supports the belief that sequential stages can be identified. Norman C. Meier tells how random scribbling gradually takes on recognizable form; how rhythm, balance and symmetry develop from primal, elemental anlage. Grady Harper describes the development of disorganized, random scribbling to organized marks that are given a name, and how geometric shapes are subsequently used consistently to symbolize important objects. Florence Goodenough finds the order of development of graphic activity to be remarkably constant. Werner Wolff notes the progression from the first stage of scribbling to the development of primitive forms and figures. Arnold Gesell offers norms for the sequences that occur in the child's ability to imitate and copy geometric forms. In the elaboration of figure drawing, stages and sequences are particularly evident and keep pace with the child's maturing concept of the body image. Viktor Lowenfeld emphasizes the need to know what to expect in modes of expression at different age levels. Herbert Read in sustaining the chance origin of art tells how the child engaged in random, kinesthetic scribbling will eventually, perhaps suddenly, detect an image in some of his chance forms, and having created a representation of an object by mere chance, will then go on drawing deliberately what he had created by chance. Rouma has outlined six stages in the evolution of representation of the human figure: the first tentative, unrecognizable attempts at representation, the tadpole stage, transitional stage, full face drawing of the human figure, transitional stage between full face and profile, profile.

In her work with preschool children, Biber noted that their graphic activity progressed in an orderly manner as earlier forms were incorporated into later ones "in an integrated developmental sequence." Biber's observations are in basic agreement with those of other investigators, including those of the present writer, that at about age three the child makes the chance discovery that his random markings suggest a head or an object. A transitional stage follows during which kinesthetic and representational elements co-exist until more consistent representation is gradually established between three and a half and four years.

Prudhommeau in his studies on the drawing behavior of French children, placed the first appearance of *"le bonhomme titard"* (our tadpole or cephalopod) somewhere between three and a half and four years, and the addition of the body and features somewhere between four and six years.

Sequences have also been observed in the development of directionality in drawing. In a study by Gesell and Ames, ability to draw the vertical precedes mastery over the horizontal. Cross, square, triangle, and diamond follow in sequence. By far the greater number of children draw the vertical downward and in copying the cross, draw the horizontal secondly.

G. H. Luquet distinguishes four stages: the first, he calls involuntary drawing during which the child is as yet unaware that the lines he is making can be used to represent an object. The second stage is the unexpected realization that he can use his hitherto random markings to represent something. The breakthrough has occurred. He has made the grade from scribbling to intentional creation. In Luquet's words, *"A ce moment, il pourrat dire: 'Anch'io son pittore'"*. But there will be many back-slidings before he is firmly established on the higher level. He will have difficulty in synthesizing, in systematizing the details into a coherent unity. The third stage of *"réalism logique"* is considered by Luquet to be the *apogee* of the child's graphic development. This stage which he subsequently called *"réalisme intellectual"* is indeed the expression of one of the most important phenomena in the mental life of the child (J. Piaget). Luquet has given us the key to an understanding of the strange drawings made between the ages of three and seven. We then reach the fourth stage of *"réalisme visuel"*. The child has now crossed the bridge into the adult world and is gradually submitted to the adult view. Its most significant manifestation is the attempt at perspective. From now on development will be a matter of technique. Many adults will be incapable of drawing any better than they did at age ten or twelve.

The schema of a person as expressed in the drawings of preschool children has fascinated investigators because of its ubiquity and timelessness. The early representations of a person are strikingly similar though greatly separated by space and time. Some have seen in this "universality" a manifestation of the collective unconscious. To Prudhommeau and Schilder, these early renditions of the human figure, this *"modèle interne"* or *"réalisme intellectuelle"* of Luquet, are projections of the child's own body image. The present writer does not share this view. Since the figure portrayed is almost invariably that of an adult, it seems more likely that the child is representing a parent. Young children portray themselves and their siblings when they draw the family.

A crucial phase in the development of graphic activity is the change from inner to optical realism. Luquet has indicated as criteria the substitution of opacity for transparency, the attempt at perspective, and the elimination of the second eye from a profile drawing of the face. Conceding that there is much variation, Luquet has located the change to occur between eight and nine years. Prudhommeau takes issue with Luquet and gives as a criterion for the attainment of visual or optical realism the attempt to depict movement and places its inception between six and seven years. During these early attempts at dynamism, the child does not abandon his internal model or schema but uses it to express movement towards an object, as in reaching out for something represented in the drawing.

Inherent in these differences of interpretation is the recognition of stages and sequences.

There is general agreement that two distinct stages can be identified in the spontaneous graphic activity of young children: an earlier kinesthetic or scribbling stage and a later representational stage. As with other developmental processes, stages form a continuum with intermediate or transitional phases in which elements of both stages may be seen side by side until the advance has been assimilated, and from then on it will appear consistently.

Once representation has been achieved, sequences are most apparent in the drawing of the human figure, which is the predominant subject of the child's endeavors. The predominance of the head and eyes, the omission of the trunk, emphasis on the limbs are some of the features that characterize early renditions of the human figure.

And lastly, sequences in the copy of geometric forms can be related to developmental age.

The validity of these beliefs underlies the inclusion of drawing situations in a variety of tests aimed at determining intellectual capacity, visual-motor coordination, perceptual functioning, emotional, and even social adjustment. To distinguish normal immaturity from retardation, deviation, or impairment, the drawings must be viewed within the framework of chronological age. The inability to copy a cross at three is not the same as the same difficulty at five; a disproportionately large head drawn at five does not have the same significance as at ten; adding the belly-button at five is not like doing the same at seven.

The second basic proposition may be formulated in terms of the question:

Are There Features in Drawings by Young Children That Are Common to All Regardless of Time, Place, or Race?

The importance of finding an answer to this question accounts for the vast literature on the subject. The issue of timelessness has led to comparisons with the art of prehistoric man. The irrelevance of place is claimed by those who have noted identical characteristics in drawings by children from far away places. Drawings by children from diverse racial groups are strikingly similar as are those by children from a variety of social environments.

Attempts to throw light on both of the crucial issues, that of developmental sequences and of universality, will be found within the body of this study. Many issues are still unresolved; others may warrant impressions rather than firm opinions; enough stands out clearly to justify the attention and respect devoted to the drawings of the young preschool child.

4

EARLIEST DRAWINGS: THE KINESTHETIC STAGE

Between the ages of thirteen months and three years, the response to paper and crayon results in avid scribbling in which the adult is unable to discern any attempt at conscious representation. The term "kinesthetic" has been applied to this type of graphic activity in order to emphasize the muscular element that is predominant. The drawing itself is the visible, abiding record of movements that were fleeting and that are now past. But like all volitional activity, these movements recorded visually are expressive of something within the individual that accounts for the differences in types of response. And since there is considerable uniformity in what is drawn, attention is more fruitfully directed to the mode of expression rather than to the content: to the "how" rather than to the "what." Graphic movements like bodily movements are influenced by physical, emotional, and intellectual factors, by level of development, by the individuality that is comprised in the all-inclusive concept of the personality. The "what" is very similar when we compare the productions of infants and young scribblers who are at the same level of psychomotor maturity. The inequalities are represented by differences in pressure, continuity of stroke, impulsivity, staccato, or sweeping movements. It is in these differences during the early period, and in others that shall be discussed later, that investigators have sought clues to the intrinsic differences that distinguish one person from another, indeed, from all others.

What Do Scribblers Draw?

Although as just stated the focus will be on mode of expression and not on content, this latter aspect of graphic activity will now be considered in what is intended to be a meaningful discussion.

The thirteen month infant may pick up the crayon and imitating his mother may bring it to his lips as she does her lipstick; or he may insert it into his mouth, a response which the Examiner will promptly deviate, as the ingestion of crayons is not innocuous. But once the Examiner demonstrates, most infants will immediately imitate and from then on scribbling and later drawing will become one of the child's most zestful and joyful activities. Graphic activity is as universal as human nature in time as well as in space. Universal, too, seem to be the sequences from earliest imitative scribble through and beyond the representational drawings of the preschool child. In the beginning, the scribble is usually a continuous to-and-fro movement represented graphically by an uninterrupted zig-zag of horizontally oriented strokes. The present writer has observed verticals and circular, skein-like scribbles to appear more consistently during the third year. This order reverses the sequence of vertical, circular, and horizontal which characterizes the child's attempts to imitate the Examiner's strokes and which represents a progressive gradation of neuromuscular maturation and visual-motor coordination. Briefly stated, the "what" is an index of the developmental level of an individual child as related to that of most of his peers. In content we observe similarity; in mode of execution we are impressed by the differences.

FIGURE 1

Her first scribble. At age twelve-and-one-half months, she has imitated the Examiner's scribble, or better, his movement.

FIGURE 2

Adopted and secure. Spontaneous drawing by a secure child, who was placed adoptively from a foster home at age 7 months. He is now 16 months. Average behavioral development. This is his first drawing. He has had no previous experience with crayon or pencil and paper. The sweep and unbroken continuity of his drawing reflects the security that he has attained in his adopting home during the course of nine months. Chronological age: 16 months. Boy.

FIGURE 3

Spontaneous kinesthetic drawing by a 25-month boy, Mainly verticals.

FIGURE 4

Kinesthetic drawing by a 27-month boy. Horizontal and circular strokes. Spontaneous drawing.

FIGURE 5

Spontaneous kinesthetic drawing by a 30-month boy. Note the variety of strokes; circular, vertical and quasi-horizontal.

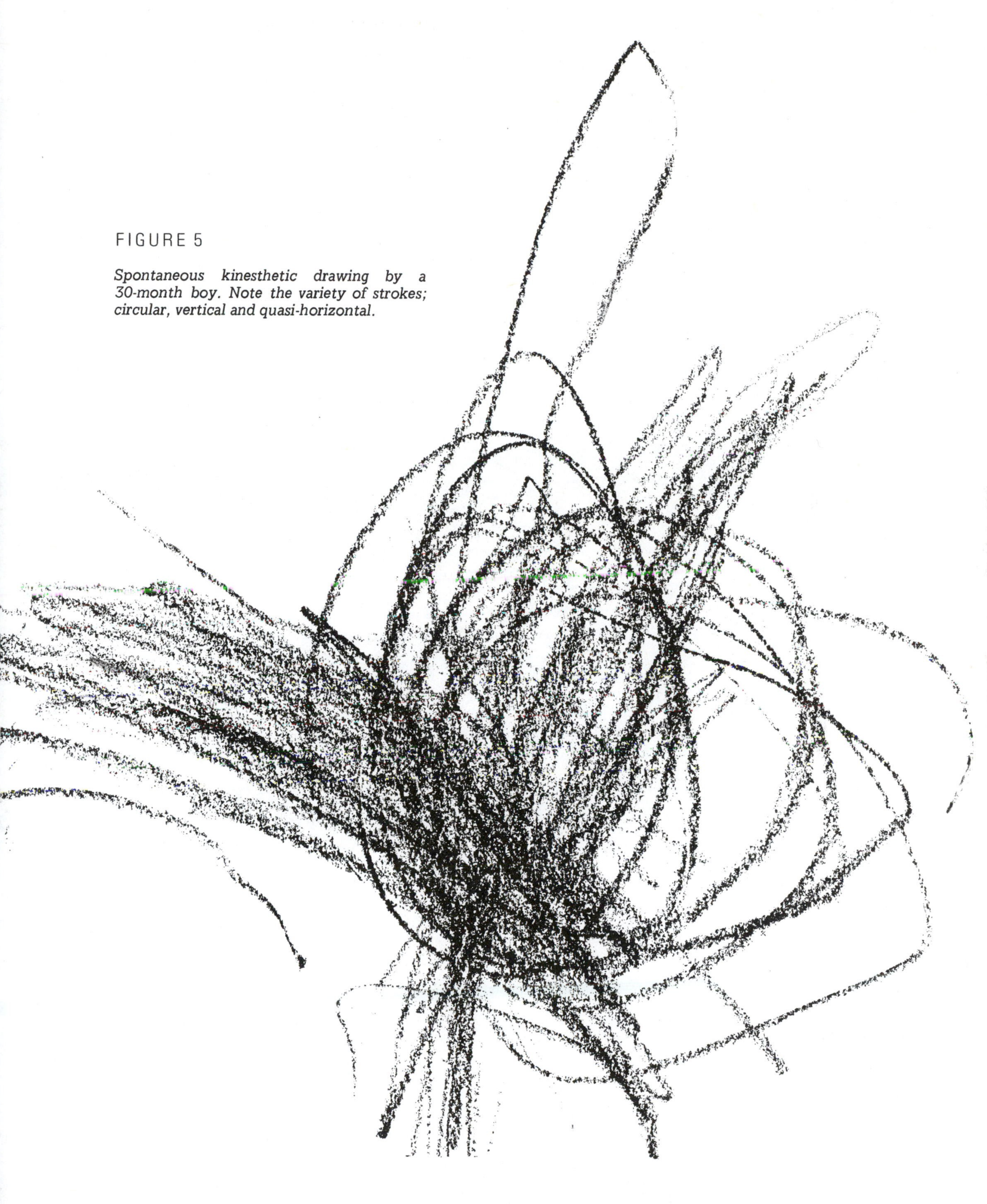

FIGURE 6

Kinesthetic drawing by a 33-month girl. All circles.

How Do Scribblers Draw?

As the infant matures and his bodily movements lose their reflex character and come increasingly under cortical control, they also become more adaptive, and more expressive of attitudes, mentation, and feelings. The early graphic activity of the child is an extension of motor play, which through the medium of the crayon leaves its record on a surface. Though there is uniformity in what is drawn, there is great variability in how the activity is approached and performed. Except for a minority who would dismiss scribbling as meaningless imitation, the variability in manner is considered a valuable clue to an understanding of the individual child's temperament and personality.

Some approach the situation with deliberation, "intellectually" observing and appraising it; others impetuously, emotionally, with facial expression, movements, and markings that reflect joy or hostility. And then there are those whose approach is cautious, hesitant, and whose small, barely visible markings express their insecurity and inhibition. If instead of dismissing scribbling as simply an uncoordinated prelude to representational drawing, and search for meanings, we shall learn to attach significance to direction of stroke, pressure, tempo, and sweep. Is the stroke directed towards the child or away? Is it strong and decisive or weak and hesitant? Does it show the freedom and sweep of the bold, or the restraint and restriction of the timid? The weight of evidence and opinion favors the view that these earliest drawings are worthy of attention and study and that they offer valuable information about the child himself. While agreeing with L. Bender that the scribblings represent motor play, done for the pleasure of motor expression, and that the scribblings are a by-product, this writer sides with the impressive majority of investigators in disagreeing with Bender's statement that the drawings have no meaning. In so doing, the writer wishes, at the same time, to express his admiration for the notable contributions that L. Bender has made to our understanding of childhood mental illness and in providing us with a valuable test of visual-motor coordination. In the bibliography, the reader will find numerous references that devote considerable attention to the subject of scribbling (W. Wolff, V. Lowenfeld, W. Grözinger, W. E. Martin and D. E. Damrin, F. Jourdain). These and other investigators have shown how the early graphic expressions of children can be studied objectively and that a relationship can be established between the mode of such graphic activity and the personality as evaluated by other independent methods. While believing that the scribblings tell us more than we are able to read in them, this writer offers only those specimens that illustrate clearly some of the points made in this discussion, refraining from interpretations that might be too subjective or even mystical.

The vast majority of young children take to scribbling avidly and with obvious delight early in their second year. The observer sees it as a pleasurable motor activity coupled with the thrill of making something that was not there before.

Its appeal is universal and abides undiminished until the child begins to express himself in writing. The child's bodily movements transferred to paper express vitality, joy, security, but also anxiety, timidity, fear. And as he progresses from stage to stage, not step-wise but in continuity, his drawings document the progressive maturation of intellect, his view of the world about him, and his feelings towards that world of persons and things. The expressive nature of his movements as they leave their graphic record behind suggests parallels with a modern expressionistic revolutionary movement that having broken with symbolism, realism, and impressionism of the past, produces a visual record of the artist's agitation, known as action painting.

In contrast to the adult who is writing to communicate, the scribbler does not seem to be trying to tell us anything. It is we who are seeking occult meanings. The scribble is non-objective, personal, and noncommunicative. The child enjoys the rhythmic, motor activity and leaves an impression on the paper: movement, rhythm, and creation.

Seriated drawings by the same child are of diagnostic value, providing the clinician with an objective and permanent record.

Usually between the ages of two and three years, an increasing variety of markings will come to be interspersed among the still predominant movement patterns until by age three to four the transition to representational drawing will have been completed. At first, the subject represented will not be recognizable to the observer, though the child may give it a name, often only to call it something else at the very next moment. The breakthrough to representation may be quite sudden, sparked by a chance resemblance of some random scribble to some person or object in the child's world. A circle may suggest Mommy's face. From then on, he will use regularly and symbolically what in the beginning was purely accidental.

TRANSITION FROM KINESTHETIC
TO REPRESENTATIONAL DRAWING

5

TRANSITION FROM KINESTHETIC TO REPRESENTATIONAL DRAWING

Now three years old, the scribbler joyfully engaged in drawing a variety of forms—vertical, horizontals, diagonals, and circles—suddenly, and quite by chance, is thrilled by a discovery. In the circle he has made, he detects a resemblance, perhaps to a person's head. What he has done by chance, he can now do by design. He can create an image.

Each child must be allowed to make the discovery by himself—unaided and undirected. This is creative activity and must remain personal if it is to live. "The creator cannot breathe with strange lungs" (V. Lowenfeld).

In the race and in the individual the origin of art can be traced to chance. A crack or a curve produced by nature in the wall of a cave suggests the contour of a bison and becomes part of the figure painted 30,000 years ago in the cave at Lascaux.

Having made the discovery that he can represent pictorially, the child does not cease to scribble. The passage from stage to stage is never abrupt. It develops by degrees, with frequent lapses into earlier levels but with an onward and upward trend into the higher level. For many months, scribbling continues to divide the field with more and more attempts at representation. Eventually an activity that was predominantly motor and emotional will become more consistently controlled by the intellect.

Recognizable representation takes time—another year. But the breakthrough has occurred. The child is now on his way to pictography, "hieroglyphics" and then calligraphy, just as his remote ancestors who made pictures and figures long before they learned to write.

Never Ask "What Is It?"

A child of three is intently at work with crayon producing a variety of lines, circles, and zig-zags not with the abandon and exhilaration that marked his earlier motion scribbling but with deliberation and control that clearly reveal an attempt at representation. Having finished, he lays down the crayon and surveys his creation. The adult, who has been peering over his shoulder, will at this point feel impelled to ask "What is it?". The question is a natural one when the child is young and the drawing is apparently representational but not recognizable. In this instance, it seems very clearly established that the natural thing is the wrong thing. Many writers on the subject of children's drawings have warned parents and teachers against "extorting" a name for the drawing by asking for it. The child will oblige by playing the game and supplying a title that is often but the first of a series of changing ones. Unintentionally, the adult has drawn the child into a trap that will tend to stifle

FIGURE 7

Transitional Stage. Kinesthetic (up and down) and representational (circular) elements are present in this spontaneous drawing by a two-year old girl. Behavioral development: average.

FIGURE 8

Transitional. Begins with the circular figure, calls it "a MOM" then reverts to the earlier type of kinesthetic drawing represented by the zig-zag lines. Transition is not abrupt; it is gradual with frequent lapses back to less mature levels but with an upward trend discernible when the observer views the activity in perspective. Chronological age of child: two years 4 months. Secure, female child living with natural parents, applicant for admission to a Montessori school.

FIGURE 9

Transitional. Begins with representation by drawing a circular figure calling it "Mommy" but soon reverts to kinesthetic drawing represented by the diagonals. Chronological age: 47 months. Institution child, fairly secure.

FIGURE 10

Transitional. Predominantly representational but not recognizable. Female of 35 months. Behavioral development average.

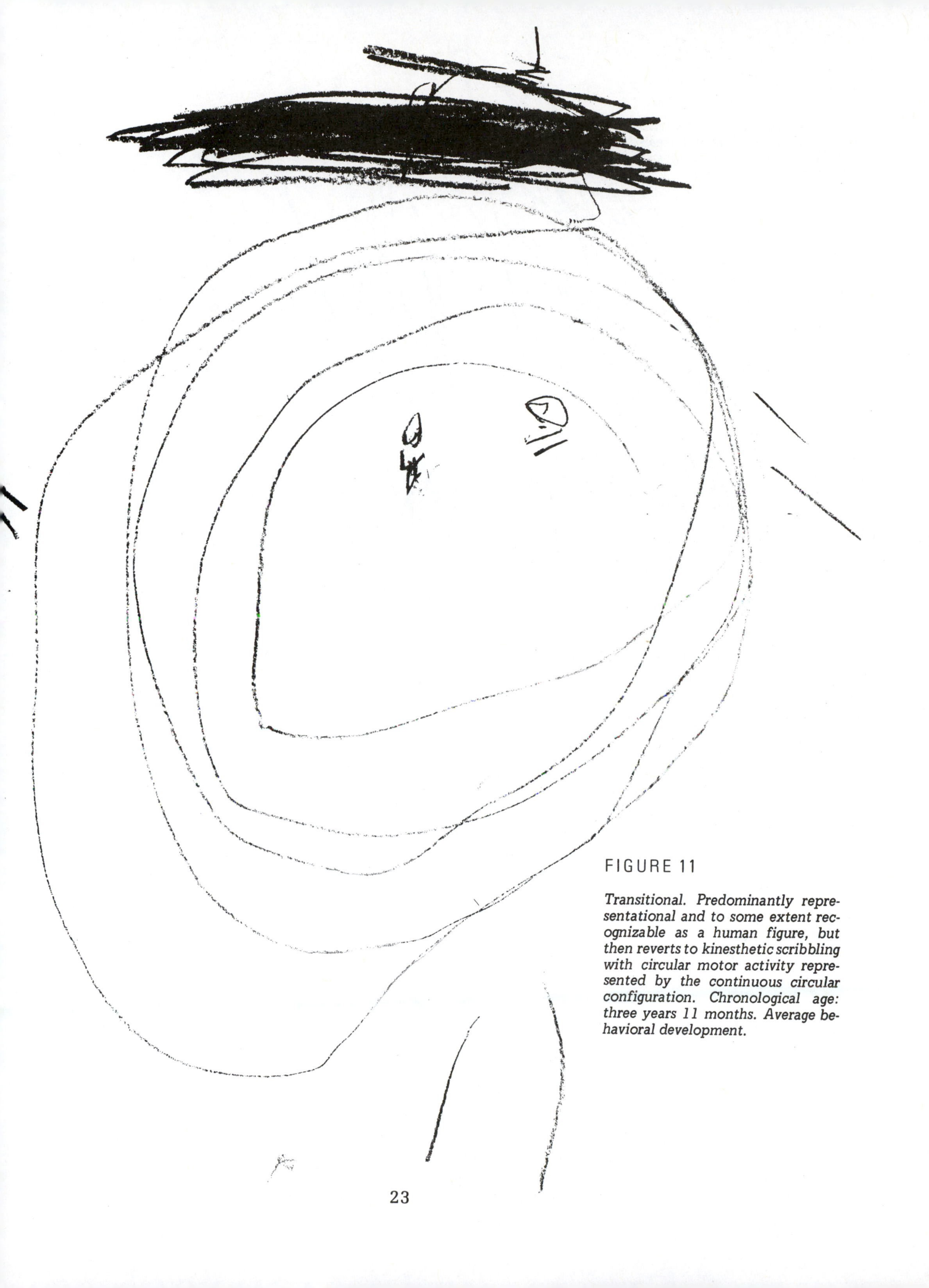

FIGURE 11

Transitional. Predominantly representational and to some extent recognizable as a human figure, but then reverts to kinesthetic scribbling with circular motor activity represented by the continuous circular configuration. Chronological age: three years 11 months. Average behavioral development.

FIGURE 12

Transitional. Both representational and kinesthetic activity is seen in this spontaneous drawing by a child of three years 11 months.

the child's pictorial and perceptual development. There seem to be grave and far-reaching effects from a little innocent question! But even if one does not object as vehemently as Grözinger, who uses terms such as "disastrous" and "laden with heavy consequences," objections to asking "what is it" are sound, well-founded, and supported by investigators and by artists. The objections are basically twofold. First, regarding the child's pictorial development, by asking for a name we are establishing a premature connection between two areas of development that are at different levels of maturity. The three-year-old is at the very threshold of graphic representation while already well advanced in language development. And since language always names things, it objectifies forms that have not detached themselves as yet from the child (Grözinger). Objectivity in drawing is a much later stage in the development of graphic activity.

Objectivity is alien to the minds of young children and should not be thrust upon them. Theirs, perhaps, is a greater reality that transcends the prosaic vision of the adult. The early stages of graphic activity are not to be eliminated or accelerated; they need to be integrated into the total developmental continuum. They are rungs on the way to the top; and the top is not objectivity, if by that we mean visual objectivity. The camera can give us that.

The second objection to "What is it?" concerns the development of perception. Interference with non-objective scribbling deprives children of the visual-motor experience that should serve as a background for the development of plastic and tactile values; those very values that elevate seeing to the level of perception, enabling the artist to communicate life and not just a resemblance. Perception is achieved and enriched by the integration of vision with touch and proprioception. Prior experience and integration of various sensory modalities permits one to actually feel what one is looking at.

The stage of unrecognizable representation that generally extends from three to four or five years of age should be respected and valued. Children should be free from adult interference, free to experiment with a variety of forms, free to perceive the outer world, free to discover and to create.

Never Let a Child Copy Anything

This should be a hard and fast rule. The only exceptions should be for purposes of evaluating mental or perceptual functioning, as there are gradients in the ability to copy geometric forms dependent upon developmental age, visual-motor coordination, and gestalt function. But except for these isolated and relatively rare instances the child should never be urged to copy anything. It is only by expressing what is within him that he can keep alive the fire of creativity that is in Everyman lest it be stifled by the powerful forces of conformity. He may achieve technical skill by submitting to the control of those who will tell him what to do and how to do it, but his product will lack the excitement and life communicating quality that only the creator can impart. Of course, not every creation will be a work of art. Not every child is gifted in that way. Very few, in fact, will continue to express themselves graphically once they are able to express their thoughts and feelings in writing. And very few, indeed, will achieve those heights of artistic perfection that unequivocally separate Man from beast. But for the multitude of lesser endowed mankind there is something other than artistic brilliance that is involved in the freedom to draw. This universally attractive activity is a means by which the child experiences the thrill of creation. He has made something that was not there before. And what he has made is unlike anything made by any other. And if his drawing evokes interest, admiration and praise, he will feel confident to continue, for what matters is the mode of expression and not the content. Judged by adult standards, the drawings will have many "wrong" features but these should not be corrected for they are not really wrong, they are the expression of a different Weltanschauung. The feelings of confidence and self-satisfaction that arise when his graphic activity is encouraged, unchanneled, and admired will tend to spread to other situations, and affect the personality as a whole.

So far, the emphasis has been on what not to do and before leaving this negative aspect something must be said against the very wide-spread practice of giving the child coloring books. These are particularly damaging to creativity. The child is presented with an outline picture drawn by someone else and is to stay within the boundaries. Drawing is thus no longer a means of self-expression, a valuable stimulus for mental growth. This type of activity is destructive of the creative impulse.

What to do is simple; what not to do is the problem. All we need do to encourage the child is to provide the simple means: crayon and abundant, limitless quantities of paper; then to admire his product as it progresses from the motor play of his earliest scribblings through representation with its fascinating peculiarities that express his changing concept of his world of persons and things.

What Do Preschool Children Draw?

The child draws that which is most significant to him. Observations made in many and varied environments are in general agreement that the human figure is most frequently represented in spontaneous drawing. And in fact, nothing is so important to the child as the people in his life. This interest in persons manifests itself in earliest infancy as the baby gradually learns to recognize his mother at four months, discriminates strangers at six months, and, if he feels secure enough, tolerates them at one year, provided mother is at hand. This overriding interest in persons is so basic to the organization of personality that failure to smile, to relate to persons, to maintain eye contact are signs of serious disorder, suggesting early infantile autism or childhood schizophrenia. As Luquet has observed, the child's figure drawings are of adults primarily and only in drawings of the family do we see children represented. This would seem to be at variance with Schilder's view that the child in drawing a person is projecting his own body image.

FIGURE 13

Representational spontaneous drawing by a girl of three.

After the person, the next object in order of frequency is some article of clothing. Gradually more apparel is added: hats, shoes, buttons. The drawings of nineteenth century children frequently showed the man to be smoking a pipe; this is rarely seen in contemporary drawings. Only older, school-age children will draw a person smoking a cigarette.

Other objects drawn are houses, trees, vehicles. These are stylized and reduced to essentials. The houses have chimneys out of which smoke issues often in impressive abundance. Animals have human faces, often smiling faces.

REPRESENTATION NOT REPRODUCTION

6

REPRESENTATION NOT REPRODUCTION

Central to an understanding of children's drawings is the recognition that the child draws his mental impression of the object and not his visual observation of it; that the product is a representation and not a reproduction; and that the representation is imbued with emotional and imaginative elements. The child does not distinguish between actual reality and his vision of it. Vision and idea are identical. The graphic statements of young children delight by their freshness and directness; they tell us far more about the artist than about the object represented. The object is distorted by the child's own feelings and thoughts. And in art, distortion is not a bad word. El Greco and Modigliani have used distortion with striking effect.

The concept that the child draws what he knows and not what he sees was first expressed by Luquet as "intellectual realism". Later writers have used a variety of other terms to signify that while the child draws what he sees—persons, houses, trees—he does not draw them as he sees them but as he knows them to be, reducing them to a fixed schematic type. W. Wolff speaks of the "optical reality" of the adult and of the "inner reality" of the child, noting that the child's perception is different and that its graphic expression is accordingly different from that of the adult. W. Grözinger writes that the child is making a statement about himself rather than about the object he is drawing. N. C. Meier notes that the child is not engaged in "naturalistic representation". Adhering to the term used by Luquet, J. Piaget considers the "intellectual realism" of the child's drawings an expression of the child's mental construction and not the fruit of pure observation. L. Levy-Bruhl speaks of prelogical mentality in discussing an attitude that finds expression in the art of the untutored as well as in that of the uncivilized.

The statement that the child draws what he knows not what he sees expresses a truth but not the whole truth. It would be more accurate to say that the child's graphic expression of his thought is colored by his feelings. It is this added dimension that renders the drawings so significant as expressions of personality.

> ...their inner eyes, those eyes with which they look through their physical eyes upon reality.
>
> from Prologue to INVISIBLE MAN
> by Ralph Ellison

The Child's World

The child is not an adult in miniature. His distinctive appearance is not due to his small size but to his body proportions. These are substantially different from those of the adult.

PLATE 1

Byzantine School, XIII Century: Enthroned Madonna and Child. National Gallery of Art, Washington, D.C. Mellon Collection.

When visiting art galleries, it is interesting and amusing to see how infants were portrayed by Medieval and Byzantine artists: a Madonna is holding in her arms the Infant Savior, whose appearance is really that of a little oldish-looking man. Realism in art came with the Renaissance, as Man directed his attention to the actual, tangible world about him. His new awareness is reflected in the art of the period. The recurrent theme of Madonna and Child now takes on a more optically realistic aspect, a different reality, an objective reality. Compare Raphael's Madonna of the Chair with the same subject as rendered by a Thirteenth Century Byzantine artist in his Enthroned Madonna and Child. (Plate 1)

But while there came a recognition of qualitative as well as quantitative physical differences between adult and child, it was not until centuries later that the child was regarded as a person in his own right. Long after he had ceased to be seen as a little man, he continued to be treated as an incomplete, deficient adult. Was not adult man the measure of all living things? Were not his standards the criteria whereby all actions and thoughts were to be evaluated? Was not all behavior to be judged in terms of the goal? Yet long before the nineteenth century, the truth had been perceived in the visions, insights, and irrational moments of poets and artists.

The recognition of two worlds, that of the child and that of the adult, is an indispensable prerequisite to an understanding of the child.

The image of the outside world is created from a confluence of sensory experiences that are gradually integrated to form perceptions. With maturation and learning the image changes. To the young infant, the world is his mother. At first, he feels and tastes her; later he will see and hear her. The perception will be strongly colored by affect. Throughout early childhood, the world image remains subjective, affect and imagination playing dominant roles. Age and experience have taught the adult to view the world objectively. He cannot avoid erring grossly if he tries to interpret the child's world in terms of his own perceptions. The child's concept of the outer world, his thoughts and feelings about his environment, find expression in his language, actions, and graphic activity. The study of the child's behavior, his verbal and graphic expressions are the most informative indicators of what goes on within him. As adults, our thoughts are mainly based on factual knowledge, even when they are speculative. Lacking facts and experience, the child's thoughts stem from sensations, imagination, and affects. The image is subjective and so, too, will be its expressions. Accordingly, the art of the young, untutored child will be nonobjective and expressionistic and symbolic, in substantial contrast to the objective, impressionistic art of most adults. The art of the adult is said to be realistic. But what is real? "More real to me, is what I see when I close my eyes." Is it not more valid to say that the adult's art represents outer reality; that the child's expresses an inner reality. And which is the truer? Judged by adult standards, the child's art is defective. There is no perspective, no proper proportions, incomplete, and lacking in synthesis. True. But let us stop criticizing and investigate with the adult objectivity of which we are so proud.

To the young infant, the world is his mother. "Only in her arms, the only place nature has assigned to him, does he find all he needs: warmth, food, and protec-

PLATE 2

Solario, A: *La Vierge au Coussin Vert. Musee National du Louvre, Paris* To the Young Infant the World is His Mother.

tion. The mother and child complement each other physically and in their function to form a higher unity of life..." (Albrecht Peiper). As the months pass, he begins to recognize her, to love her, to trust her, to take her for granted, and to reach out confidently to explore the outside. His world continues, nevertheless, to be primarily a world of persons as he extends his relationships to include father, siblings, other children and adults. His concept of the physical world is at first limited to the immediate space which he can touch and, to a lesser degree to what he can see. Until about nine months, the world is two-dimensional; only then does he discover the third dimension into which he will now poke and pry, put things in and take them out.

With the attainment of locomotion, the child projects himself further and further into the environment, integrating a variety of sensations, visual, tactile, and kinesthetic, fusing them into the higher realm of perception.

His drawings reveal what is important in his world: primarily people, later and secondarily things. His physical world is circumscribed within the radius of a few yards. The parent should not be disappointed if when sailing through the Strait of Gibraltar his three-year-old refuses to look at the Rock. Out of the myriad things that surround him, the young child will probably select trees, houses, and pets and these will appear in his more elaborate drawings. But far beyond his physical world, the child will be fascinated by those things that have been and continue to be the wonder of all mankind: the sun, the moon, the stars. The sun will appear in many of his scenes; and it will be represented as a circle with rays. Children widely separated by space and time and culture have used and continue to use the same symbolic, stylized version of the sun, as though they had all agreed to do it that way.

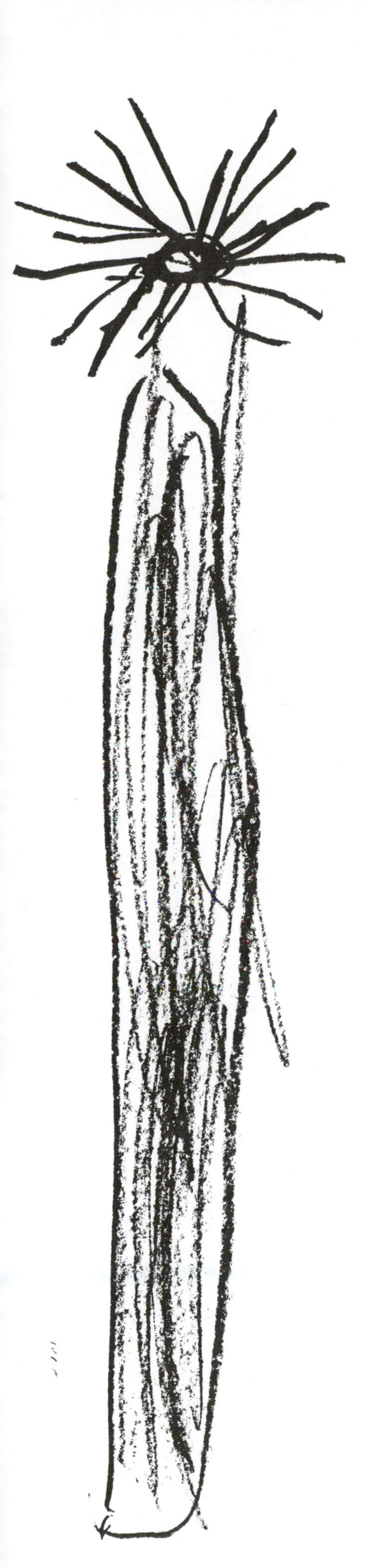

FIGURE 14

"Cloud and sun". Drawing by boy of five years 8 months.

FIGURE 15

Drawn by a boy of six years 10 months.

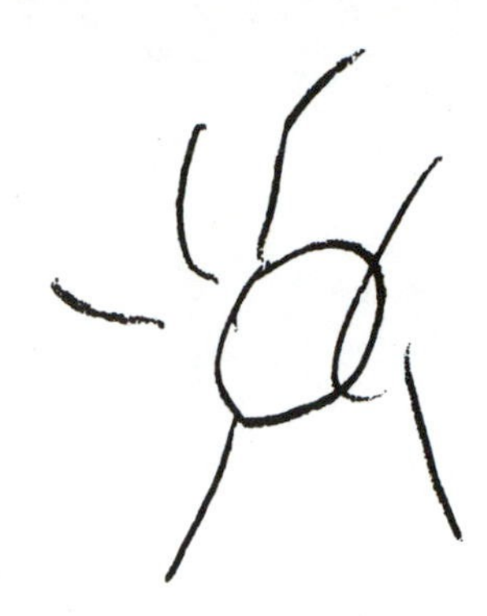

FIGURE 16

Drawn by same six year 10 month boy.

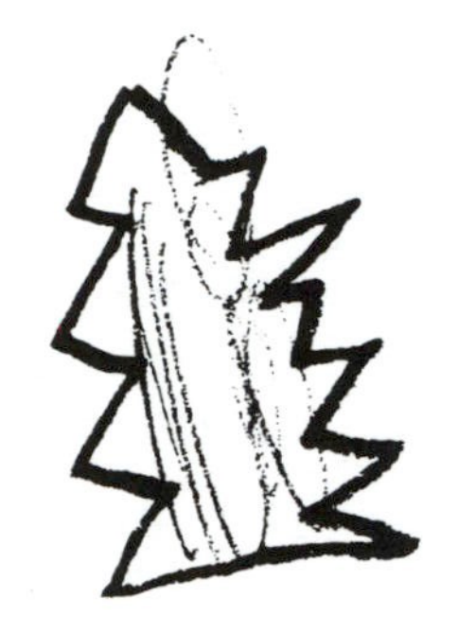

FIGURE 17

Drawn by a boy of seven years

THE HUMAN FIGURE EVOLVES: PRIMACY OF THE HEAD

7

THE HUMAN FIGURE EVOLVES: PRIMACY OF THE HEAD

Earliest Recognizable Representations of the Human Figure

Somewhere between the ages of three and four, the child's attempts at representation become recognizable to the adult. As the child tends to draw what is important and significant to him, most of his subject matter is human; and with his ability to perceive the essentials, there occurs a reduction of the human being into what is actually basic: the head, the arms, the legs. For it is in the head that we see and hear and eat and speak. And it is with our limbs that we grasp and hold and hurt and love. And with our legs we come and go. The pictorial result of this basic concept of man is a figure likened to a cephalopod in which the dominant element is the head out of which issue the limbs. This stage is an expression of Everyman's basic concept of the body image; it is drawn by the child of rich or poor, white or non-white, in the New World or in the Old, today as in generations past. The body is ignored, for though essential, its function is primarily vegetative, while the head and limbs are the means by which we relate to the world of people and things.

The Primacy of the Head

Early in embryonic development, a major portion of the pear-shaped embryonic disk is set aside for the formation of the head. At the termination of the embryonic period, the head is one-half of the total length; at birth one-quarter. At age six, the head has achieved nine-tenths of its adult size. The head takes an early lead in development and is destined to maintain that dominant role throughout life. Little wonder then that it assumes such priority in the thought of the young child. The importance assigned to the head is manifested in his earliest attempts at representational drawing. He draws what is most significant to him: a person. And he represents the person by making a large circle; the person is represented by a head. Soon, he will add lines that issue from the head; these are the limbs. The head will promptly be fitted with conspicuous eyes and other features. For a long time it will continue to dominate the figure as it does in the living person.

Artists, past and present, have selected the head as the part of the body most representative of the whole. The cherubim is represented as a head with wings. In modern art, reduction to essential elements often resorts to the same device of depicting the head alone as representing or suggesting the total person.

Eyes Like Goggles

The cephalopod will soon be provided with a pair of conspicuous eyes. Children are fascinated by eyes. Even in earliest infancy, nothing will engage the baby's attention like the human face; but within the face it is the eyes that spellbind and activity subsides.

PLATE 3

Boucher, F: Cherubim. The Pierpont Morgan Library, New York.

FIGURE 18

Spontaneous drawing by a three year 2 month old girl. The person is represented by what is most important, the head and features.

FIGURE 19

FIGURE 20

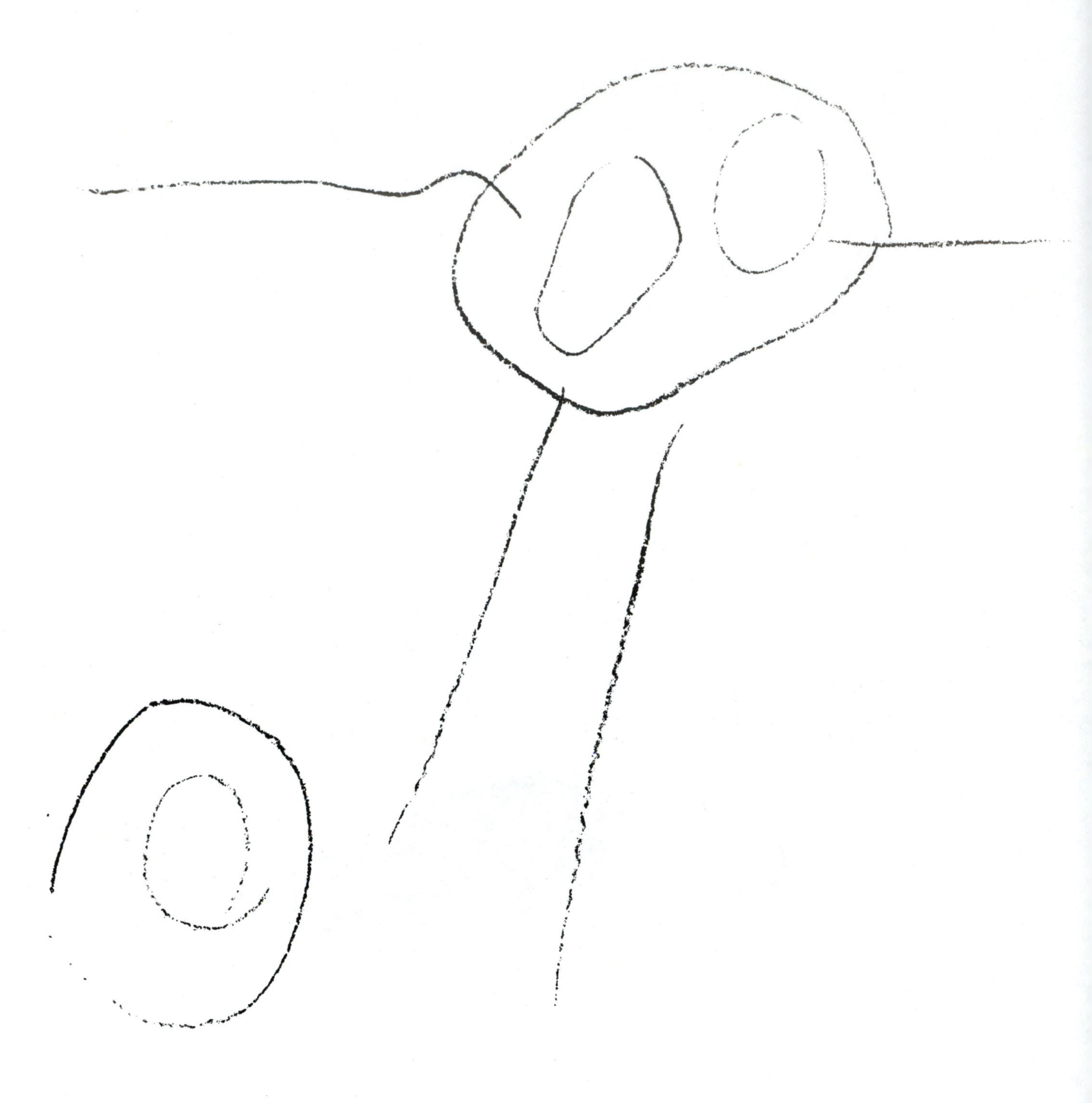

FIGURE 21

Spontaneous drawing. *Evolution of human figure. At first, this 52 month girl drew a series of circles. She then turned the paper over and drew the human figure above by adding eyes then legs and finally arms.*

FIGURE 22

Drawn by a boy, age four years 7 months.

FIGURE 23

Drawn by a bright girl at age three years 5 months

FIGURE 24

Drawn by a girl age four years 5 months.

FIGURE 25

Drawn by a bright child age three years 8 months.

And indeed, the failure to show interest in a face, the failure to establish and sustain eye contact, the failure of the smiling response to appear are warning signals of personality disorder. Observe an infant at breast. He stares continually at his mother's face, especially at her eyes unwaveringly, until satiety and relaxation flow to heavy-lidded sleep. That is why it is so important that the baby who is bottle-fed be held facing the mother so that he can see her instead of the ceiling and wall. He will thus become more quickly aware that the creature comforts emanate from a person and not just from a lifeless gadget of rubber and glass.

Other Features

In due course, mouth, nose, and ears, even fingers will be added and yet no body. Its function is hidden and archaic and so it is low in the hierarchy of human parts. In line with the child's omission of the body in his early drawings is the observation that young children will not detect the changing contours of mother's increasingly pregnant abdomen but will immediately call her attention to a person minus a leg or arm.

FIGURE 26

Drawing by a girl of four years 6 months. The drawing expresses fully average mentation. Eyes, nose, mouth, ears and legs are represented but no trunk.

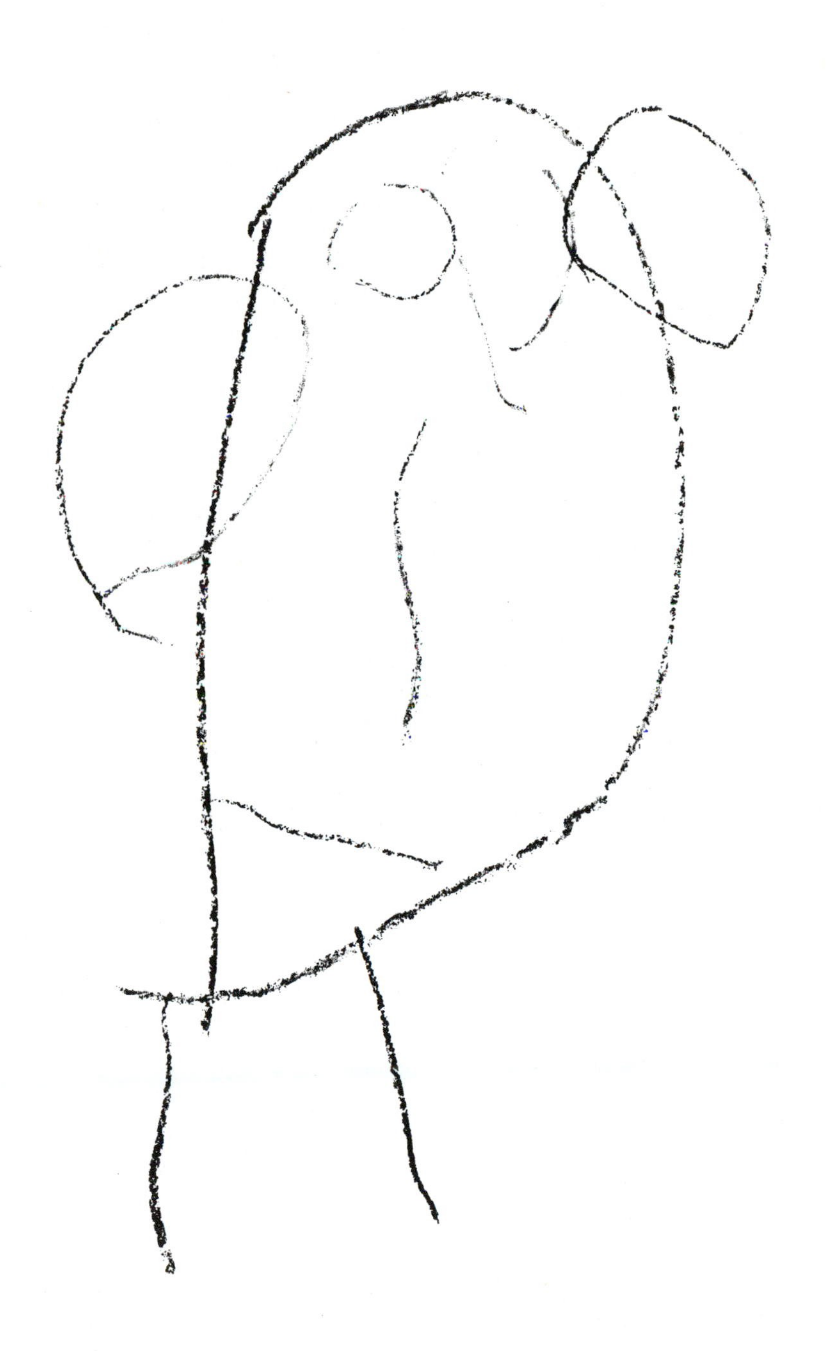

FIGURE 27

Drawing by a girl age four years 7 months. No trunk.

FIGURE 28

Drawing of "Mommy" by a boy, age four years 10 months. No trunk.

FIGURE 29

Drawn by a girl age five years 1 month. No trunk.

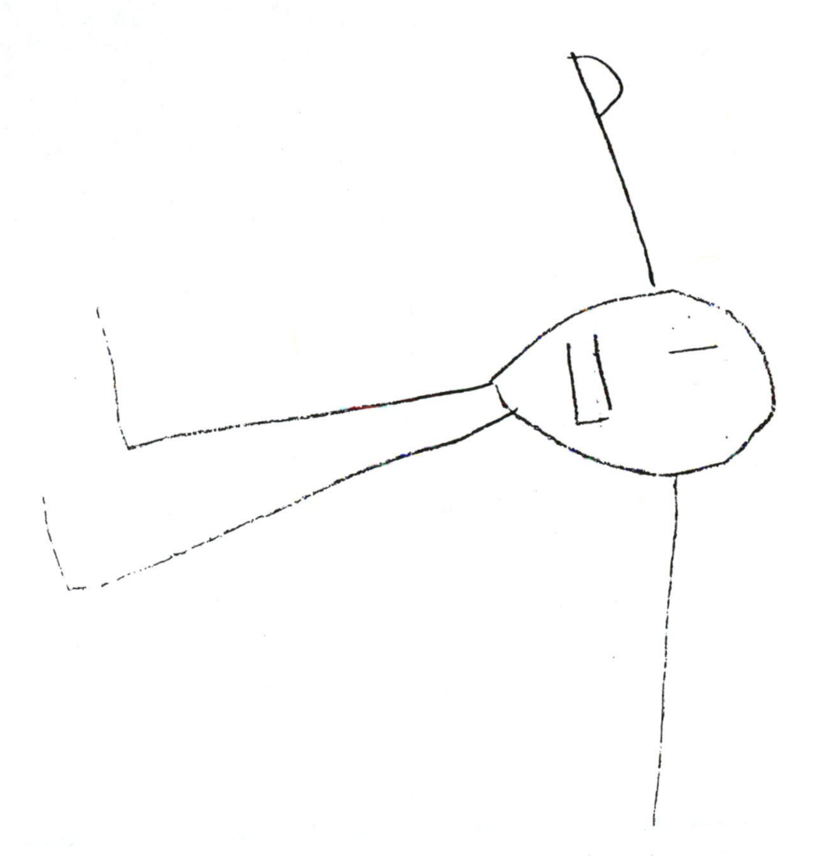

FIGURE 30

Drawn sideways by a girl of five years 1 month. No trunk.

FIGURE 31

Drawing by a girl, age five years 2 months. Although the drawing expresses fully average intelligence, there is no trunk.

FIGURE 32

Drawing by a girl age five years 7 months. No trunk. The number of body parts expresses average intelligence.

FIGURE 33

Drawn by a bright child of four years 10 months. No trunk.

8
THE HUMAN FIGURE EVOLVES
THE TRUNK APPEARS

At about age five, the trunk is added and the limbs no longer issue from the head, but are more or less properly located at upper and lower regions of the little circle beneath the large head. Some children will represent the trunk by a line. In more mature portrayals, the trunk is longer than it is wide and larger than the head.

FIGURE 34

Drawn by boy of four years 1 month, wh
behavioral development is in advance of norms
his chronological age. Head larger than trunk.

FIGURE 35

Drawn by a bright child of four years 1 month. Head larger than trunk.

FIGURE 36

Drawing by a bright girl of four years 6 months. Head larger than trunk.

FIGURE 37

Drawn by boy, age four years 7 months. Head dominates trunk.

FIGURE 38

Drawn by a girl of four years 6 months whose behavioral development expresses superior intelligence. Head smaller than trunk.

FIGURE 39

Drawn by a girl of five years 8 months. Head smaller than trunk.

FIGURE 40

Drawn by a boy. Chronological age: four years 10 months. Head smaller than trunk.

FIGURE 41

Drawing by a boy. Chronological age: five years 11 months. Head smaller than trunk. Ears appear.

The Belly Button

At age four, the child may become extremely conscious of the navel and may add it to drawings of the human figure. The navel is an enigma (Gesell and Ilg). Having learned that babies grow in mother's tummy, the child may spontaneously conclude that it is through the navel that they come out. Concern is tinged with amusement as the child laughingly calls out "belly button" when adding it to the drawing.

This absorbing interest generally tapers off as the child reaches age five. Persistent involvement with the navel and continued inclusion in figure drawings are considered evidences of immaturity. Most children do not add a navel to their drawings. Though infrequent, its presence is by no means rare in drawings by preschoolers.

In the examples that follow, the presence of the navel in the drawings by preschoolers are within a wide range of normal drawing behavior; while in the family drawn by a twelve-year-old, addition of a navel to each figure is just another item in the immature, stereotyped concept of the body image expressed in the child's drawing and reflected in the child's learning difficulties.

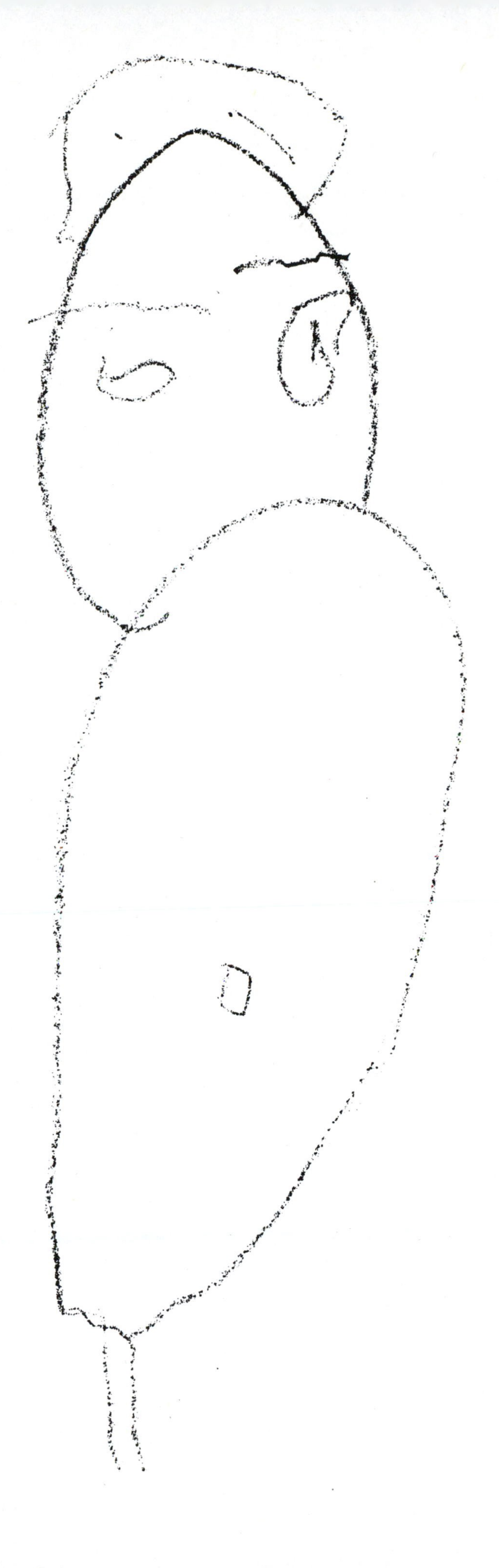

FIGURE 42

Drawing of a person by a boy of above-average intelligence, at chronological age three years 5 months. The "Belly-button".

FIGURE 43

Drawing of a person by a bright boy age three years 11 months. The navel has been added below the body.

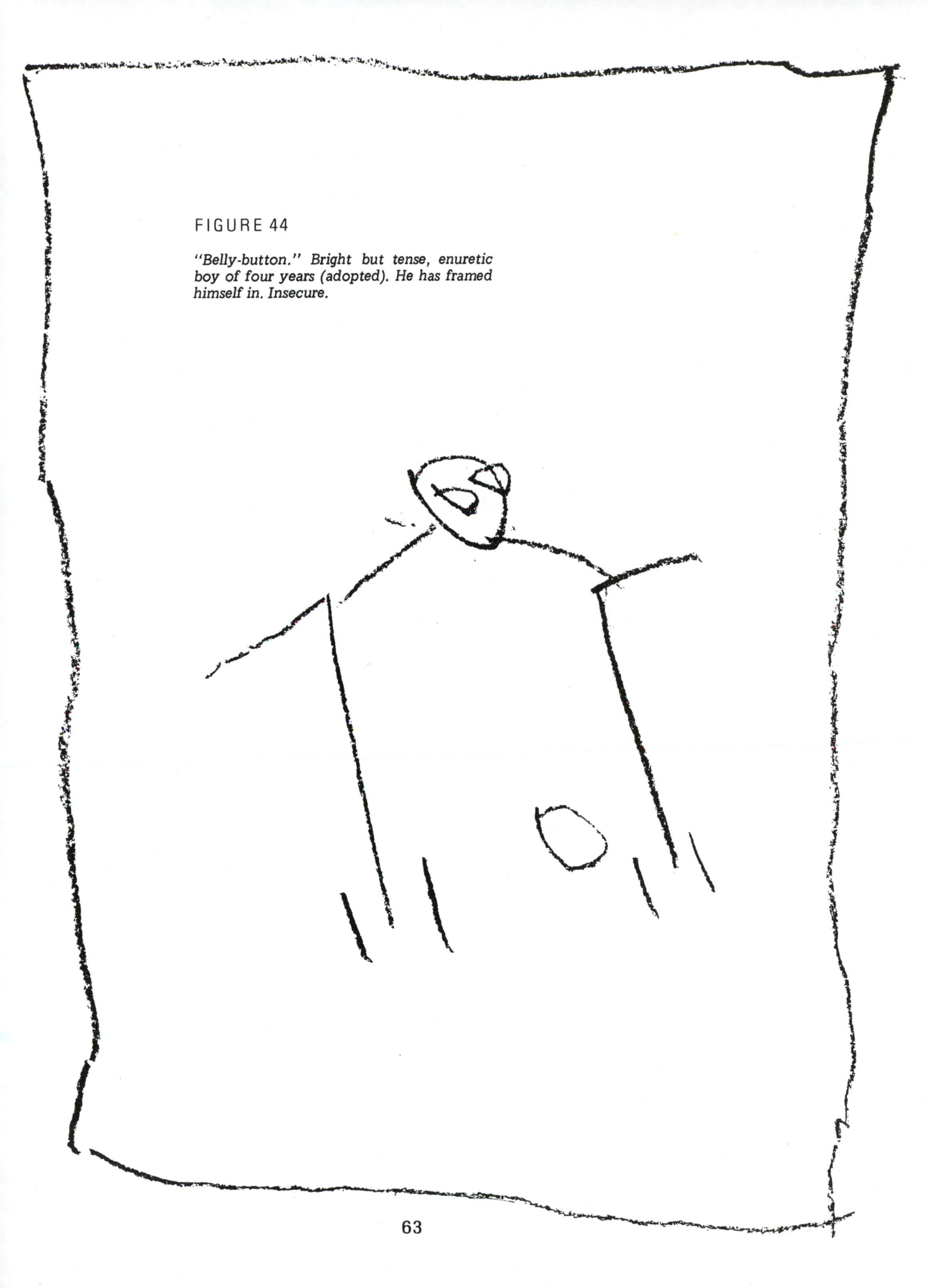

FIGURE 44

"Belly-button." Bright but tense, enuretic boy of four years (adopted). He has framed himself in. Insecure.

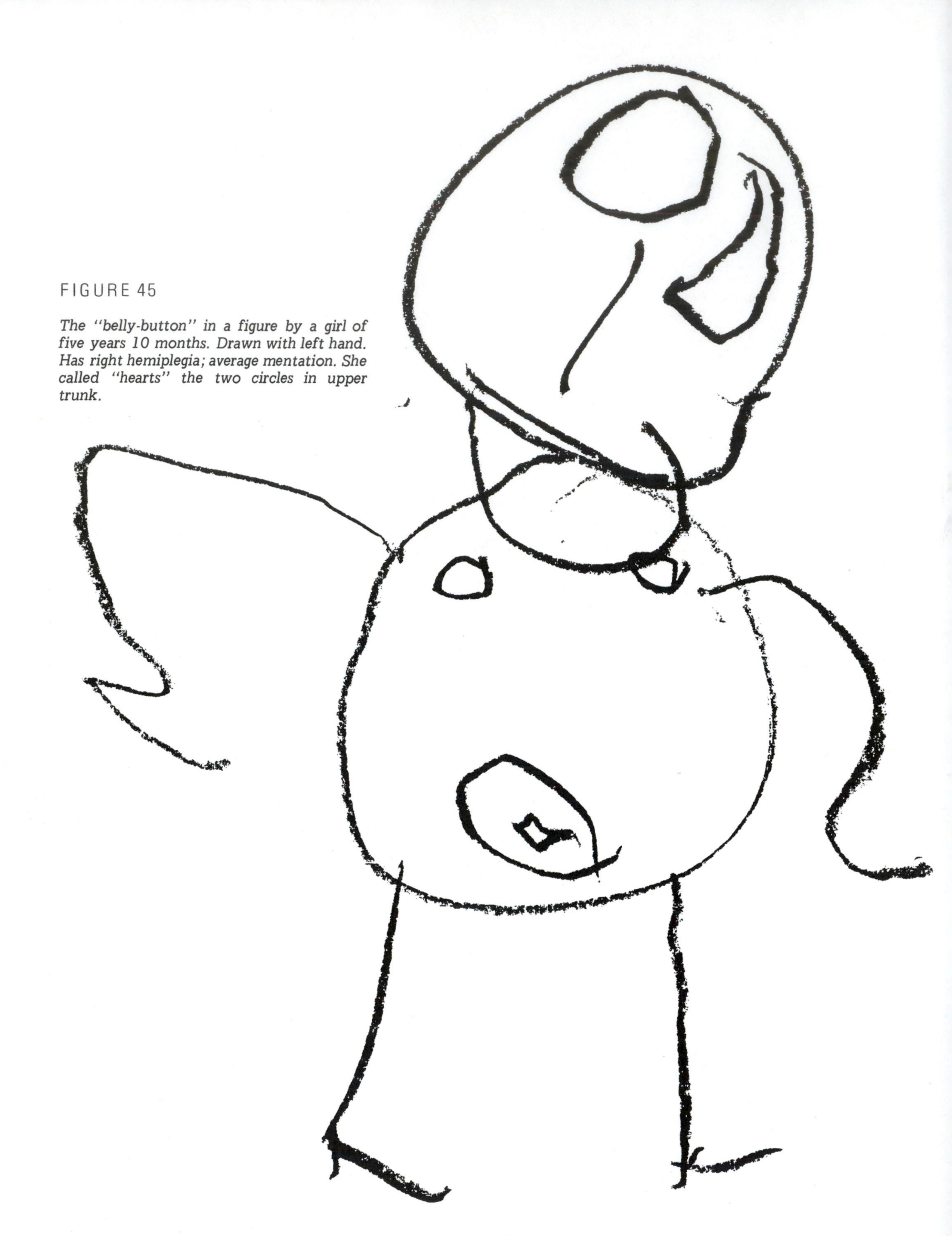

FIGURE 45

The "belly-button" in a figure by a girl of five years 10 months. Drawn with left hand. Has right hemiplegia; average mentation. She called "hearts" the two circles in upper trunk.

FIGURE 46

Drawing of family by immature adopted child of twelve years. Dyslexic. Note stereotyped figures.

FIGURE 47

The Genitalia

In reviewing thousands of figure drawings by children, this writer has been impressed by the rarity of any attempt to represent the genitalia. Apparently, the genitals are not considered important enough to be included in the child's parsimonious reduction of the human figure to what he considers its essentials. Or is the child reflecting cultural taboos? Possibly. Yet the generalized neglect of the genitalia by the vast majority of children from the most diverse environments, the rigid as well as the most casual, suggests that the reason is within the child himself, in his concept of the body image. Perhaps the explanation is to be found in the sexual latency that prevails during early childhood, in the differential growth pattern of various systems, the head growing rapidly to reach nine-tenths of its adult size by age six while the genitalia remain infantile until the teens, when they develop rapidly and cannot be ignored.

In some cases in which the penis was added, the child had been made conscious of it because of a recent operation, herniorrhaphy or circumcision.

Three drawings are presented in which the boys who made them added the genitalia.

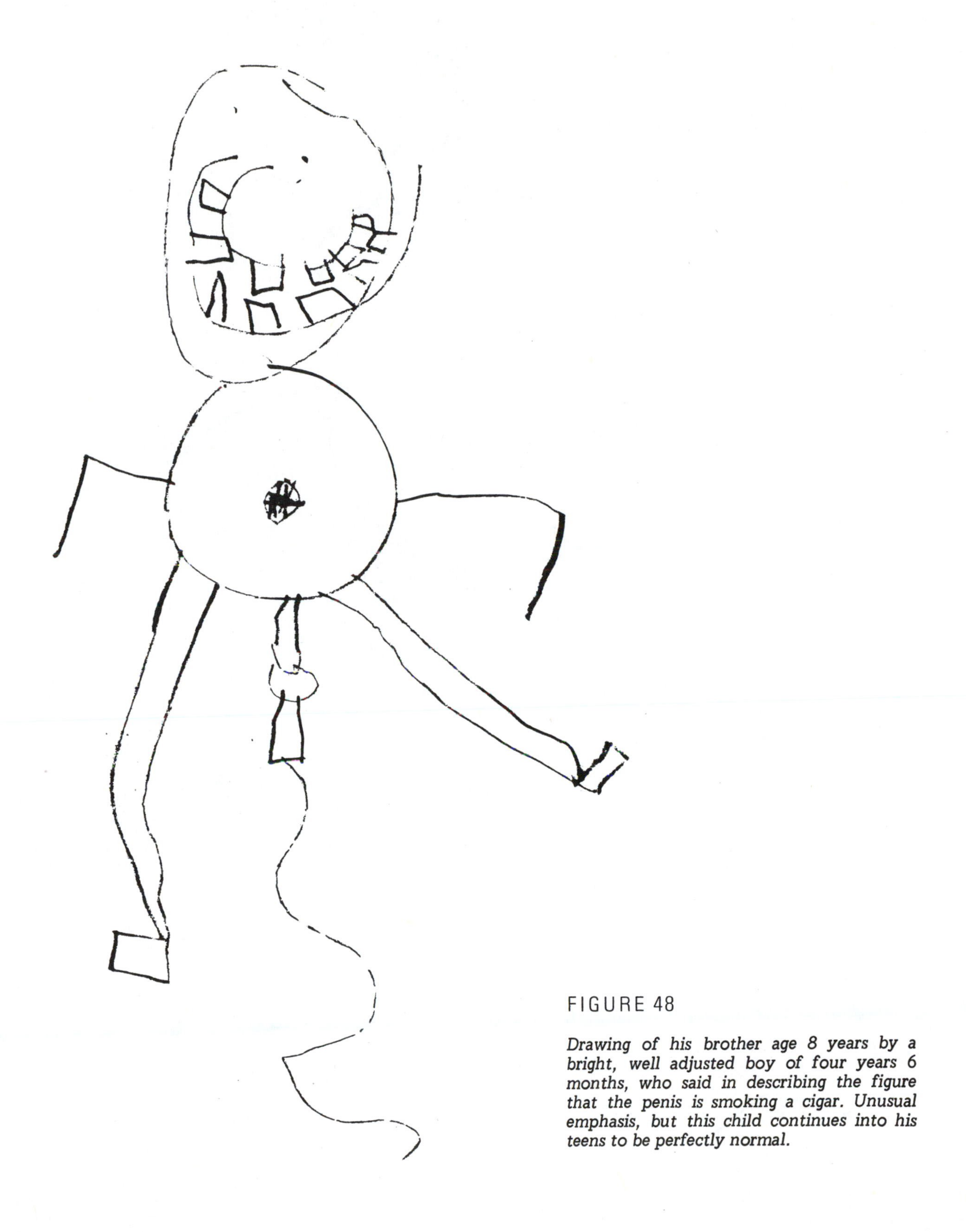

FIGURE 48

Drawing of his brother age 8 years by a bright, well adjusted boy of four years 6 months, who said in describing the figure that the penis is smoking a cigar. Unusual emphasis, but this child continues into his teens to be perfectly normal.

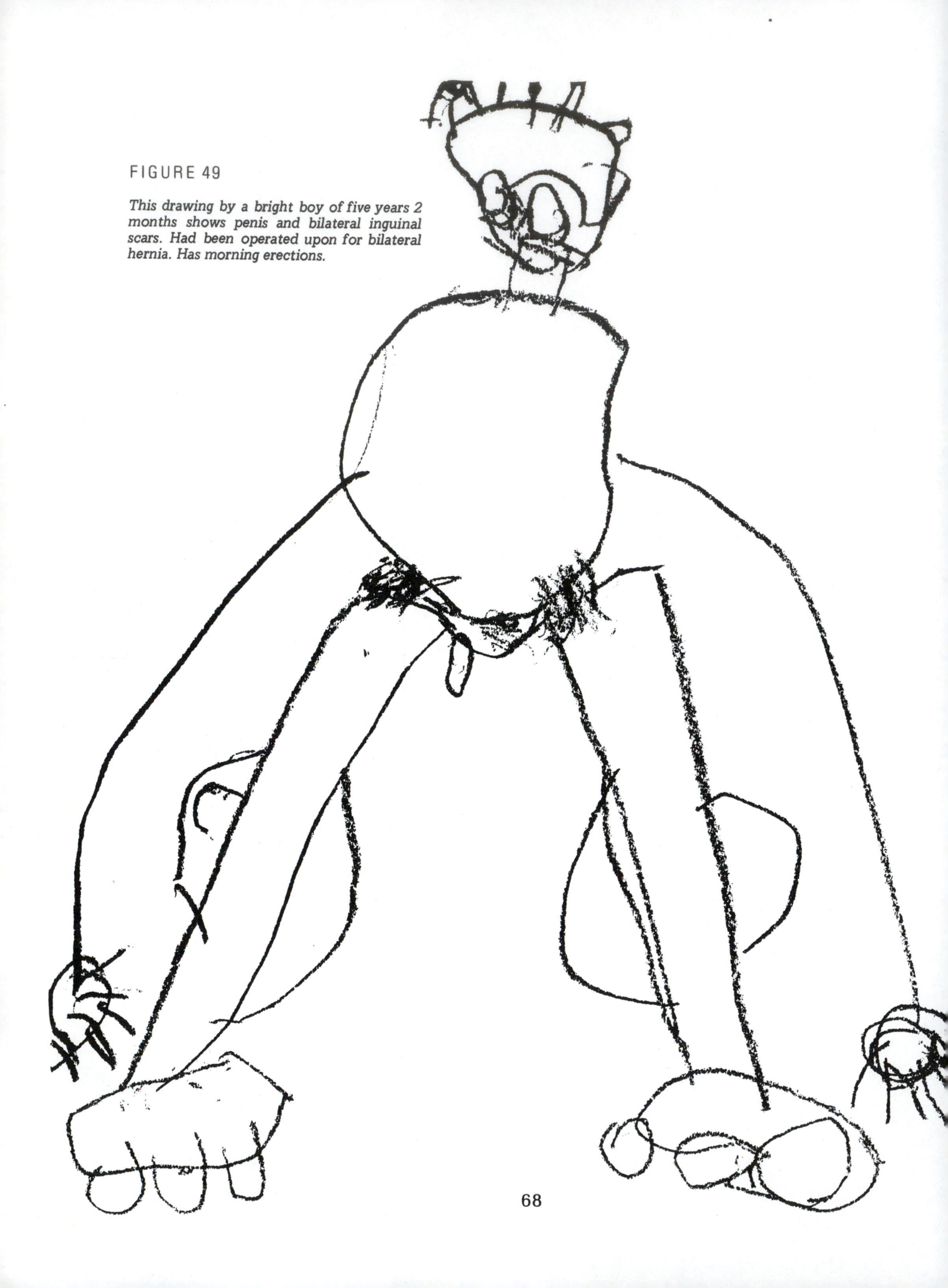

FIGURE 49

This drawing by a bright boy of five years 2 months shows penis and bilateral inguinal scars. Had been operated upon for bilateral hernia. Has morning erections.

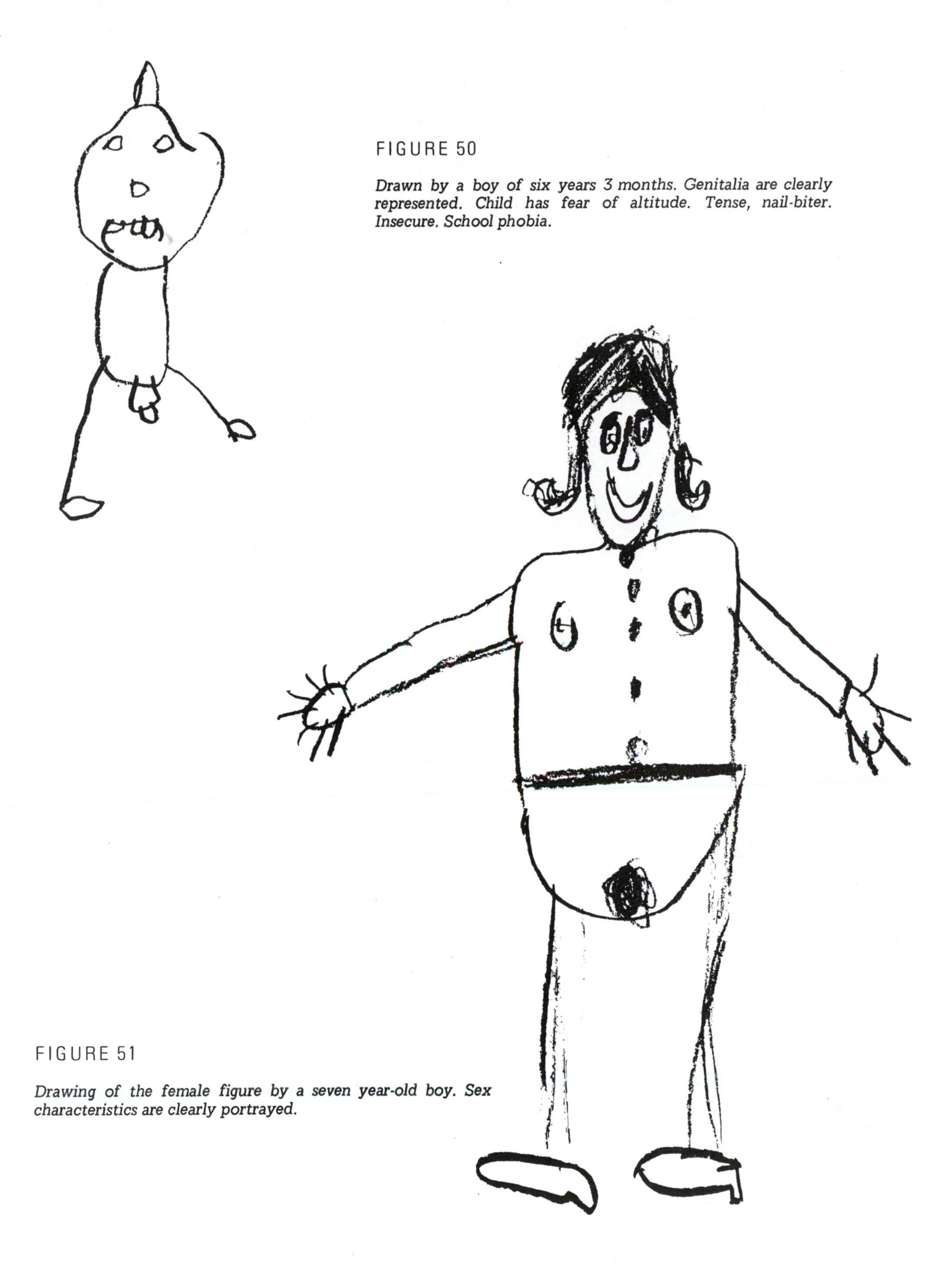

FIGURE 50

Drawn by a boy of six years 3 months. Genitalia are clearly represented. Child has fear of altitude. Tense, nail-biter. Insecure. School phobia.

FIGURE 51

Drawing of the female figure by a seven year-old boy. Sex characteristics are clearly portrayed.

9

THE HUMAN FIGURE EVOLVES

The Mixed Profile

In discussing sequences in drawing the human figure, mention was made of the fact that early representations are always full-face and that a transitional period may be observed before profile portrayal is established. During the transitional stage, the child may draw an outline profile of the face but with two eyes and even with a second nose. This confusion is an expression of the underlying change that is taking place in the child's mind, from intellectual to visual realism, from the child's to the adult's perception of reality, from the natural to the cultivated vision, and, as some say, from the greater to the lesser. Profile drawing is a prelude to the depiction of movement. Then, when the child eliminates transparencies from his drawings and attempts perspective, the transition has been completed. The child has accepted visual realism, he has conformed.

The attempt to draw distant objects smaller, the substitution of opacity for transparency, the elimination of the second eye from a profile have been singled out by Luquet as the criteria that document the change from subjectivism to objective reality. He has located its attainment between seven and nine years. Goodenough placed it generally at eight to ten years. Prudhommeau selected the attempt to depict movement as the basic criterion of the transition and set the time at six to seven years.

Careful examination of a large number of drawings has led the present writer to conclude that there is a wide range of variability in the time factor and that bright children will not only achieve visual realism earlier but that they may never show in their drawings the confusion that is expressed in the mixed profile.

It is interesting to note that mixed profiles appear in the drawings by psychotic adults. Machover interprets the peculiarity as indicative of regression and collapse of judgment.

The mixed profile has been used deliberately and with striking effect by modern artists, notably by Picasso.

The Profile

A relatively late development in the art of childhood, the profile was an early stage in the childhood of art. The cave art of our paleolithic ancestors is typically profile representation.

Although profile representation is maturational in that it is not attempted by the very young, it falls short of being universal, since only 80 to 85 per cent of mature persons draw the human figure in profile (Goodenough). The same author noted that the transition from frontal to profile view was achieved earlier and more consistently by boys and that it was related to the desire to express movement by the more active sex. As already mentioned, the profile lends itself to graphic expression of movement.

The cave paintings of Altamira probably represent the highest point artistically and aesthetically in the art of prehistory. As man progressed into the New Stone Age, his art became more conventional, more geometric. A further reduction in pictographic elements resulted in the evolution of symbols, pictography was being replaced by written language. A survey of these developments strongly suggests "that the art of writing evolved from drawing in profile" (Mégroz).

Young children draw profiles much like the ancient Egyptians. Body parts are shown in their clearest aspect: face in profile but eye frontally, trunk in frontal view as well as arms but legs and feet in profile. Later on, the child will attempt to draw what he sees from where he sees it and the profile will be a truer one from the optical point of view. But Gauguin would not be happy; he disdained the naturalism of Periclean Greece. For him, Truth lay in pure cerebral art, in primitive art, and the wisest of all were the Egyptians.

PLATE 4

PICASSO, Pablo. The Necklace. Collection, The Museum of Modern Art, New York. Acquired through the Lille P. Bliss Bequest.

FIGURE 52

This mixed profile reproduced from Corrado Ricci's book shows both eyes and is strangely evocative of Picasso. (Plate 4)

"Now, if you had the two eyes on the same side of the nose, for instance—or the mouth at the top—that would be some help." Humpty Dumpty to Alice.

Lewis Carroll: THROUGH THE LOOKING GLASS.

FIGURE 53

Profile with two nostrils. Drawn by a boy of six years 6 months. School phobia.

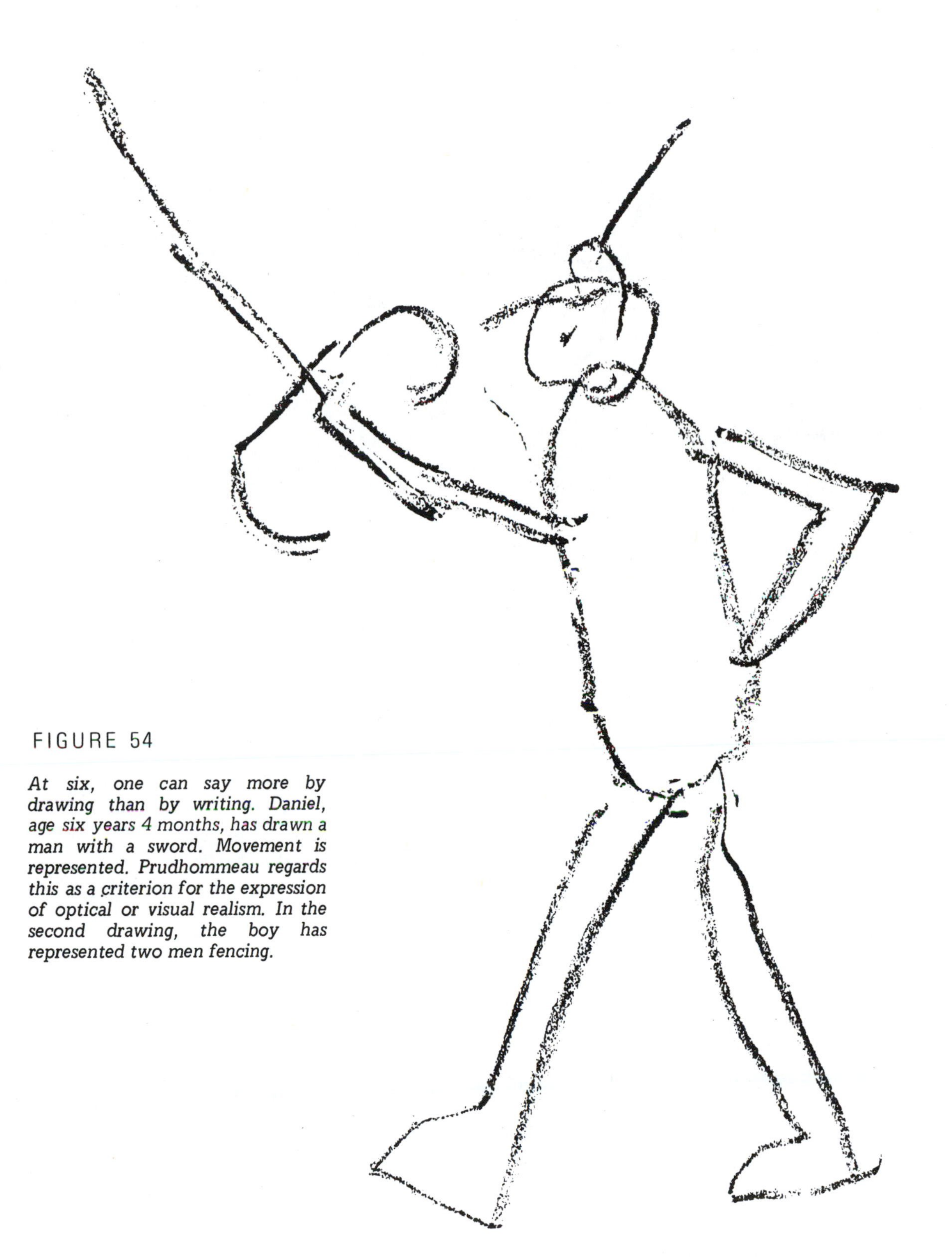

FIGURE 54

At six, one can say more by drawing than by writing. Daniel, age six years 4 months, has drawn a man with a sword. Movement is represented. Prudhommeau regards this as a criterion for the expression of optical or visual realism. In the second drawing, the boy has represented two men fencing.

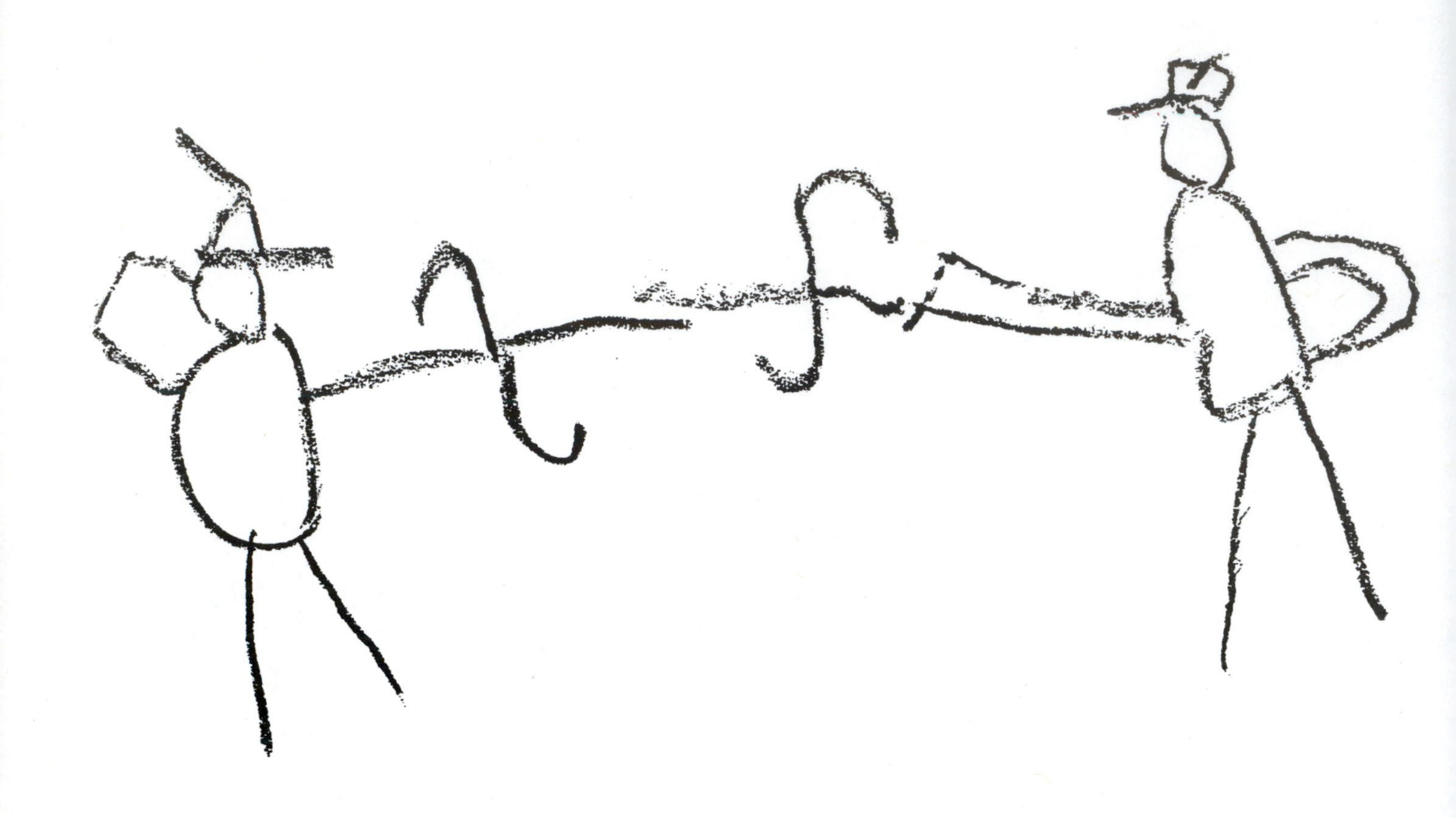

FIGURE 55

Dynamism: The representation of movement. Men fencing. Drawn by a boy of six years 4 months.

FIGURE 56

Profile: head in profile, trunk and limbs in frontal view. Drawn by girl, age 7. Superior intelligence.

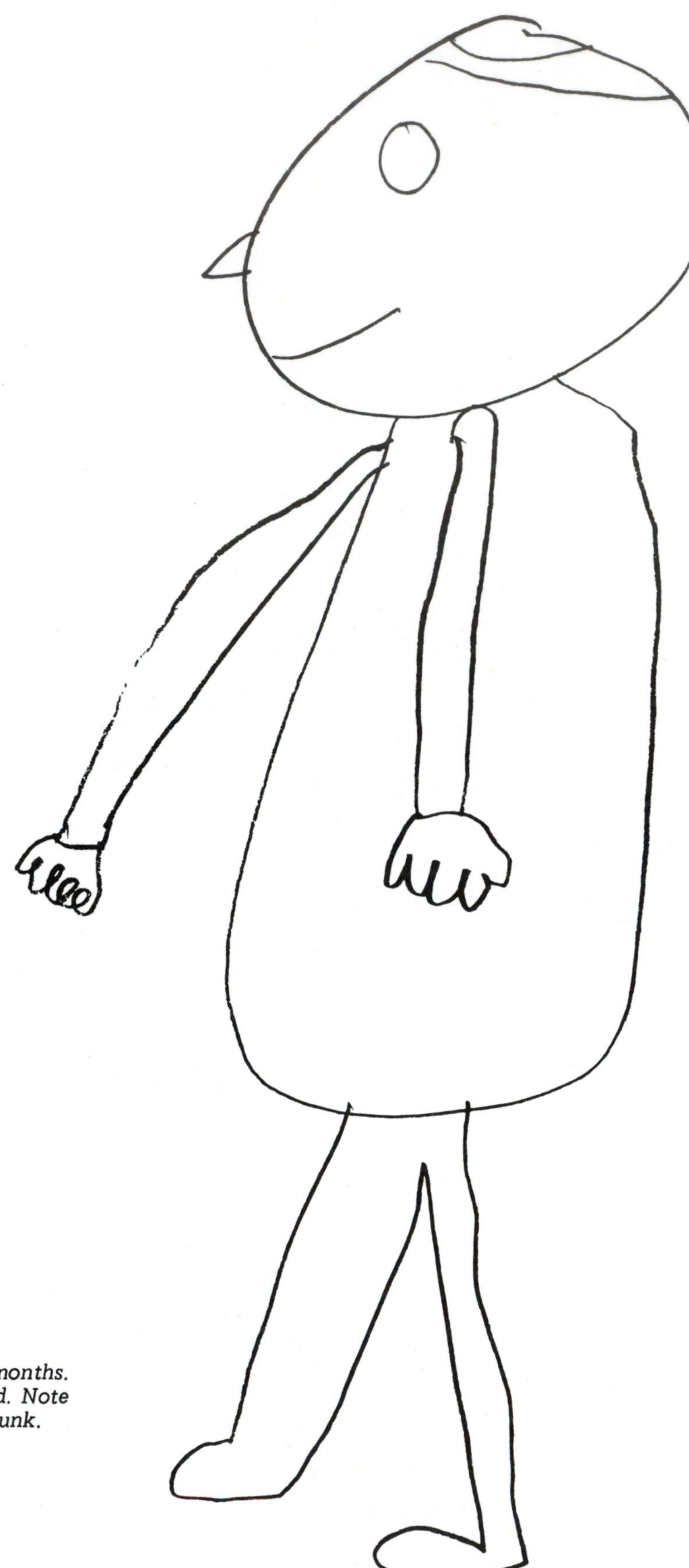

FIGURE 57

Profile by a boy of seven years 6 months. Average intelligence but unmotivated. Note attachment of right arm to front of trunk.

FIGURE 58

Profile of head; rest of person in frontal view.
Drawn by boy, age 10 years 6 months.

FIGURE 59

Representation of movement. Drawn by a boy of 10 years 9 months. He said "the man's running, going to say good-bye to his wife". "I drew also a muscle; all boys on my block say I don't have any muscle."

FIGURE 60

Profile drawing depicting motion. Drawn by boy of eleven years. Unmotivated, functioning below capacity at school, reacting to family tensions. Called the figure a beatnik.

FIGURE 61

Body and limbs in frontal view; face in profile. Drawn by boy. Age eleven years. Disruptive.

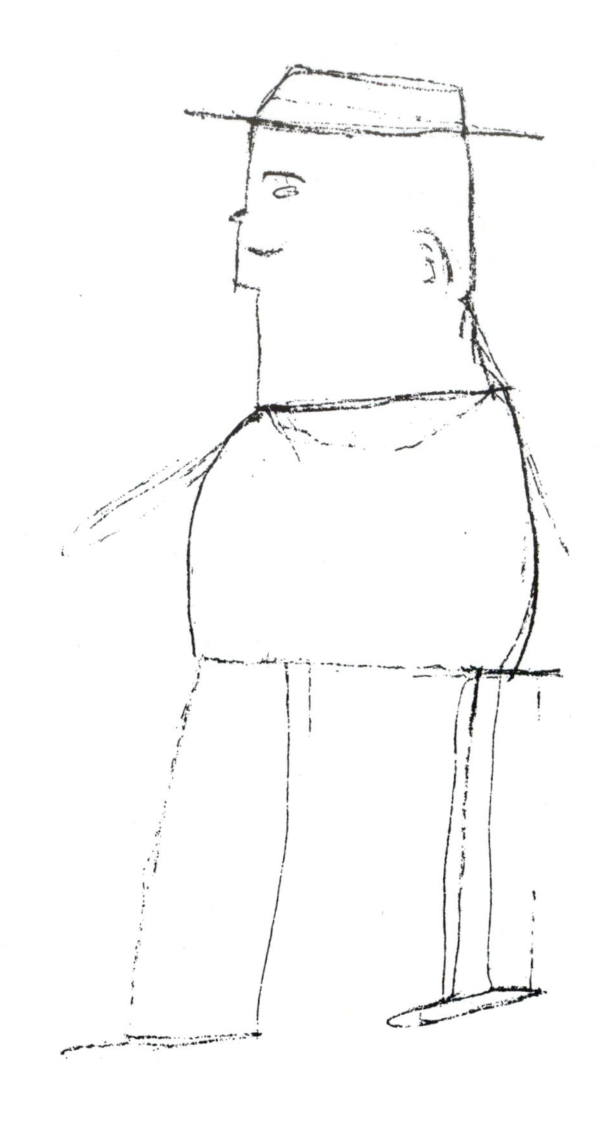

FIGURE 62

Profile by boy age twelve years. Educable retarded.

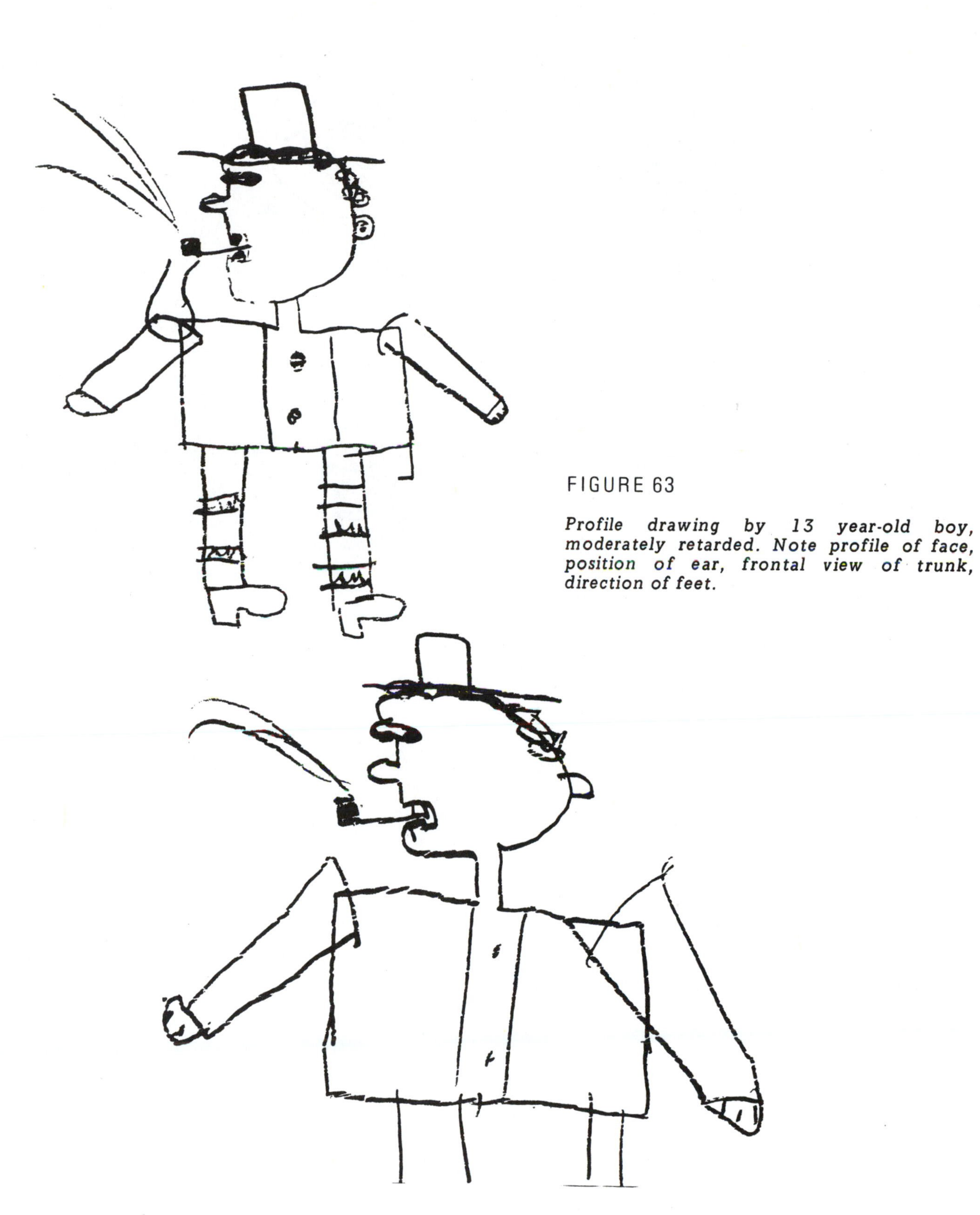

FIGURE 63

Profile drawing by 13 year-old boy, moderately retarded. Note profile of face, position of ear, frontal view of trunk, direction of feet.

FIGURE 64

Drawn by boy of 15 years. Expelled from school because of aggressive behavior. Has broken into a house. Has stolen. He is a foster child.

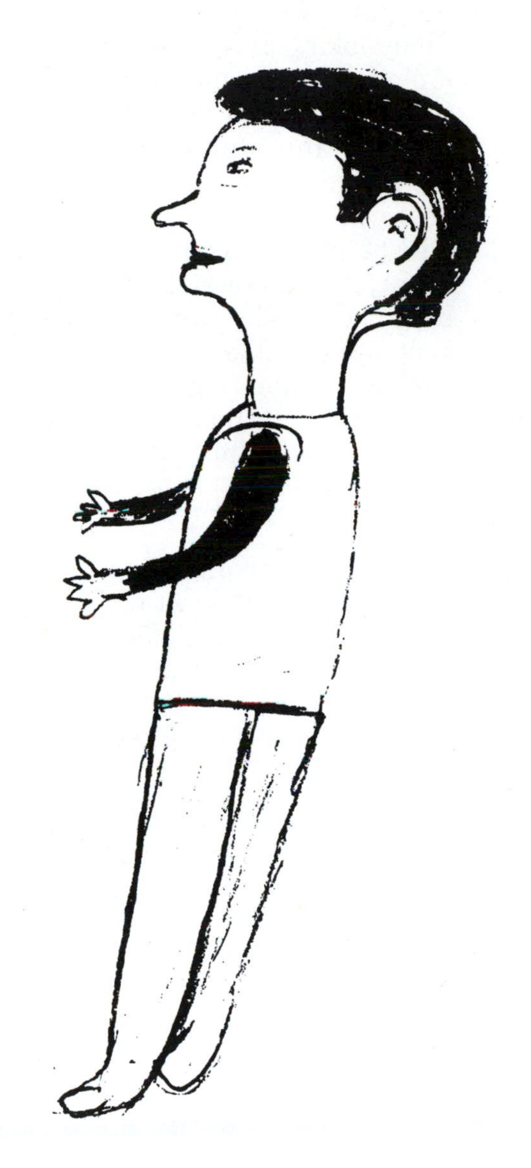

FIGURE 65

Profile by boy age 16 years. Compulsive eater. Obese. Note attachment of right arm correctly to side of trunk.

10

FLUCTUATIONS

Viewed in perspective, development of behavior advances towards maturity, but its course is not straight and even. In every field of behavior there are forward thrusts, backward slides, pauses, and renewed thrusts. Only the broad view will reveal the advance. Development is a dynamic process in which may be distinguished phases of equilibrium and disequilibrium, advance, recession, integration of the newly acquired pattern, and again a forward thrust. The year-old infant taking his first steps does not suddenly discard creeping. The same principle applies to the development of graphic activity. The four year old, who typically draws a man as a cephalopod, may now and then endow him with a body but the addition will be only inconsistently present until the body will have become assimilated and integrated into the child's slowly maturing concept of the body image. Incidentally, this view of developmental fluctuations will be of great help to the adult who may be disappointed or disturbed by behavior or regressions that are in reality phasic deviations in a normal course of growth. Under stress, behavior may regress to an earlier level. The regression becomes the object of justifiable concern when it is of extended duration, suggesting a serious emotional disorder or personality deviation. In drawing a person, those parts that are drawn consistently have been integrated into the child's concept, while those parts that appear irregularly are in the process of becoming integrated.

Again, it is essential to a valid interpretation to know what can be expected at various ages and levels of development. The absence of the trunk at four is to be expected. Its inconsistent appearance is generally the case between four and five. But its disappearance, or loss after it had become a constant feature of figure drawing may be a clue to the diagnosis of a behavior disorder. Fluctuation must not be confused with loss.

While on the subject of fluctuation, this writer would like to add the following observation that he has made repeatedly, and of which he has numerous examples: There is often a discrepancy between the child's drawing of an isolated person as compared with his more primitive rendition of human figures when asked to draw his family. The superior quality of the individual figure is interpreted by the writer as indicating a more intellectual response to this task in contrast to the more emotionally influenced response evoked by the request to draw his family. In fact, the value of the family drawing as a projective technique is considerable, for by this means the child often expresses his feelings and attitudes towards individual members of his family, as well as his own status within the family group. The more emotion, the less intellect, hence the discrepancy between the two renditions of the human figure. The gap seems to be greater when negative feelings are more intense and where there are greater problems of assimilation and adjustment within a family.

FIGURE 66

The drawings on this page are by a boy of seven years 4 months. In this figure he has drawn the trunk, in the next he has omitted it. Both renditions of the human figure were drawn on the same day. The one with the trunk yields a mental age of six years, the other a mental age of five years 3 months but must be considered immature because it has no trunk as well as for the failure to add more parts.

FIGURE 67

He has omitted the trunk

Fluctuation: An Example of Striking Variability in Level of Performance Within a Period of Minutes

Figures 68 and 69 were made by a girl of six years, 8 months. She first drew a man, then turned the paper over and drew a lady. The "man" expresses a mental age of four years, 6 months, while the lady is what would be expected at chronological age six years, 6 months. If one were to judge from the first drawing alone, one would say that the child was retarded.

Besides illustrating fluctuation, the marked difference between the two figures reflects the strong emotional tie that bound this particular child to her mother.

Fortunately, such striking disparity is not the rule or it would render the appraisal of intelligence from drawings extremely tenuous. That it may occur should guard against too hasty a conclusion from a single specimen.

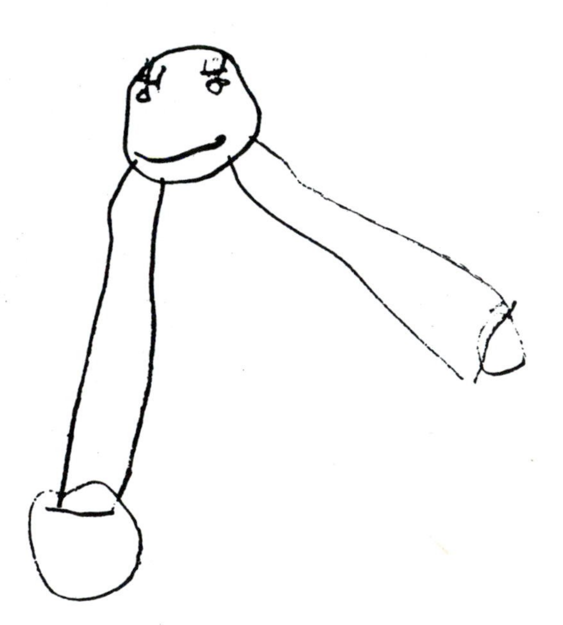

FIGURE 68

FIGURE 69

FIGURE 70

Compare these figures with the drawing of a single person by the same child on the same day, on the following page. The drawing of a single person has more parts (neck, shoulders, better ratio of head/body size, arms in two dimensions). Age of child: seven years.

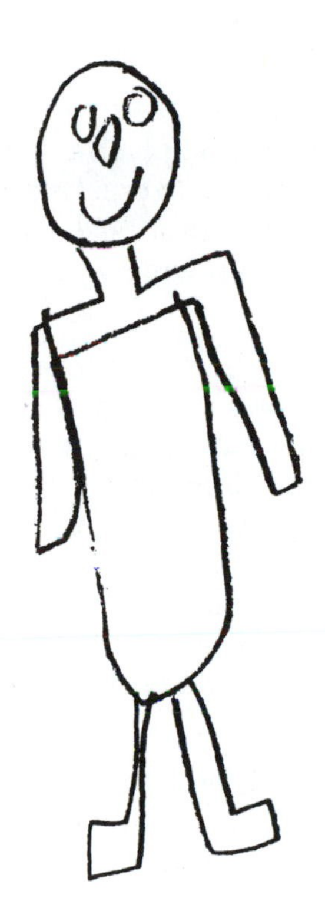

FIGURE 71

11

DRAWING WHAT IS KNOWN TO EXIST

Though what the child draws is suggested by something or someone in his environment, he does not make a copy but a representation, that is, a mental impression not a visual observation. In fact, if an adult stands before him and says "draw a person" the child will begin to draw without once looking up at the model standing in front of him. It is said that he draws what he knows to be there. It is more correct to say that he draws what impresses him, for there are many more things that he knows about the object than will appear in his drawing. Of the things he knows, he draws only those that have impressed him not only mentally but also emotionally. And these he tends to emphasize according to his own scale of values usually by drawing them first and larger, the result being an optical distortion: enormous heads, eyes like goggles, threatening arms and hands, huge savage teeth.

When the object is not invested with strong feelings, his drawings are accordingly more intellectually than affectively expressive. There is more knowing than feeling in his rendition of "a man in a boat". In contrast, there is more emotion than intellect involved when drawing a picture of his family.

What he knows leads the young artist to draw those parts that are invisible to the objective viewer because they are behind an obstacle. This does not deter the child from showing the men inside the house or the legs inside the trousers. These transparencies characterize the drawings of children until they are eight or nine. But optical realism comes on by degrees. It seems as if the child is reluctant to surrender his own inner realism to the prosaic objectivity of the adult, for even after he has outgrown transparency, he places his man on top of the boat and continues to draw the whole person. Eventually, the man will get back inside and only the upper part of him will appear in the drawing.

A striking demonstration of the principle that young children draw what they know to be there is afforded by the experiment conducted by Clark at Stanford University and described by Goodenough in her book on the Measurement of Intelligence by Drawings. A large group of children were asked to draw an apple with a hat pin running through it. All that they could see was the hat pin entering the apple on their side; yet, almost all of them drew the apple with the hat pin entering and emerging horizontally, while most of the younger children showed the entire hat pin even as it traversed the interior of the apple. The model served simply as a cue to express what they knew to be there.

Herbert G. Spearing tells of a little girl, who on being shown a profile picture of a bird, asked why it had only one eye. Dissatisfied with the explanation, she "seized the pencil, turned the paper round and gave the bird its other eye on the back of the drawing".

FIGURE 72

Drawing of a "cow" by a boy of three years 10 months. Turn it over and see the tail on the back side.

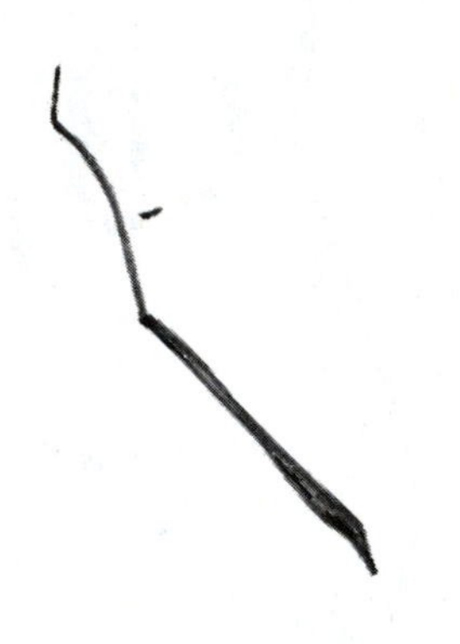

FIGURE 73

The tail of the cow.

In a similar vein the preceding drawing by a boy of three years, 10 months. He called it a "cow." The animal is represented by a recognizable head, eye, and legs. Knowing that cows have tails, the boy proceded to turn the paper over and drew on the back side. (q.v.)

The child knows what is there and draws it regardless of whether it can or cannot be seen. His drawings are ideographic and not a "light report" of the appearance of an object (C. Biederman).

12

PAST AND PRESENT

As expressions of the developing concept of the body image, drawings by contemporary children are strikingly similar to those by children of past generations. These drawings reproduced from Corrado Ricci's volume published in 1887 are not only similar but identical with those by our own children.

1885 FIGURE 74

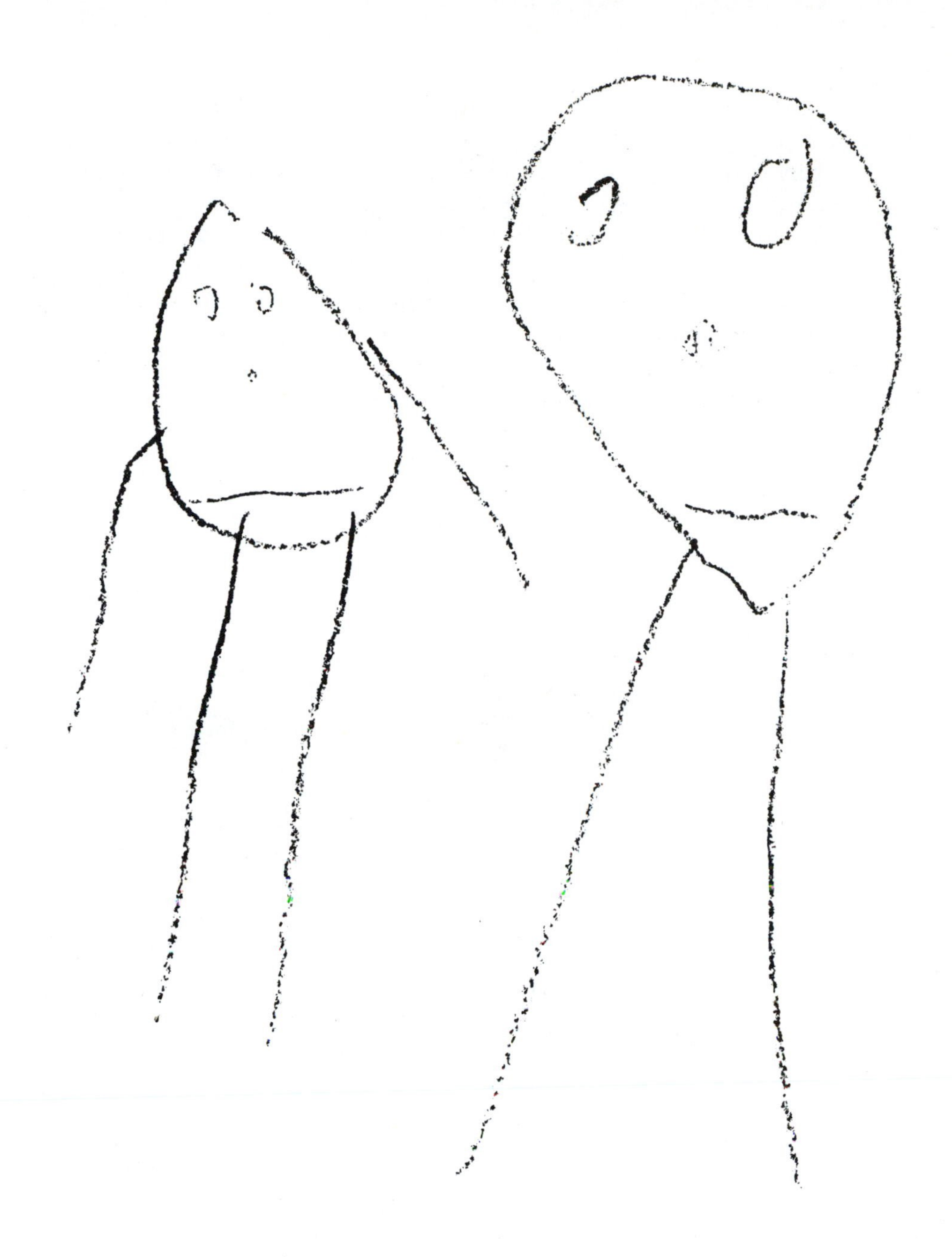

1967

FIGURE 75

The Cephalopod or Tadpole Stage in the Evolution of the Human Figure. Drawing by a child of four years 6 months.

And like his twentieth century descendant, the child of the past saw the world in his inner eye and drew what he knew to be there not simply the retinal image—a perception, not a mere photograph. A century apart and we observe the same "see-through" or "X-ray" technique. "I show it because I know it to be there" and so the men in the boat are visible through its sides, the men in the house are visible through its walls. "I can't actually see the sacristan in the campanile but I know he's there because the bell is ringing."

1885

FIGURE 76

1885

FIGURE 77

Men in a boat (from Corrado Ricci's L'ARTE DEI BAMBINI).

1967

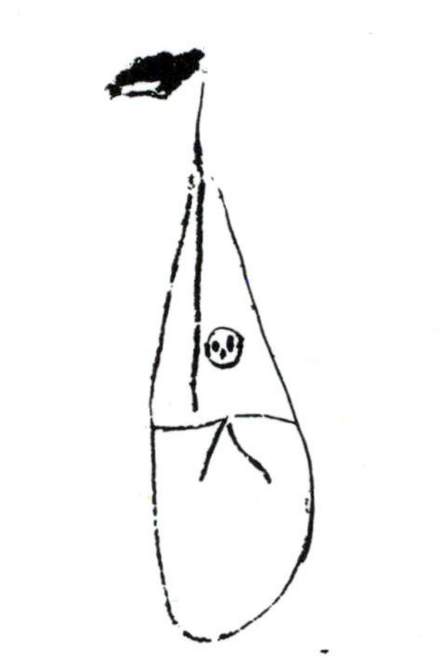

FIGURE 78

Drawing of man in a boat by boy age six years 6 months, contemporary. The man is visible through the hull.

FIGURE 79

Drawing by a girl age six years 9 months. Contemporary. The man is visible through the hull.

1967

1885

FIGURE 80

The sacristan can be seen ringing the bell in the campanile. From Corrado Ricci's L'ARTE DEI BAMBINI.

1967

FIGURE 81

Drawn by a boy of five years 8 months. People visible through walls of house.

Body parts that cannot be seen are drawn nevertheless. The child knows what is there and draws it. The child's realism is not **visual** like the adult's but **intellectual.** Both legs are shown of the man on horseback. The whole man is seen though he is in the boat. Both eyes may be shown in a profile. Four sides may be shown in drawing a cube. The term "X-ray technique" is used to designate this.

1885

FIGURE 82

FIGURE 83

Drawn by a girl age four years 6 months of superior intelligence, contemporary. Both legs of the rider are shown.

1961

FIGURE 84

Disparity between immature concept of body image and average mental age. X-ray technique. Transparencies. Limbs visible through clothing. Drawing by a boy of nine years 1 month. Female figure. Child was cyanotic at birth.

In the following drawings there are no transparencies but the man is on deck and all of him is shown. This transitional stage will gradually merge into the more realistic portrayal in which only parts that can actually be seen will be represented.

1885

FIGURE 85

FIGURE 86

"Man in a boat" drawn by boy of six years 1 month.

1967

FIGURE 87

Drawing by a girl of seven years 9 months. Getting around the problem of portraying the man in a boat, there are no transparencies but the whole man is shown on top of boat.

FIGURE 88

"Man in a boat" drawn by girl of eight years 6 months.

1967

1967

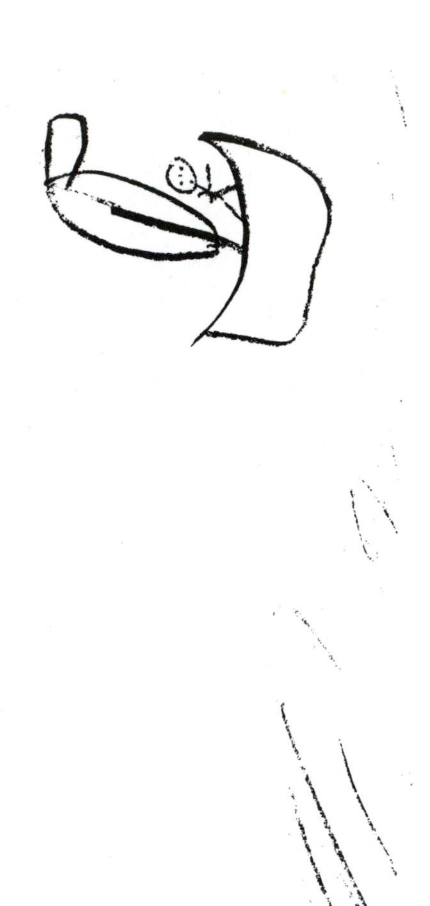

FIGURE 89
"Man in a boat" drawn by boy of nine years.

"At what age can the child be expected to outgrow the 'X-ray technique' and to make drawings that are free from transparencies?" At nine years, Goodenough states that 36 per cent of the accelerated but only 7 per cent of the average and none of the retarded succeed. She considers the correlation with school success "usually good."

1967

FIGURE 90

"Man in a boat" drawing by a boy of ten years of average intelligence. There are no transparencies.

13

WHAT IS "WRONG" IN CHILDREN'S DRAWINGS

Enthusiasm for children's drawings though widespread is by no means universal. Negative attitudes towards the drawings fall into two main categories: the drawings are meaningless; the drawings are defective.

They are dismissed as meaningless because they are said to be imitation. Nothing could be farther from the truth. The open-minded critic need only observe a room full of young children who have been asked to draw a man. Each child will be seen to engage himself busily in drawing without the least interest in copying from his companions. Nor will any of them draw inspiration from the real person standing in front of them. No two productions will be identical though a common denominator—the mind of a child—will be expressed in each.

It has been objected that the child copies himself. Serial drawings of the same subject made by the same child at six month or yearly intervals show such a variety of forms and styles that it is not possible to establish a common source. In contrast, the style of an artist—even when as in the case of Picasso it has passed through a variety of forms and isms—bears within it a thread that permits attribution of authenticity without need of signature or document.

The drawings are said to be defective because there is no perspective, because the proportions are all wrong, because there is no feeling for beauty. These objections will be discussed individually. They are valid only if the adult is taken to be the measure of all things. Such an attitude leads inevitably to the conclusion that the child is defective because he is an adult in the making or that the child is simply a miniature adult. This prejudicial viewpoint fails to see that there are two worlds, that of the young child and that of the adult, that there are two world concepts, that there are two ways of perceiving reality: one's own and the culture's. School is the bridge for most children.

The "Wrong" Proportions

It has been said that the child has no sense of proportion; that he draws a man taller than the tree in front of him; that the man's head is twice the size of his body. These statements are obviously correct from our adult sense of objective proportions. But if we try to see the world through the child's eyes, we can interpret the meaning of the "incorrect" proportions. The child's frame of reference is not the same as ours. The meaning is clear if we bear in mind that the child does not copy what he sees. His are affective proportions. The drawings are expressions of an inner realism; the relationship between object and expression is not a direct one as in the adult. Once we begin to understand the language of the child's graphic expression, we are impressed by how much the child is telling about himself through his drawings, and how worthy they are of our attention, and how revealing they may be of the child's attitudes, feelings, and intellect. The child's drawings are not imitation but personal projection (W. Wolff). The child emphasizes what is important to him and omits or contracts what he considers minor or undesirable.

FIGURE 91

The head is disproportionately large. It is the most important part of the person.

FIGURE 92

The neck is disproportionately long and distorted. A similar device has been used by great artists with striking effect; notably, by El Greco and Modigliani.

This drawing was made by an intelligent boy being treated for idiopathic grand mal epilepsy. The long neck, separating the head from the trunk–mind from body–may be interpreted as symbolizing the boy's anxiety and dissatisfaction with his unruly body.

The Lack of Perspective?

Perspective is defined as the art of picturing objects as they appear to the eye. We have been taught to represent distant objects as smaller, thereby giving the illusion of depth. But are they really smaller? The child knows that the man fifty feet away is just as big as the one five feet away. So why draw one smaller than the other? The child's drawings are not reproductions of an optical image. He uses size to impart emphasis and significance. He draws his concept of the object. His drawing is consequently more meaningful than a faithful reproduction. Objectivity can be achieved by photography. Many true artists use distortion, exaggeration, or reduction to essentials. The child draws the man bigger than the tree in his front yard because to him the man is more significant. For the same reason, we see the person bigger than the house. Medieval artists were not bound by our laws of perspective; in fact, they did not appear to be even aware of them, but this did not prevent them from creating magnificent works of art.

FIGURE 93

Drawn by a boy age nine years. The man is larger than the tree.

FIGURE 94

Drawn by a four and a half year old girl of superior intelligence. The girl is larger than the house.

FIGURE 95

Drawn by a boy of eight. The child is as tall as the tree.

FIGURE 96

Drawn by a girl of six years. A tree, a house, a girl too big to get through the door.

FIGURE 97

There is a seeming lack of perspective in children's drawings. To the child, size is an expression of significance. This is perspective of a different order that is not bound by the rules that guide the adult.

PLATE 5

Chagall, M: At the Easel, from the series. *Mein Leben*, 1922 Collection, The Museum of Modern Art, New York.

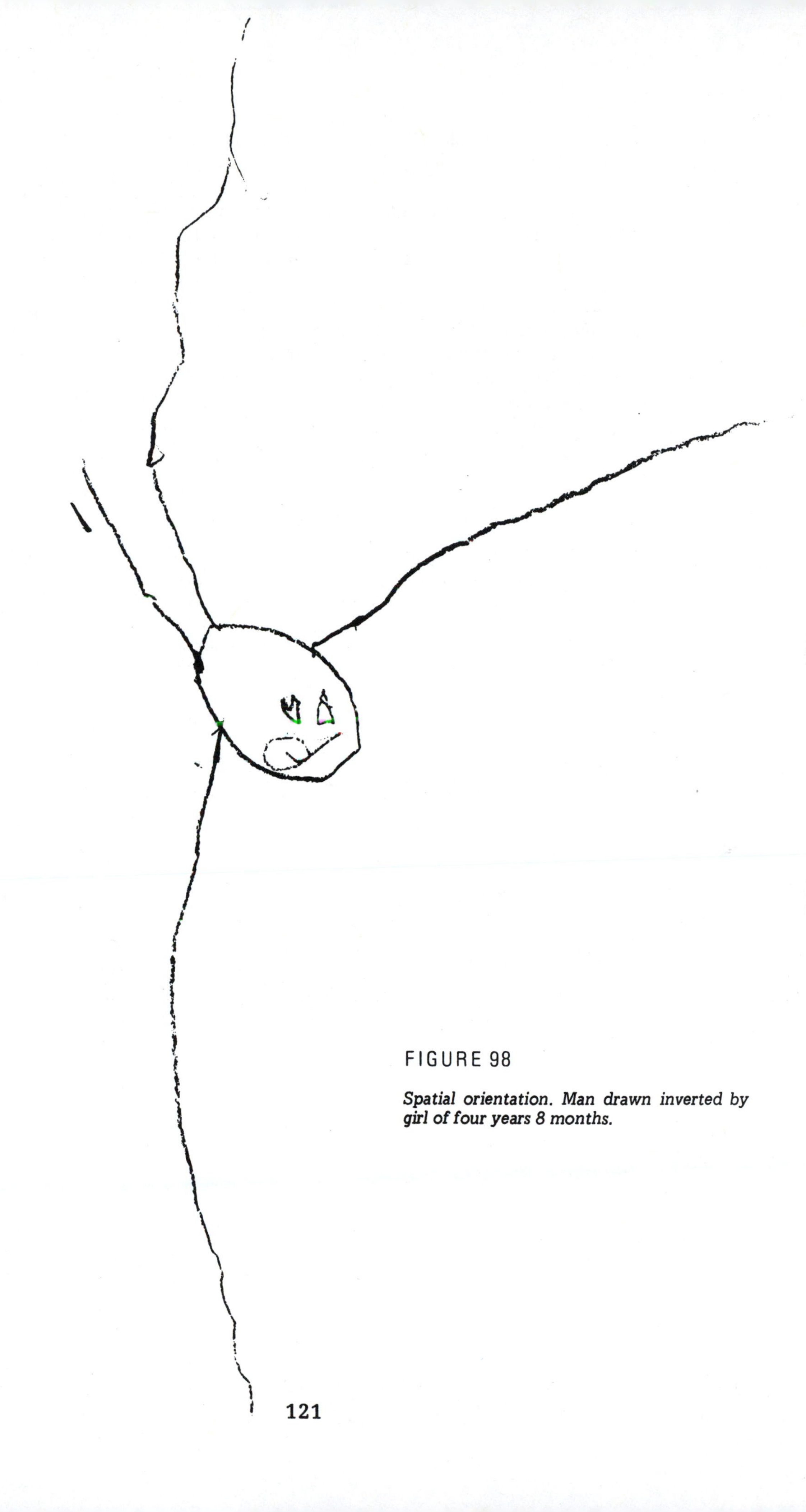

FIGURE 98

Spatial orientation. Man drawn inverted by girl of four years 8 months.

Lack of Spatial Orientation?

Another criticism directed at children's drawings is that they reveal defective concept of space, that the figures are incorrectly oriented in space. Drawings by three and a half and four year olds may indeed show the person drawn upside down or sideways. But this "incorrect" orientation will not be considered to be defective if one is willing to admit that the world may be perceived differently by the child who has not yet been taught how to see it "correctly." Reference will be made in a subsequent chapter to Chagall. Shall we say that he has no sense of spatial orientation because many of his people are upside down or sideways? Is Chagall incorrect in rejecting the conventional rules of spatial orientation for a more subjective, vivid, expressive representation in which all earthly heaviness falls away as his people begin to float? (Plate 5)

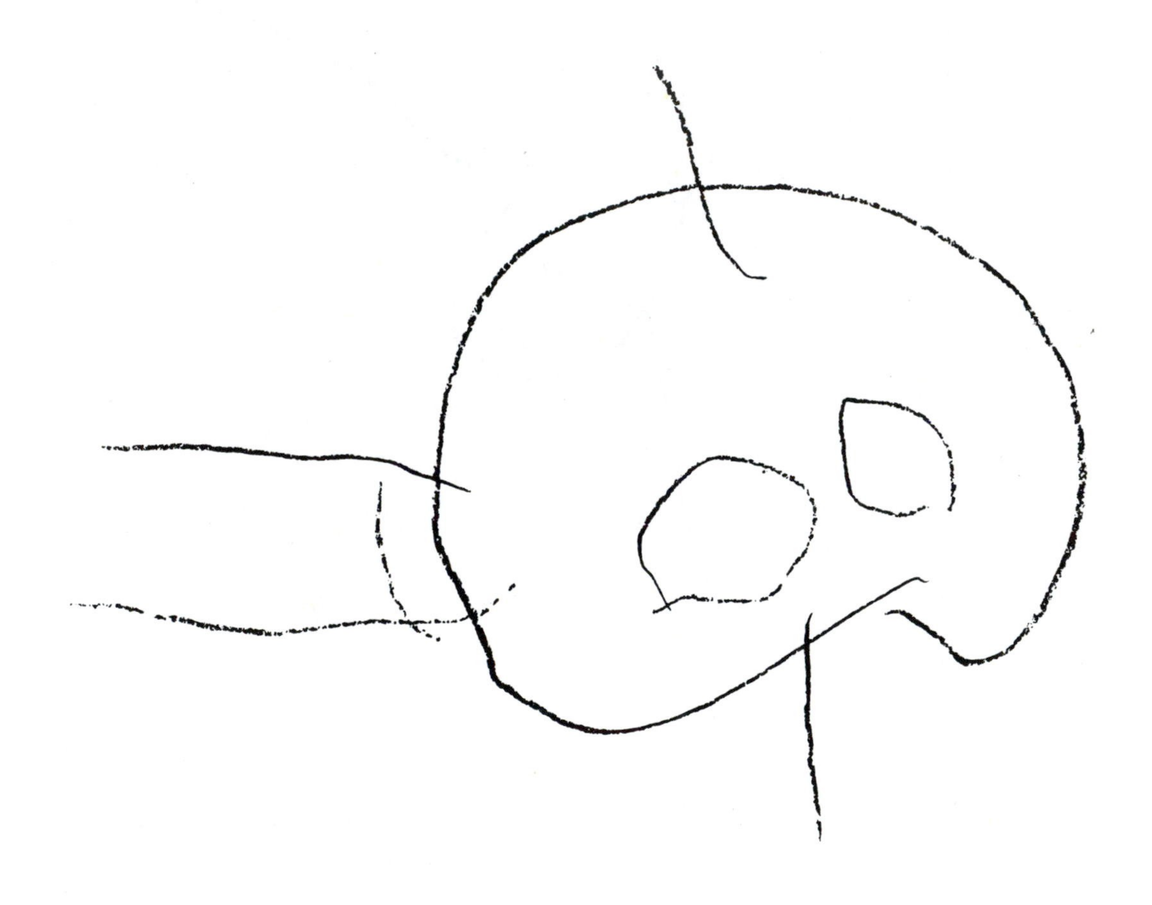

FIGURE 99

Man drawn sideways by boy of four and a half.

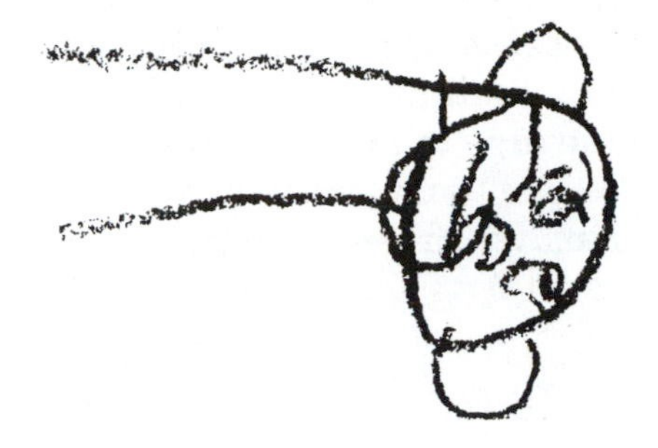

FIGURE 100

Man drawn sideways by boy of three years 5 months.

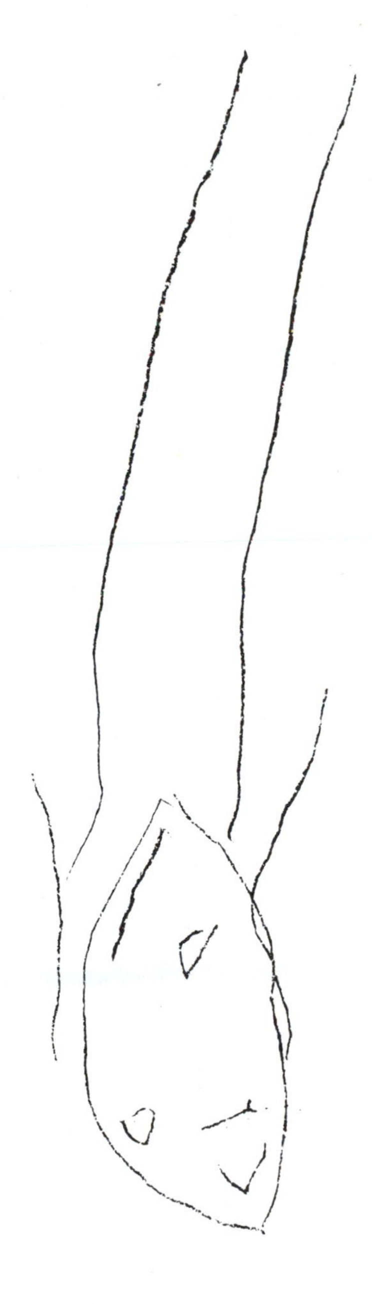

FIGURE 101

Drawing by 4 year-old. No trunk. Man upside down. Started drawing from the head.

No Aesthetic Sense?

The aesthetic sense—interpreted as a capacity to see, hear, feel, appreciate, perhaps to create beauty—is something distinctly human, deep-set, and primal. Its development is influenced by the environment. The sense of rhythm, balance, and symmetry are innate; they are found in all mankind, though not possessed in the same measure by all men. Universal, too, is the urge to express one's self graphically. All children draw, but only a few will eventually impart to their drawings those tactile values and movement, that elusive life—communicating something that Berenson calls the very essence of great Art.

The sense of symmetry can be detected in the child of three. If an adult makes a vertical stroke along one side of the paper, the child may balance it by a symmetrical stroke along the opposite side.

By the time he is four and a half, the child is able to make an aesthetic judgment when presented with three pairs of faces. He will surprise his mother by selecting the prettier of each pair of girls, reflecting the aesthetic standards of his culture.

Is not the aesthetic sense revealed in the child's ability to suggest reality with the greatest economy of means? (W. Wolff).

Paul Klee wrote that children are quite capable of artistic expression and that all of us could learn from them.

Norman C. Meier notes how good art is possible at any age and that "the absence of the trappings of civilization may partly explain the attainment" in young children.

Cizek believed that any child could express his experiences creatively unless stifled by the pedagogy.

Though technically unskilled, the child is gifted with insight. His drawings are expressive of a viewpoint that is fresh and direct. In the opinion of many eminent artists, the drawings are by no means devoid of aesthetic sense. They must not be judged by conventional adult standards any more than one should apply a Renaissance yardstick to Medieval art. Impressionism says little and Expressionism nothing to the Objective Realist. Likewise, children's drawings are meaningless unless one tries to view them in context and as expressions of the child's view of his world. Otherwise, one sees the drawings as lacking sense of proportion, "proper" orientation in space, perspective, and aesthetic sensitivity. True that important parts of the body are missing, that persons may be seen through the walls of a house, that figures may be upside down. Judged by objective adult standards the drawings are certainly defective. But when one approaches the matter with a positive attitude and searches for meanings it will be discovered that the child is expressing another view, another concept, an-

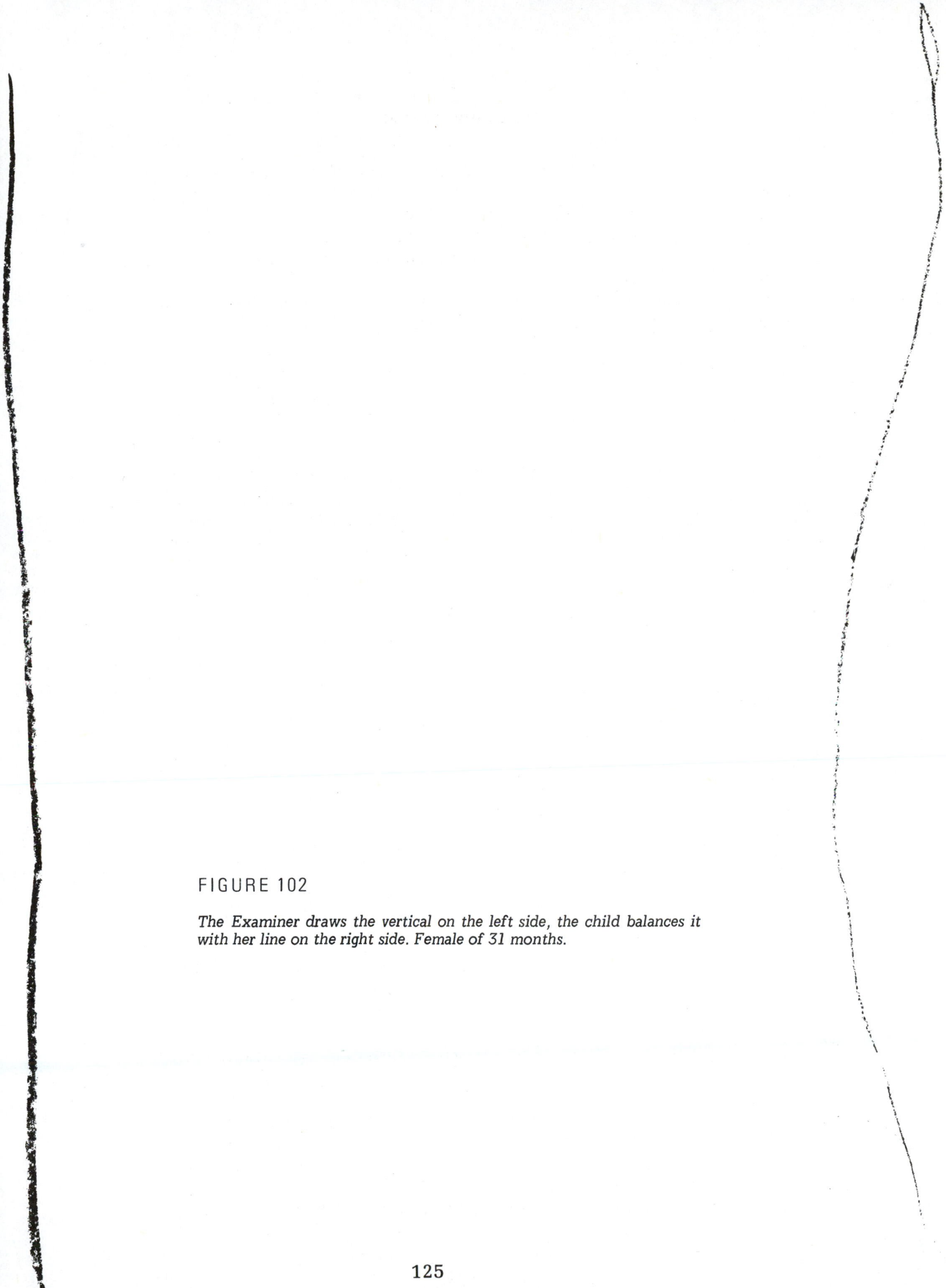

FIGURE 102

The Examiner draws the vertical on the left side, the child balances it with her line on the right side. Female of 31 months.

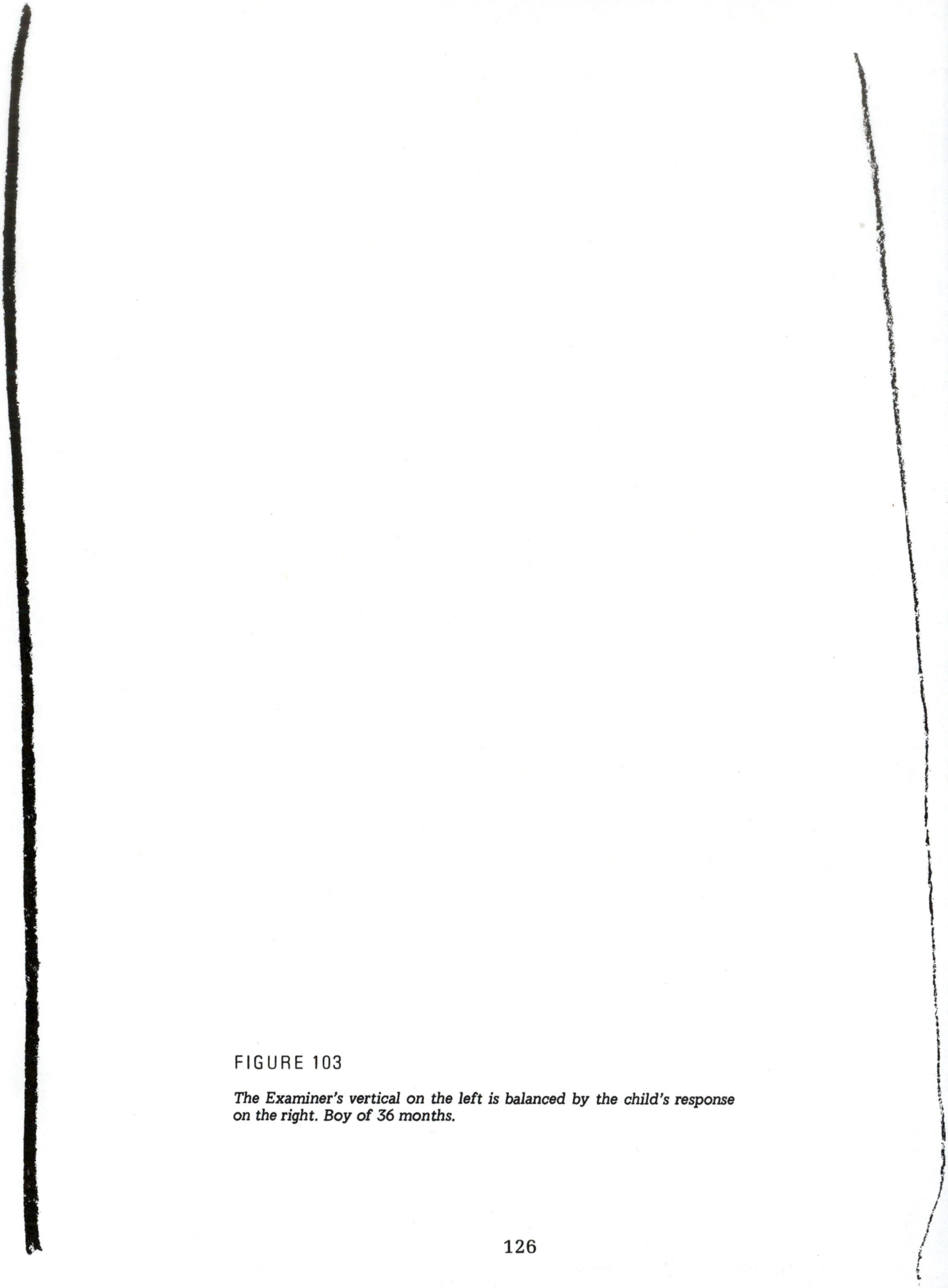

FIGURE 103

The Examiner's vertical on the left is balanced by the child's response on the right. Boy of 36 months.

FIGURE 104

Same 36 month female as on other side of paper. This time she balances the Examiner's horizontal along the upper margin with her own along the lower margin.

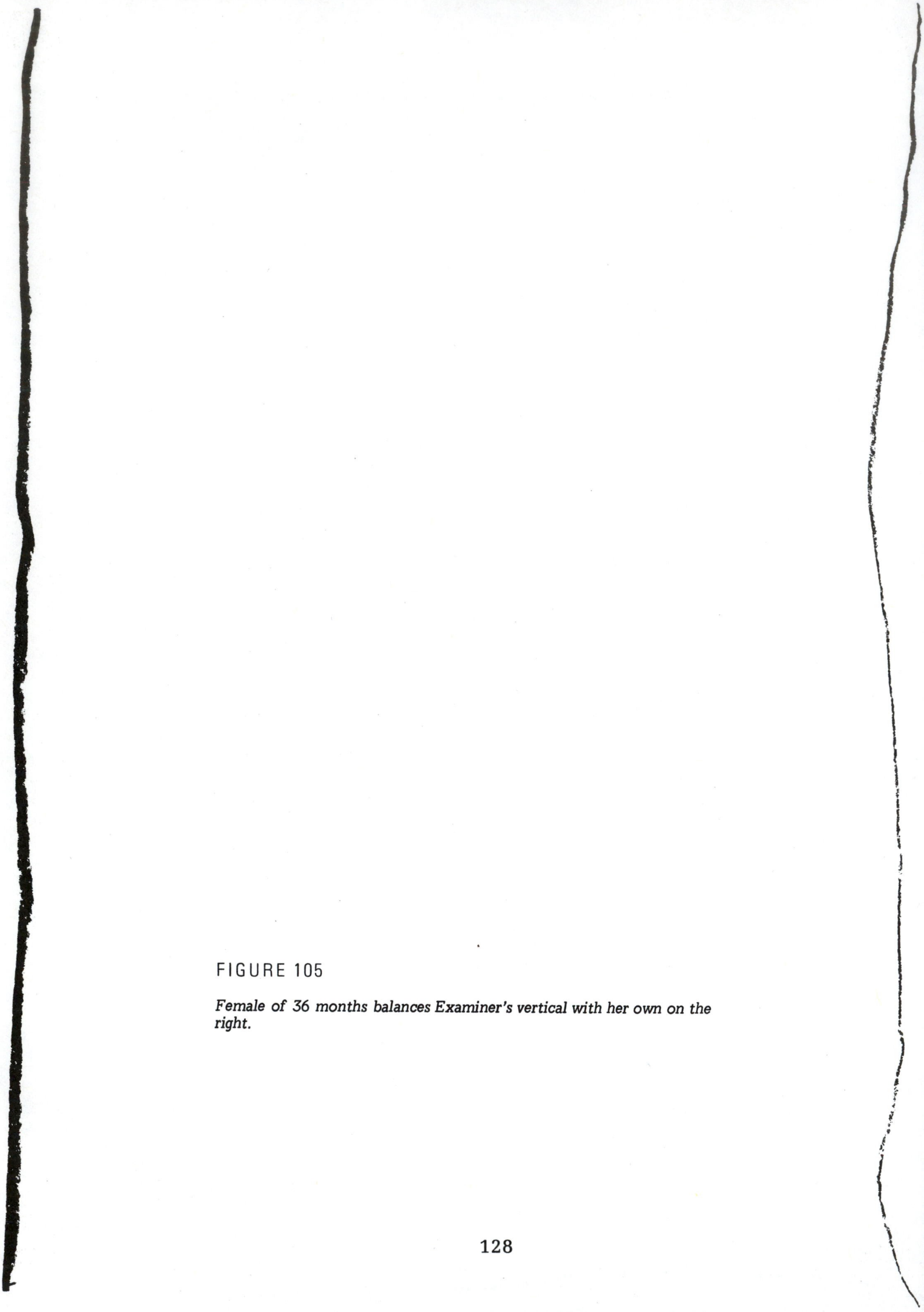

FIGURE 105

Female of 36 months balances Examiner's vertical with her own on the right.

FIGURE 106

Spontaneous drawing in which markings are made symmetrically at the four corners of the paper.

other set of values, stemming from a world in which feelings and imagination have dominant roles. In drawing a person, the child is telling us about himself, not about a man. His proportions, omission, sequences, orientations in space, transparencies, and even the pressure of his earliest strokes are talking to us in language more primal than the spoken word, more natural than the written. Herbert Read considers the essential elements of art to be irrational and intuitive, and that the artist in his creative phases dips down into "a cauldron of timeless and intensely vital entities and in some manner brings to the surface one or more of these entities." The concept is Freudian, the cauldron being the id, with the artist free for the time being from the restricting power of the superego. Similarly, the young child still unrestrained by an undeveloped superego, still close to the origin and realities of Life, still finds the timeless, vital entities readily accessible.

Viewed in this light, the drawings of young children no longer appear defective. The search for meanings reveals the significance of certain peculiarities that far from being meaningless are the expression of a universal mind as yet untutored, still free from the mold into which the culture will try to compress it. The peculiarities cut across all barriers of time, place, and race; they are present in the drawings of all young children no matter when and where. The large head, the conspicuous eyes, the omission of the trunk, the different perspective, proportions, and spatial orientation, these are seen in the drawings of the children of yesterday and today, of deprived and favored, of Caucasoid, Negroid, and Mongolian, for they are the expression of a universal mind, of universal feelings reacting to the important things in life: people, a tree, a house, an animal. After the preschool years, the child will cross the bridge into our world. He must leave childish things behind. He will be told not only how but also what to do, to think, to draw. Creativity, the gift to Everyman, will be stifled. Instead of blank paper and a crayon—an unstructured situation—he will be presented with a coloring book—someone else's drawing—and told to stay within the lines. By this time, his pictorial development will have been arrested. Only those endowed with strong drive and manifest talent will be able to successfully resist the pressure to conform. Grözinger says that as with a lasso, the adult tries to catch the child and pull him over to our side. By now, the reader is certain that this writer is strongly biased. Yes, against coloring books and all forms of interference with free graphic expression by the young child.

DRAWING BEFORE WRITING

14
DRAWING BEFORE WRITING

In 1879, on a visit with her father to the caves at Altamira, a little girl of five suddenly cried out "TORO, TORO!" and discovered prehistoric man's painted ceiling—"the Sistine Chapel of Stone Age Art." Archeologists and art historians are in agreement that this art was not intended as communication but that its purpose was magical; it was almost completely confined to animal representation. Its aim was by creating an image of the animal to gain power over it. These pictures were to be found in hidden places, in caves, not where they could be seen by others. In a way, the child's drawings are similar in that they, too, are a personal affair and not a communication, at least not an intentional one. The use of graphic means for communication begins with the stylization of art during the New Stone Age, a development that is to culminate with historic man's reduction of the picture to a symbol. The basic identity of drawing and writing is inherent in the Greek "graphein" which comprises both drawing and writing and which in our own day is a component of such widely divergent fields as calligraphy, stenography, and iconography.

In attempting to communicate by means other than the human voice, our ancestors resorted to drawing. Pictographs served an immediate and a long-term function. These pictures could be understood by all, for they employed a universal language. The Egyptians devised a system of hieroglyphics in which the picture was barely suggested in a symbolic figure that could serve to convey ideas as well as mere facts. Further cultural evolution of the human species resulted in the development of writing by the use of symbols which could be deciphered only by the educated.

These developments of writing in the race are paralleled by their development in the individual. The child of three begins to discover in his random markings a suggestion of something in his environment. Increasing control over the medium will permit him to gradually express graphically his interests and concepts by drawing pictures. At five or six he learns to use symbols. He learns to print his name and to use the symbols for communication. As he becomes more adept at expressing himself by writing, the avid interest in drawing tends to decrease. There occurs a parting of the ways as only the artistically gifted will persist in further developing their graphic skill. The others, without special talent, will abandon drawing and only when writing has become an accomplished fact and taken for granted, may they begin to decorate the margins and inside covers of their school books with a variety of figures, doodles, and arabesques, deliberately or unconsciously created. Biographies of great artists tell of no falling off of interest in drawing. Possessed by the Spirit of Art, they evolved as intellectual maturity added depth and insight to brilliance. It is interesting to note that musical genius has manifested itself in early childhood—Mozart is an outstanding example—while masterpieces of visual art are all the work of mature individuals. The drawings of children may tell us many things but not who among them will become the great artist—not until the intellect has been more fully developed.

Drawing and writing, two forms of graphic activity, related but different in origin—the first expressive the other communicative—are both valuable indices of the child's psychological development. Both can contribute to our understanding of the developing child. Both may reveal his intellectual or perceptual difficulties.

FIGURE 107

Spontaneous drawing by girl age 46 months. Attends nursery school in institution. Left-handed. Drawing is imitative of writing.

FIGURE 108

Spontaneous graphic activity by a girl of four years. She said she was writing the Examiner's name and the names of other persons. Foster-child.

FIGURE 109

Spontaneous graphic activity by a boy of three years 3 months. First attempts at printing.

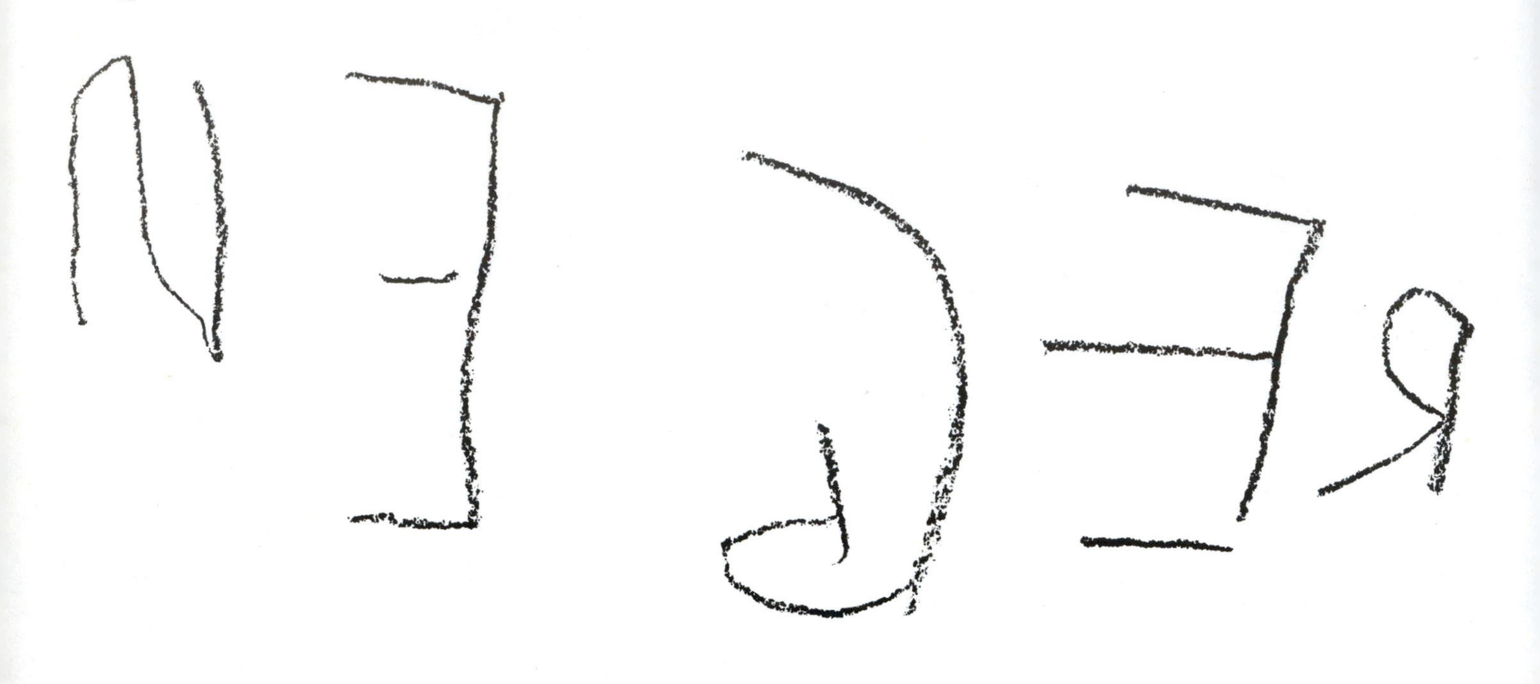

FIGURE 110

"Mirror writing" by a bright boy of 4 years 6 months. Left-handed. Direction of printing: from right to left.

FIGURE 111

Bright boy. Mirror writing. Crossed dominance: Scores above age on Goodenough Draw-a-man test. Chronological age four years 4 months. Left-handed, right-eyed.

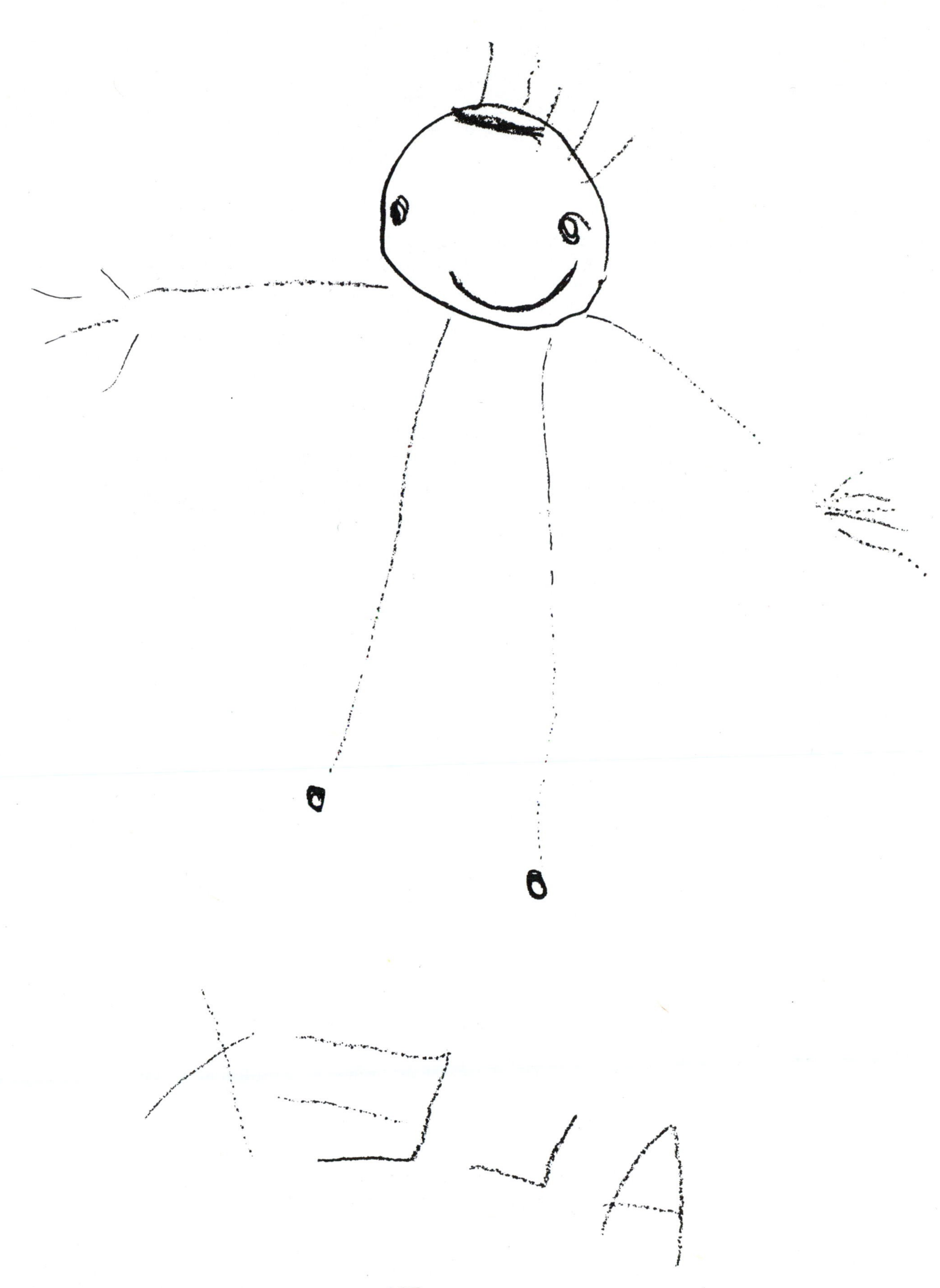

15

DEVELOPMENT OF GRAPHIC EXPRESSION IN MANKIND AND IN THE INDIVIDUAL

Recapitulation

Though often discredited, the recapitulation theory of G. Stanley Hall has a way of reappearing in diverse guises whenever organic or cultural evolution is discussed. It is an attractive, fascinating formulation which sees the ancestral history of the race reproduced condensed in the development of the individual "Ontogeny recapitulates phylogeny. Every animal in its individual history or ontogeny climbs up its own genealogical tree." Originally intended for structural and biological evolution, the theory has been extended to cover cultural evolution as well. Structurally, as well as culturally, there are facts that seem to support the theory. Viewed organically, the person begins life as a single cell and passes prenatally through stages of development that are similar to those of his subhuman ancestors. But critical analysis of the apparently striking analogies reveals differences so basic that only in its broadest sense can the theory be accepted as having any validity. For at no time is man an amoeba, a fish, a reptile, or a subhuman mammal even though he is progressively unicellular, aquatic; even though he will crawl on his belly like a reptile and subsequently creep on all fours before he stands and strides like a man. From the very beginning, his DNA bore the stamp of humanity as it destined him to fashion tools, to ask "why", to admire beauty and to create it, to strive to realize his dream of a better world.

Nor does the growing child really repeat during his development the stages of cultural change that fill the wide gap separating modern man from his remote cave-dwelling ancestors. Nor can he be identified with contemporary humans living under primitive conditions. Though there be similarities in the graphic expressions of the uncivilized and the young, untutored child, the differences are so basic that analogy is more attractive than valid.

What are the similarities and what the differences?

Similarities

The expression is fresh, direct, vital, and reduced to essentials. The subject matter depicts what is most significant. It is a representation not a reproduction. It is drawn from a mental impression and not from a model. It is expressive and emotionally motivated rather than communicative. In both instances, it expresses the interests, and also the feelings of the "artists."

In both primitive man and child, art appears to have had a common accidental origin. Just as our cave-dwelling ancestor saw in an artifact in the wall a curve that suggested the hindquarters of a bison stirred in him an urge to complete the picture; so, too, does our child of today suddenly perceive in his casual scribble the outline of a head and from then on, he will draw by design what he had portrayed by chance.

The Differences

But does a similarity necessarily mean the same thing? There is an over-all similarity in that both child and primate man draw what is most significant. But the subject matter is quite different. Children draw persons; primitive man drew animals. One study by Maitland, another by Lukens and others (cited by Anastasi & Foley) estimate the frequency with which human beings appear in children's drawings at about 75 per cent whereas animals appear in about 7 per cent. The reverse is probably true for primitive man.

The drawings of children, like those of our remote ancestors are strikingly direct, fresh and vital. The analogy cannot be carried further. The paleolithic paintings in the caves of Altamira and Lascaux are truly artistic and reveal a mastery of technique totally lacking in the crudely drawn forms of the child.

In drawing his predominant subject, a person, the child emphasizes the head by exaggerating its size. On the rare occasions when paleolithic man included human beings in his scenes, the heads were small, just a ball surmounting a crude stick figure. Incidentally, this crude elemental portrayal of the human figure is in sharp contrast to the strikingly fine portrayal of the animal forms.

In both child and early man fantasy and emotion play their roles but in different contexts. The paintings of the caves, located in places where no one might easily find them, seem to have had a religious significance. Animals were the fears and needs of man. Man was a hunter. Many scenes are devoted to the hunt. Bison, deer, horses, and wild boars are represented with artistic stylization yet with zoological accuracy. In the child, graphic activity does not have the same magico-totemistic significance; it is more an expression of play, and that is the work of children.

In brief, the often referred to similarity between the child and his earliest ancestors would, if it were demonstrated, equate our early years with the early ages of the species, another way of saying that ontogeny recapitulates phylogeny. Closer examination, however, shows the similarities to be more apparent than real, and the differences to be substantive.

The Development of Graphic Expression in History and in the Individual: Similarities and Differences

The development of art is closely related to cultural, religious, social, and political changes, in a word, to history. Art is in fact an expression of the historical climate prevailing at a given time. From its apparently accidental origins in the caves of Lascaux and Altamira, the art of Western man has evolved through the stylization of the Egyptians who represented what they knew, to the Grecian mastery of synthesizing the best of what they saw into an ideal of unsurpassed beauty, then to the Medieval artists who ignoring what they saw conveyed the sacred message with a symbolism so inspiring that their product itself took on some of the spirituality of the subject represented, culminating in the ikon with its rigidly dogmatic concept of art. Another thousand years were to pass before artists would awaken to the observation of nature. A different perception of the world led to the realism of the Renaissance, the rediscovery of beauty in Man and his world. And so on to the vagaries, glories and fiascos of the Modern Age.

These currents have their points of similarity with certain phases in the development of graphic activity in the child, especially regarding those periods during which artistic expression was less concerned with objective reality and more with its symbolic representation. No value judgment is intended. Artistic perfection has been achieved in many styles. A work cannot be properly evaluated in terms of another style, another historical context. While similarities are sometimes striking, they do not attain the level of analogy. There is danger of being overly impressed by similarities to a degree that ignores substantial differences.

Like the Egyptians

While resisting the view that the maturing child recapitulates in ontogeny the cultural as well as the biological development of the race, this writer is impressed by certain similarities with the art of the ancient Egyptians. Underlying the art of this highly civilized, sophisticated people and that of the untutored child there seems to be the same basic principle that gives graphic expression not to what can be seen but rather to what is known to exist. What are the characteristics of Egyptian art that are perpetuated in that of today's young children? These are most strikingly apparent in figure drawings. The parts of the body are shown from their most evident aspect: though the face be in profile, the arms and trunk are in frontal view; the feet always in profile usually pointing in the same direction; the importance of a figure is expressed by emphasizing it, by making it larger, so that the king is greater (larger) than the queen, and the queen larger than the diminutive (insignificant) servants. There is no objective reality. Foreshortening was unknown to the Egyptians. In a profile of the face, the eye is in full frontal view. All parts were represented in their most clearly visible aspect. The Egyptians based their art on rigid formulas which were adhered to with remarkable persistence and conservatism. This is not surprising, since their art was predominantly religious in nature and was destined for their temples and tombs. This formalism spreading beyond the frontiers of Egypt into Crete influenced artistic expression until it was broken by the Greek masters with their discovery of foreshortening, enabling them to portray what they saw from where they saw it. The earliest examples of foreshortening are in Greek vases of about 500 B. C. As Gombrich has pointed out "in all the thousands of Egyptian and Assyrian works which have come down to us, nothing of that kind had ever happened...."

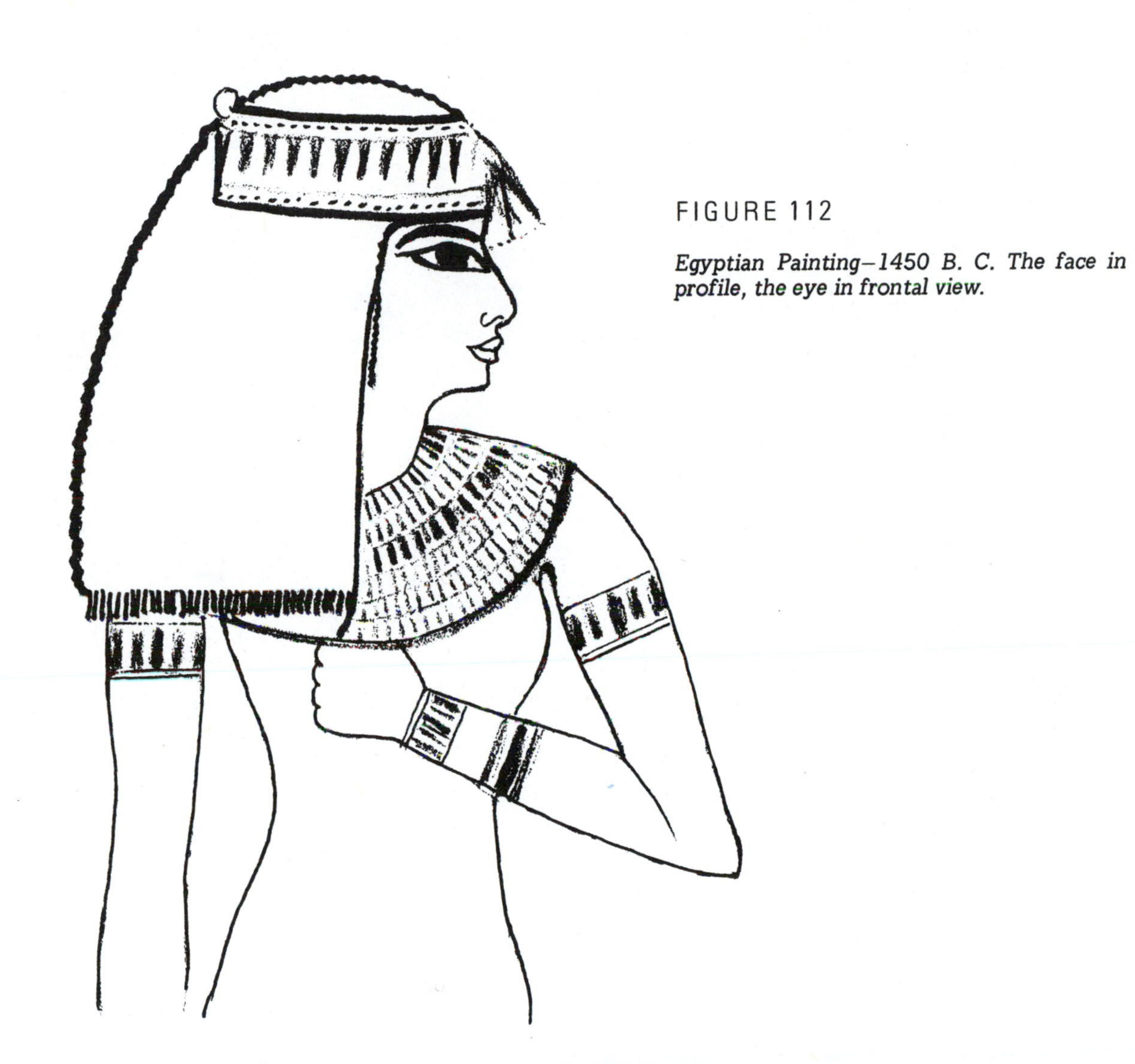

FIGURE 112

Egyptian Painting—1450 B. C. The face in profile, the eye in frontal view.

drawn by the author

FIGURE 113

Like the Egyptians, face in profile, full-face eye.

FIGURE 114

Profile of face, frontal view of arms and torso, side view of feet. Drawn by boy of 11 years in sixth grade near the top of his class.

FIGURE 115

Egyptian Painting—V Dynasty about 2490 B. C. Head in profile, eye in frontal view, shoulders, trunk, arms in frontal view, legs and feet in profile. The parts of the body are represented in their clearest aspect, as they are known to be, not as they are seen at a given moment from a given place.

drawn by the author

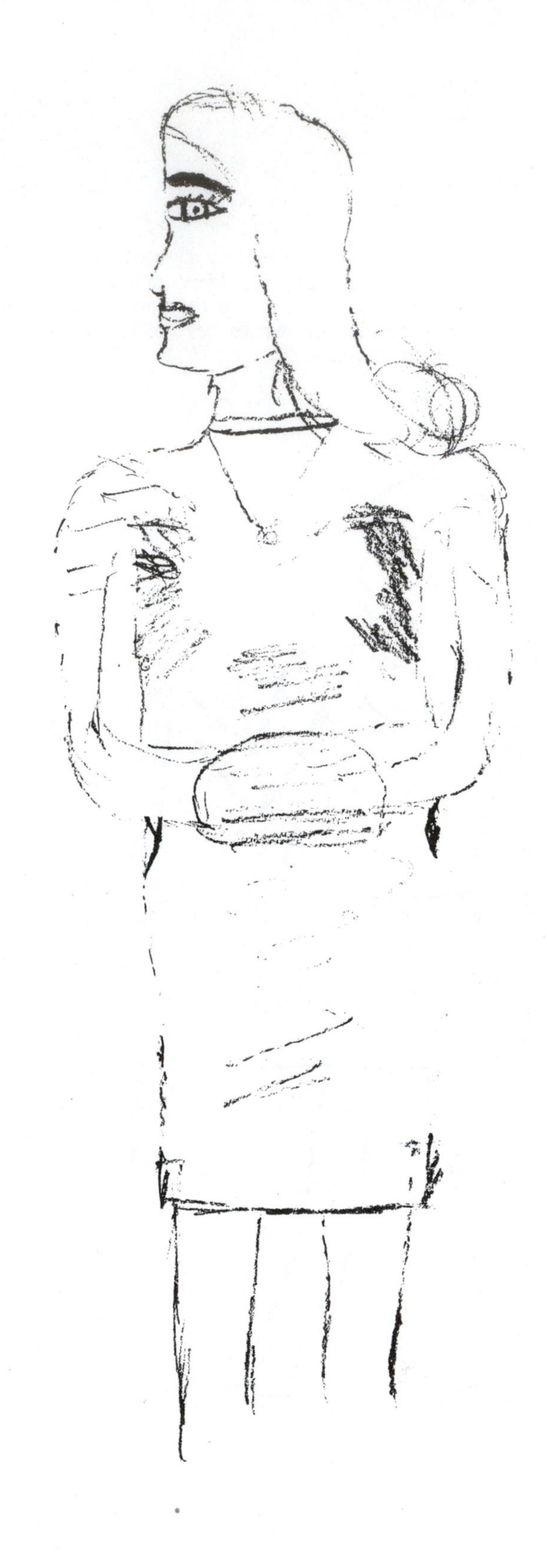

FIGURE 116

Face in profile, eye in strict frontal view, arms and trunk in frontal view. Drawn by a boy, age fourteen years 10 months.

PLATE 6

Egyptian: XI-XII dynasty Stela of the Count Indy. The Metropolitan Museum of Art, Rogers Fund, 1925
Importance represented by size: wife smaller than husband; servant tiny.

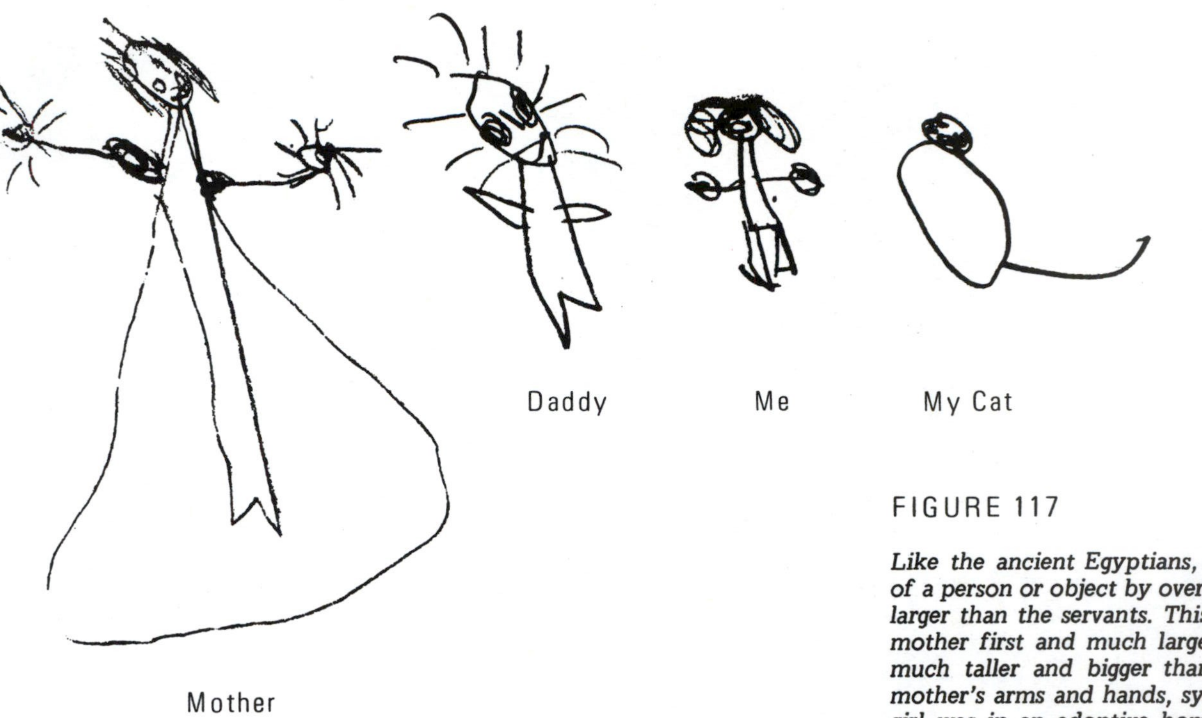

FIGURE 117

Like the ancient Egyptians, the child tends to express the importance of a person or object by over-emphasizing. The Egyptians drew the king larger than the servants. This child of six years draws her domineering mother first and much larger than daddy, who is reality is physically much taller and bigger than mother. Note also the emphasis on the mother's arms and hands, symbols of power and aggression. This little girl was in an adoptive home and had to be removed because of the poor relationship between mother and child. This drawing is an eloquent expression of the problem. Age of child: six years 2 months.

FIGURE 118

Importance represented by size. Subjective concept of body image. Only four years 7 months but draws himself larger than his brother who is eight years 3 months. Currently, 1967, the artist is a bright assertive, highly verbal, creative child of ten. The youngest and one of the smallest in the 6th grade but a leader. He is very affectionately attached to mother and in good, warm rapport with the other family members. Enjoys life and manages to have things his way, generally. Note how he has made mother first, himself next to her and larger than his older siblings.

My Family (1961)

Mother | Me 4 Yrs. 7 Mos. | Eddie 8 Yrs. 3 Mos. | Suzy 11 Yrs. 10 Mos. | Daddy

Unlike The Greeks

The transition from the rigidly stylized art of the Egyptians with their full-face eye planted in a profile and their full-front torso and side-view of the feet, was finally effected by the Greeks in the fifth century B.C. Now the art is lifelike, their gods and goddesses almost breathe. The harmony, refinement, and beauty of this art have never been surpassed. But this development marks the parting of the ways with the art of Egypt and with that of the young child. The threads uniting children's art with that of civilized man will be resumed again during a period when art again becomes rigid and formalized and subservient to the image itself.

Childhood and the Middle Ages

The council of Nicea meeting in 787 attempted to settle once and for all the question of whether images could be used in Christian churches or whether their use was not a carryover from the idolatrous practices of the Hellenistic world. Dissension became acute over the significance, indeed over the propriety of ikons, and erupted in what is known as the Iconoclastic Controversy. The Council in proclaiming the value of images as effective media for the instruction of the faithful intended to clarify its purpose and to support the charge of idolatry levelled at those who endowed the images with intrinsic holiness and power. In the Eastern Church the only images allowed had to be stylized according to set formulas. Within the narrow restrictions imposed, artists succeeded in creating magnificent mosaics which adorn the walls of Hagia Sophia in Istanbul, San Vitale in Ravenna, the cathedral at Monreale, and the jewel that is the Cappella Palatina in Palermo. No statues were permitted. A much freer interpretation of the Nicean Councils formulation prevailed in the Western Church.

Rigid, unrealistic, and formalized, Byzantine art expresses religious symbolism and feeling as never before or since. Its symbolic nature and unconcern with the real shapes of things, its lack of perspective, the way figures are planted in frontal view all remind us of children's drawings. Similar, too, is the lack of any attempt at portraiture, so that the child, like the Medieval artist, distinguishes his figures by the name that he will print underneath each.

While these features invite comparison, one must not carry the analogy too far. A similar effect may have quite different causes. The Medieval artist's motive was to communicate and to instruct; the child has no such purpose though he may be telling us a good deal about himself.

The Byzantine artist's approach is direct and clear. Only essentials are represented. The aim is to convey the sacred message to the illiterate masses. The child's representation is also direct and clear and shorn of superfluities. But the Byzantine mosaics are the work of gifted, highly skilled artists whose simplicity is deliberate and sophisticated, and whose use of foreshortening, shadows, color, and treatment of draping reveal the Greek and Roman influences from which they cannot disengage themselves. This classical heritage is totally absent in the drawings of the untutored child.

Yet, despite these reservations, the fact remains that the actual observation of nature that characterizes the art of classical antiquity is set aside by the Medieval artists until the great awakening 1000 years later in the Florentine Renaissance. It is precisely in the lack of any attempt to check their work against objective reality that a common bond exists between the symbolism of the Byzantine masters and symbolism of the child.

FIGURE 119

Drawing of his family by a boy, age 10 years 9 months.

FIGURE 120

Drawing of his family by a boy age nine years 8 months. Full-face and lined up like medieval saints. Rigid, unrealistic, formalized. Distinguishable by the name printed underneath each figure.

FIGURE 121

Drawing of her family by a girl of eight years. Lined up in strict frontal view.

Renaissance

The rebirth that from Florence was to spread over the countries of Western Europe influenced every aspect of thought and action. Drawing its inspiration from the philosophers, dramatists, writers, and artists of classical antiquity, it strove to create a realistic image of Man. Observation, objectivity, correct representation of the human form, the discovery of the laws of perspective, perceived and expressed by a stunning flowering of genius have given to the world a priceless heritage. This magnificent era in the history of art has no corresponding phase in the child's graphic development. Renaissance art is an expression of a refined, cultivated mentality that can have no parallel in the nature-bound thinking of the young child. Renaissance artists combined science with art in their detailed study of anatomy and in their great attention to correct human proportions. And yet, their realism is not photographic. The intangible qualities of great art speak out from the works of the masters.

Recapitulation in ontogeny—to a point, but with many gaps. An engaging theory, but not to be accepted without reservation. "Se non è vero, è ben trovato."

Modern Primitives

Weary of the hollowness of modern mechanized life, many gifted modern artists have turned to the vivid fantasy of children in an attempt to recapture the essence of life as perceived through the innocent eye. Convinced that *"qui peut le plus peut le moins,"* they set out deliberately to forget what they had accumulated since childhood and to shed the accretions of a civilization that obscured "the greater reality."

"The things which I have seen I now can see no more" (W. Wordsworth). Paul Klee regarded the drawings of young children as visual documents wherein lay concealed the secret of childhood, which, once deciphered, could lead us back to the wonderland of spontaneous poetic creation.

Wassily Kandinsky believed that the artist, who in many ways resembles the child, could attain to the "inner core of things" more easily than other men. He coined the term "greater reality" to express the naive vision.

Paul Gauguin, gifted also as a writer, gave verbal as well as graphic expression to his credo. Reacting to a statement by a horse fancier that, thanks to photography, painters had at long last come to understand the action of the horse, Gauguin, who detested the optical realism of photography, wrote: "As for me, I have drawn back, beyond the horses of the Parthenon, back to the rocking horse of my childhood."

To a degree, the "naive artists" succeeded in transcribing graphically a vision strikingly similar to that of the innocent eye of the child. With studied artlessness, they produced delightfully charming works of art. Notable examples of this trend are paintings by Rousseau, Klee, Miro, Gauguin, and Chagall, while sculpture is eminently represented by Constantin Brancusi. But can one really eliminate learning, training, and experience? Can one really reenter the world of childhood? Things are not so simple. It is not within the power of man to forget, much less to eliminate from the deeper recesses of one's mind the innumerable events and influences that separate the man from the child. The vision of the adult cannot be innocent; it is modified by unconscious forces.

Among the modern primitives, Chagall stands out as having been especially successful in resisting the academic compulsion that has stifled creativity in so many artistically gifted students. Rejecting the influence of schools and "isms", he has retained the clear vision of the innocent eye to a considerable degree. Like his friend, J. Maritain, Chagall believes that the artist does not produce his work for people. Neither does the young child.

In several of his works (Death 1908), Chagall discards perspective foreshortening in favor of vital expression, making the dominant background figures larger than the closer but less important ones. He uses color for emotional effect and not to reproduce optical reality, as in "Banks of the Seine" (1953) in which his mother and child have red bodies, she has violet hair, and the Chagallian cow-like animal is green. His soaring figures are not bound to earth by gravity. In the art of children, color, orientation in space, and neglect of the laws of perspective and gravity are similarly, though unintentionally, used for expressive purpose. The child will express love for his mother by coloring her "beautiful" which may be with the serenity of a blue face and green hair.

Chagall's work, like that of the child, has a liberating effect from the tyranny of time and space. It expresses a greater reality and that is why "children and lovers most readily find access to Chagall's pictures as manifestations of their world" (W. Erben).

Another trend in modern art is to go even beyond those artists mentioned by eliminating all representational elements and returning to the even more primitive stage of kinesthetic drawing. The works of these "action painters" are at times indistinguishable from the scribblings of the very young. This writer has shown three action drawings made with "magic markers" to interested adults, requesting that they select among the three the one made by an adult. The selection made, it was then revealed that all three were the work of children, whose ages were two years 9 months, three, and three years 10 months.

Understandably, the quest for "the greater reality" goes on. Enough of the child remains in most of us to intimate where the treasure lies hidden. The search is worthwhile.

quand nous ne sommes plus enfants, nous sommes deja morts.
C. Brancusi.

16

MALE AND FEMALE: THE AWARENESS OF SEX

The first and most consistent item selected to indicate sex is the hair. Even in 1968, the young child continues to express his concept of sex differences by adorning the female figure with long or more abundant hair. The present tendency to obliterate this differentiating feature has not affected the traditional concept. There is no telling what may happen if long hair becomes more universal and abiding. In discussing the evolution of the human figure (Chapter 7), mention was made of the fact that the genitalia are rarely represented in children's drawings, even in those by the most uninhibited children. One shall have to look for the symbols of sex in lieu of its outright "graffitic" representation. As will be seen from the drawings that follow, differences in clothing are generally the ways in which further differentiation of the sexes is represented by the young child. The widespread addition of trousers to the female wardrobe explains their presence on both parents in one of the drawings. Here, too, there is no certainty that the dress will remain as a sexual symbol in the child's concept of femininity. At the time of this writing, the skirt is approaching the vanishing point. Only an heroic action by some prestigious fashion designer can save it as ornament and symbol. The hat and tie are currently used to adorn the male figure. After age five or six, most children enter a period of latency unless events have occurred to disturb the modus vivendi with which the Oedipal strivings are temporarily resolved. Machover has found that the drawings of children who have been consistently repressed reveal a great deal of sexual agitation during what would ordinarily be the latency period. She tells how in one child's drawings, the libidinized role of the hair was unmistakably portrayed by having a baby come out of it. The drawings by older children have been included to show how they express interest and preoccupation with sex. Girls tend to draw the male first. Cultural influences are obvious in drawings by preteen and teen-age children.

In line with her earlier attainment of puberty, the girl's drawings tend to show evidences of sexual and social awareness at an earlier age than the boy's. Attention to the crotch area, zippers on trousers, shading over the genital area are some of the more obvious manifestations of sex interest.

Towards the end of the latency period, boys will often reveal contained hostility and aggression in their selection of articles with which they adorn their figures: guns, knives, swords.

The ability to verbalize one's sex is generally established at age three, when in response to the question "are you a little boy or a little girl?" the boy will answer correctly. (In asking a girl, the order of questioning is reversed in order not to be misled by those children who may simply be repeating the last word of the question). The following are the usual answers given when the examiner on being given the correct answer asks "Why?"
"Because" is very common at age three.

Other replies between ages two years, nine months and four years were:
"'cause I'm three"
"I don't know"
"Because my mommy said so"
"Because I want to be a big boy"

The following reasons were given between ages four and five:
"Because I have a dress on"
"Because I'm a boy"
"Because I'm the same as mommy"

Between ages five and six the replies were often:
"Because God made me a girl"
"Because I have a dress; boys don't have dresses"
"Because I like boys" (boy speaking)

In young school children between the ages of six and nine the replies varied as follows:
"Because I have long hair"
"Because I want to be" (male twin). "Because I skip on the sidewalk" (female twin, 7 1/2 years)
"Because I can have more fun with my friend's boat"
"I don't know"
"Because God made me a boy"
"Because God made me that way"
"Because God wants me to be a little girl"

Many assertive boys will answer the question, "Are you a little boy or a little girl?" by stating "a big boy." One little boy of two years, seven months replied, "Nobody." Most children between two and three will reply by giving their first name: "I'm Bobby."

FIGURE 122

"MAN" Drawn by a girl of five years 9 months; note trousers, tie, and hat. The figure of a woman on the following page has long hair, a ribbon and a dress. She has shown her preference for the female by embellishing the picture with flowers, radiant sun, and a tree.

FIGURE 123

FIGURE 124

"Man" drawn by a girl of six years 7 months. On the reverse she has drawn a "lady". The only difference is in the hair with which she has adorned the female figure.

FIGURE 125

FIGURE 126

"MAN" drawn by a boy of six years 10 months. On the reverse, he has drawn a "lady". The sex difference is indicated by the longer hair of the female figure.

FIGURE 127

FIGURE 128

Drawn by a girl of six years 10 months. Sex of figure is indicated by the long hair.

FIGURE 129

Drawn by a girl of seven, functioning in the high average range. Sex differences are represented by different treatment of hair and by traditional differences in clothing: pants and dress.

FIGURE 130

FIGURE 131

This drawing of a male and that on the following page of a female show considerable awareness of sex differences. The artist is a girl of superior intelligence. Seven years, 1 month.

FIGURE 132

FIGURE 133

This and the drawing of a female are by a girl age seven years 4 months of superior intelligence.

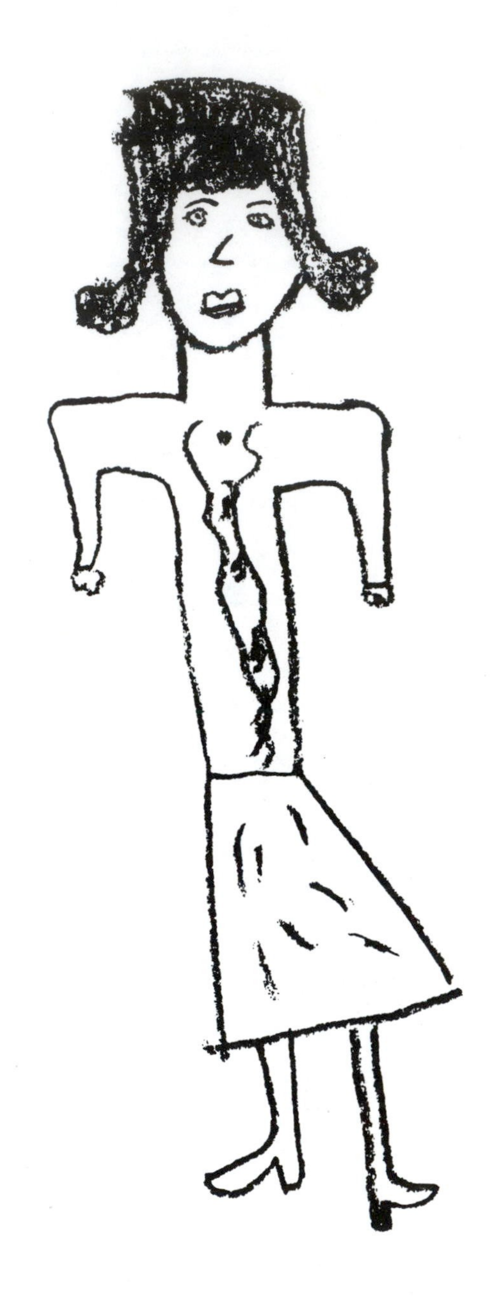

FIGURE 134

FIGURE 135

G. G., a bright girl of seven and a half, has drawn a picture of her family. Note zipper on the male figure and also his full lips. The second figure has long hair and breasts. The large figure represents mother; she has abundant hair and shading over the genital area. The fourth figure is the child herself: "my behind is sticking out". Mother has been drawn disproportionately large; she is an authoritarian figure with whom the child is in conflict.

FIGURE 136

Drawn by a boy of seven years 7 months. This figure and that of a female on the following page are distinguished by the shape and length of hair.

FIGURE 137

FIGURE 138

Sex difference is indicated by different treatment of hair: curly hair for girls, straight hair for boys. Chronological age: seven years 11 months. He has omitted himself from the family group of children and has drawn himself on the reverse side of the paper, isolated. This child is functioning below capacity at school. He is disruptive and is getting remedial reading. His drawing supports the view that he is lacking in self-esteem.

Me

FIGURE 139

FIGURE 140

Male and female figures by a boy of seven years 10 months. Sex difference is indicated primarily by the hair length. Both wear pants.

FIGURE 141

Drawing of a man.

FIGURE 142

The female has a different hat and high heels. Drawn by a boy of nine years 4 months.

FIGURE 143

Male figure by a boy of nine years 8 months. His drawing of the female is distinguished by longer hair and a dress. The man has a hat.

FIGURE 144

FIGURE 145

The artist is a girl of ten years one month. Bright. The figure is unmistakably male.

FIGURE 146

This drawing of a man has a beard. It is also more elaborate and at a higher level than the boy's drawing of a female on the following page. This boy of 10 years 6 months is obese (compensatory gratification) and resists direction from mother.

FIGURE 147

FIGURE 148

Sex differences are obvious (hair, body contour, clothing). Drawn by a boy age thirteen years 4 months.

FIGURE 149

FIGURE 150

This drawing and the female figure are by a boy of thirteen years 8 months.

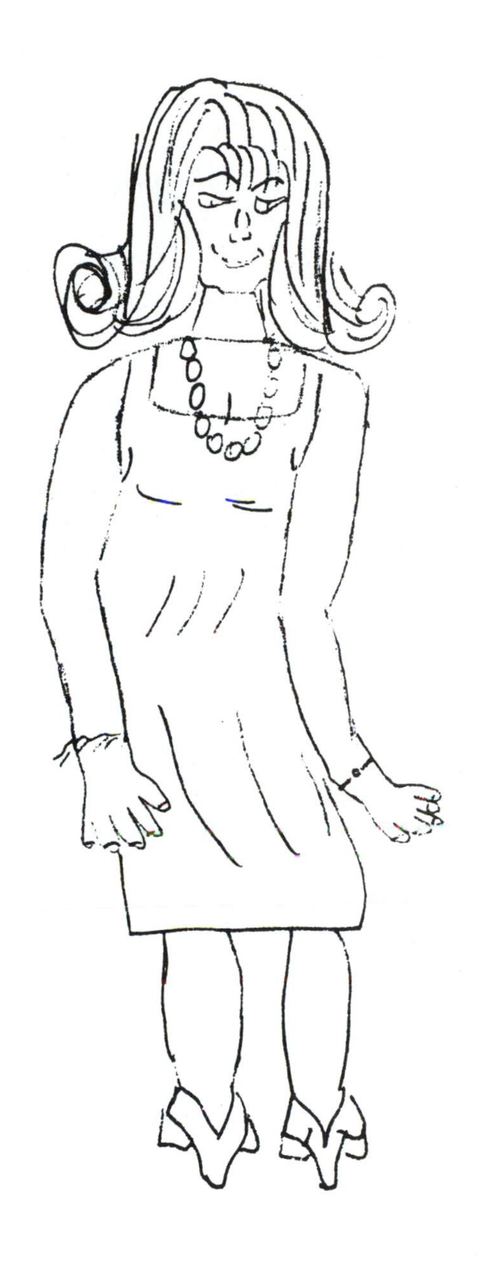

FIGURE 151

Part Two

THE UNUSUAL AND DEVIANT

17

DRAWINGS AS DIAGNOSTIC AIDS: DRAWING THE FAMILY

> Normal children are basically all alike; each abnormal child is abnormal in his own way. (With apologies to Leo Tolstoy for this paraphrase of his unforgettable opening to Anna Karenina.)

Thus far in this volume, an attempt has been made to present material that expresses the basic unity of mankind during the early years, before the universal mind of the child has been modified by the many and varied cultural influences that tend to deviate and even destroy the natural bonds that unite child to child and that find vivid expression in the universal sequences and similarities of graphic representation.

Yet, even within this universal kingdom of early childhood, damaging influences may have been at work altering the normal course of development. These influences may have been intrinsic or environmental, prenatal, circumnatal or postnatal, man-made or unavoidable, resulting in a variety of abnormal conditions that render the child different from the normal and different from other abnormal children but still a child like every other. It is to a consideration of abnormalities as they are manifested in drawings that the remainder of this volume will be directed.

The greater share of space has gone to a presentation of normative drawing behavior in the conviction that a familiarity with what most children do will make the observer more sensitive to deviations. The writer is well aware that discussion in depth of any single abnormal condition deserves a volume all to itself. The most that he can promise the reader at this juncture are some remarks on how the drawings may assist in diagnosis and then some examples to show how drawings are affected in specific handicapping conditions.

More Than Words Can Tell

Children's drawings are of great value diagnostically as projections of the personality, of the fears and hostilities at the basis of many behavior disorders. But just as deviant child behavior cannot be properly diagnosed except in terms of what is normative at a given age or stage, so too, the interpretation of drawings must take into account the changes that occur normatively in the development of graphic expression. In the area of personal-social behavior, hand inspection is normal at four months but rapt fascination with one's hand at one year is indicative of mental retardation.

As has been shown, the concept of body image as expressed in figure drawings develops gradually, becoming more differentiated and more complex. Until the child adopts our adult point of view, his drawings express a mental concept influenced by affective elements that result in a subjective rather than in an objective portrayal, substantially at variance with that of most adults. It is, therefore, essential to know as much as possible about what is usual or normative in the graphic activity of children at successive stages of their maturation. A man drawn with limbs issuing from his head is normal at four but questionably so at five. In accordance with this view, much of this volume has dealt with what could be expected of most children at various and progressive stages in their development. Parallelisms have been drawn between drawings of children past and present, and between the development of graphic expression in the individual and in the race.

Armed with a knowledge of what is normative, the investigator is able to detect significant deviations and, in many instances, to decipher what the child is telling about himself and his difficulties.

Drawing the Family

This situation, of universal interest and appeal, evokes responses that are highly revealing of the child's personality. They provide both student and diagnostician with a most valuable aid for knowledge and understanding of a child's attitudes and feelings as an individual acted upon and reacting to the most powerful forces in his environment—the members of his family. The situation is presented to children four years and over. Exceptionally, a revealing response may be obtainable from younger children as in the case of a child of three years 7 months, whose drawing is included in the specimens that will be offered for the reader's consideration.

The family drawing is not a test of mental ability; it should not be used in place of the Goodenough Draw-a-Man test. In drawing an isolated figure, the child's response tends to be predominantly intellectual, so that he will produce a more complete figure with more parts than those he draws when portraying his family. When asked to draw his family, the product is highly colored by the child's feelings; as a result, the response is predominantly emotional. He tells us how he feels about himself and his family and less about what he knows.

Procedure

The child is invited to seat himself on a small chair at a table of appropriate height. His feet are resting on the floor; his arms as well as his hands are free to move. A sheet of letter-sized paper (green-tinted for easy finding among so many white sheets) is placed on the table directly in front of him. The crayon (red lumber crayon: Dixon No. 520) is placed in the center of the paper, pointing away from the child, who is then asked to draw a picture of his family. No further instructions are given. Every kind of suggestion must be avoided. Some of the younger children will mechanically say "I can't." These will generally comply after a little cheerful encouragement. Noncompliance is so unusual that it should be made a matter of record.

The situation is terminated when the child indicates verbally or by gesture that he has finished. Many will lay down the crayon; others will hand the drawing to the examiner. There is rarely any difficulty in determining the end-point of the situation.

The drawings presented in the following pages were all obtained by the writer from children individually, not in group sessions. The possibility of copying or of being influenced by other children was thereby excluded.

Particular attention is directed to the following features: size of individual figures (like the ancient Egyptians, the child uses size to express importance, power), order in which the figures are drawn (those that most impress him are drawn first), his position in the family group (as an expression of his status), is he present at all? (feelings of not belonging), has anyone been excluded? (desire to eliminate), who is he next to? or between? is the sex of family members distinguishable? whom has he embellished by addition of extra clothing or ornamentation? who has accentuated arms and hands? (symbols of force, aggression), what has he added other than persons? (pets, trees, houses, sun).

Feelings of Inadequacy

In many family drawings by children with minimal cerebral dysfunction, there are evidences of the low regard in which the child considers himself. At times they draw themselves last in the family group or not at all; or they may draw an admired sibling much larger even though younger and in reality smaller than themselves. This lack of self-esteem further complicates and aggravates the child's difficulty by eating away at his motivation so that he functions decidedly below capacity. At the root of the problem is the parents' failure to recognize the child's difficulty as a handicap. As a result, the parent, describing the behavior to wilfulness, is likely to use harsh or inappropriate disciplinary measures, criticism, and unfavorable comparison with siblings. Where the handicap is more evident, as in visual, orthopedic, or auditory impairment, the parent is more likely to see the child as needing help rather than psychological or corporal punishment.

FIGURE 152

Drawing of family by a boy of 8 years 6 months. No one has been omitted, all are in chronological order.

FIGURE 153

"MY FAMILY" by a girl of six years. The last figure is a child as yet unborn.

FIGURE 154

Pets included in family drawing. Drawing by adopted boy of seven years.

FIGURE 155

Drawing by a child of eight years. Has added cat, bird, and turtle.

Sibling Relationships

Sibling rivalry may be manifested in a variety of ways. Some will attack, others will withdraw, others will imitate the intruder, the new arrival with whom they will henceforth have to share parental attention. Accordingly, the child's graphic expression of his altered status will vary. In drawing the family, the child may reveal his feelings more clearly than in words or actions. Feelings of jealousy are not limited towards the new arrival; they often arise as the result of parental comparison with a more admired sibling. At times feelings of envy develop between siblings of the same sex when the younger is more attractive, as in a problem that came to the attention of this writer, in which the younger girl had attained obvious pubertal development before her one year older sister.

The child may omit the rival from the family drawing, as in the first drawing.

In the second drawing by a boy of five, he has assertively drawn himself first and larger than his seven and a half year-old brother.

In the third drawing the seven and a half year-old boy has drawn his three-year-old sister like a worm.

In the fourth drawing, a nine and a half year-old boy has drawn his sister last, after the dog.

In the fifth drawing, a girl of nine years, 11 months is expressing positive feelings for her brother. She has drawn him first and placed herself next to him.

FIGURE 156

Sibling Rivalry. Family drawing by a boy of seven years 1 month, low average intelligence. Has omitted an 18 month sibling.

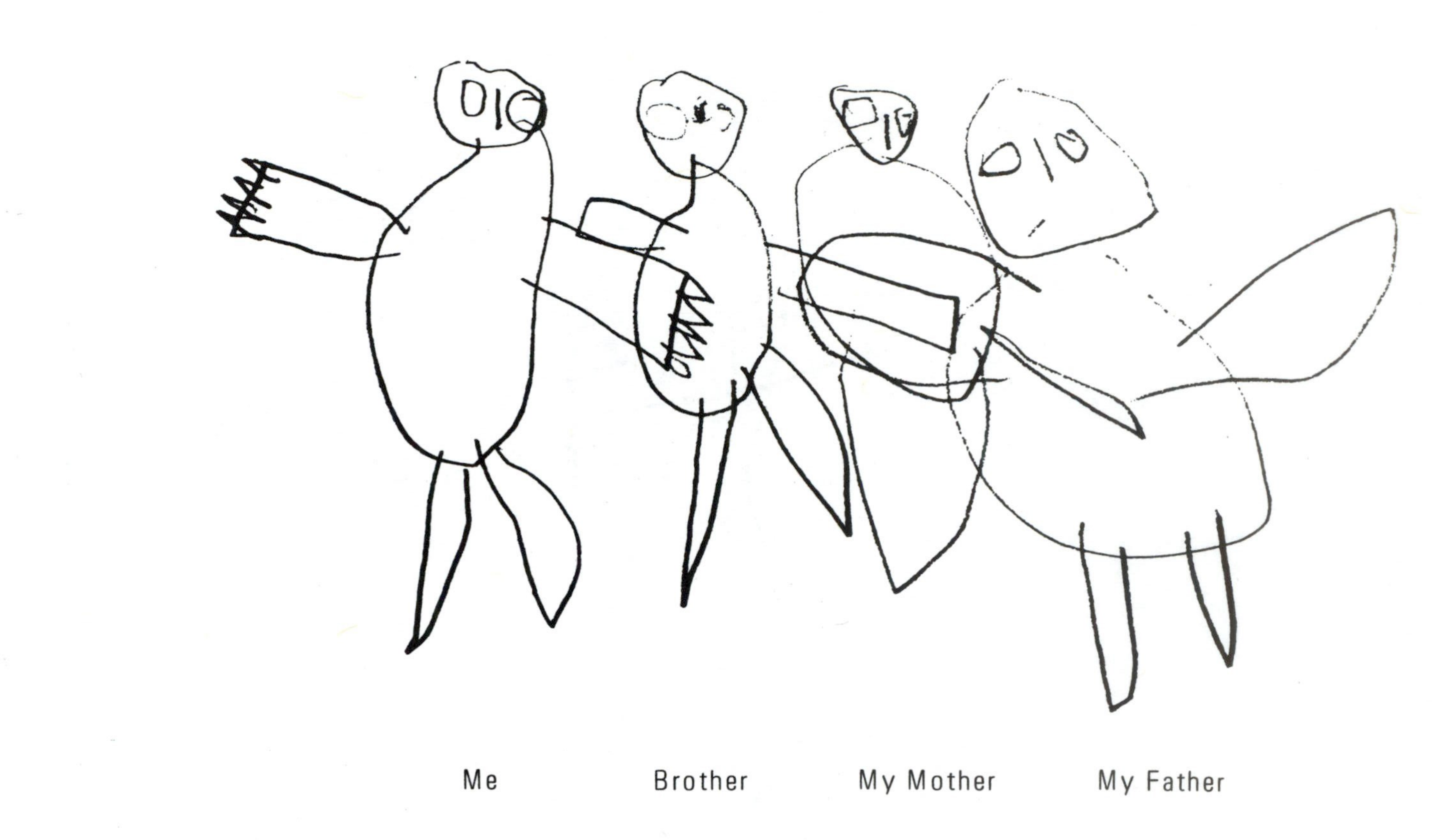

FIGURE 157

Family drawing by a boy of five years 2 months. Disruptive in Nursery Schools. Assertively drew himself first, larger than his brother who is seven years six months of age. Both parents are professionals whose activities keep them out of the home a great deal of the time. The boy has an unsatisfied craving for affection and demands attention from the teacher. While waiting to be seen by the writer, he attempted to sit on the secretary's lap. Measurable IQ is 140. Goodenough mental age is average. He attends half-day sessions in 2 nursery schools.

FIGURE 158

Family drawing by a boy of seven years 6 months of dull normal intelligence. He has drawn his three-year-old sister like a worm.

FIGURE 159

Family drawn by a dyslexic boy of nine years 6 months. He has excluded no one but has drawn his sister very last, after the dog. Average intelligence but immature concept of body image. Bleeding during first trimester of pregnancy. Midforceps delivery. Hyperthermia at 18 months.

FIGURE 160

The Preferred Sibling. Family drawing by a girl of nine years 11 months. She has drawn the preferred sibling first and next to him, herself. She is constantly bickering with the others. She has stolen to buy candy for her favorite.

FIGURE 161

In drawing the family, the figures are generally drawn at a lower cognitive level than the isolated figure. Family drawing should not be used as a substitute for the Draw-a-Person test if the purpose is to measure intelligence. The drawing of his family by a boy of six years 3 months would yield a lower score than the drawing of a person on the following page done by the same child at the same session.

FIGURE 162

Drawing of a person by the six year 3 month boy who drew his family on the preceding page. Note the higher level of intellectual response as compared with the figures in the family drawing.

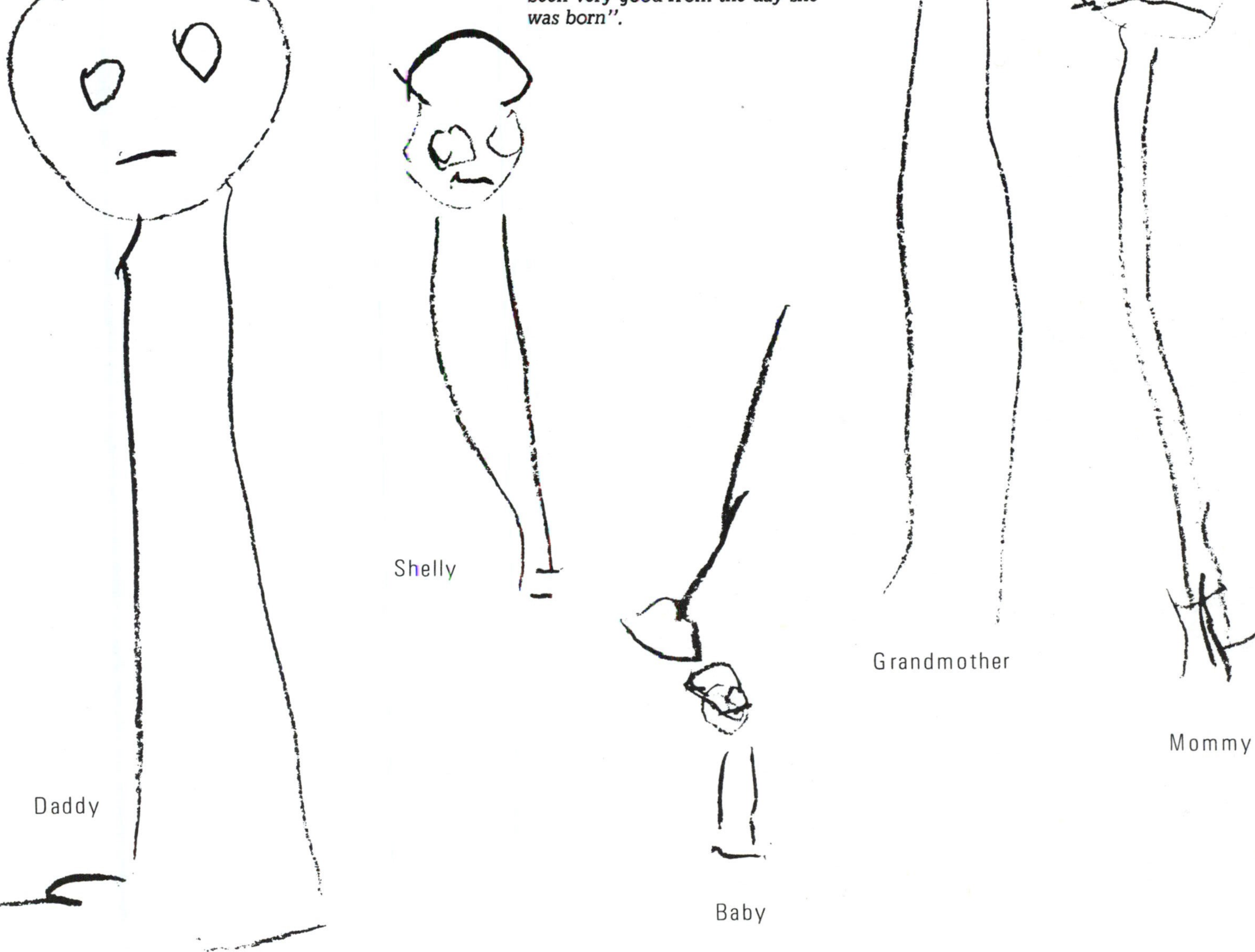

FIGURE 163

Parent Preference: *This girl of three years 7 months, has drawn Daddy first and placed herself next to him. Note that she has drawn mother last. Mother describes her as stubborn, hard to handle, difficult; unlike her 11-month sister who "has always been very good from the day she was born".*

FIGURE 164

Lack of Self-Esteem in Reaction To Parental Disapproval. Drawn by a girl of six years 10 months. School work below capacity. "I don't care" attitude. Parents critical, make unfavorable comparisons with siblings. In drawing her family, C. L. has drawn herself last and omitted her father. The females have longer hair, no other distinguishing features.

FIGURE 165

Lack of Self-Esteem. Drawn by a boy of six years 10 months. School work below capacity. This drawing of his family is revealing in that he has drawn himself after his sister and brother Jimmy, who although only 3½ years of age has been drawn larger than himself. As he gave me this drawing, he commented, "I'm the last one". Jimmy is admired by all, parents, relatives, and friends, who consider him attractive and delight in his performances. Father is drawn last. Only more hair distinguishes the females. The figures are stereotyped and below the level of mental ability as revealed in other situations. He shows signs suggestive of minimal cerebral dysfunction, viz., gross motor awkwardness, inability to tie shoe laces, distractibility in a group, crossed dominance (left-handed and right-eyed), immature concept of body image. History of "spotting" during 7th month of pregnancy.

FIGURE 166

Family drawing by a girl (me). Feels rejected by her mother who favors the sister of whom she is jealous. The "artist" is five years of age, her younger rival, whom she has drawn larger than herself is only 18 months old. Note the accentuated extremities of the mother as contrasted to their absence in the figure of the father.

FIGURE 167

Mother Disciplinarian. Family drawing by a girl of seven years.

FIGURE 168

Oedipal Situation. Family drawing by a boy of nine years. He has drawn himself next to mother, has omitted his stern father from the group and has later drawn him dressed as a military man on a separate page. (Figure 169)

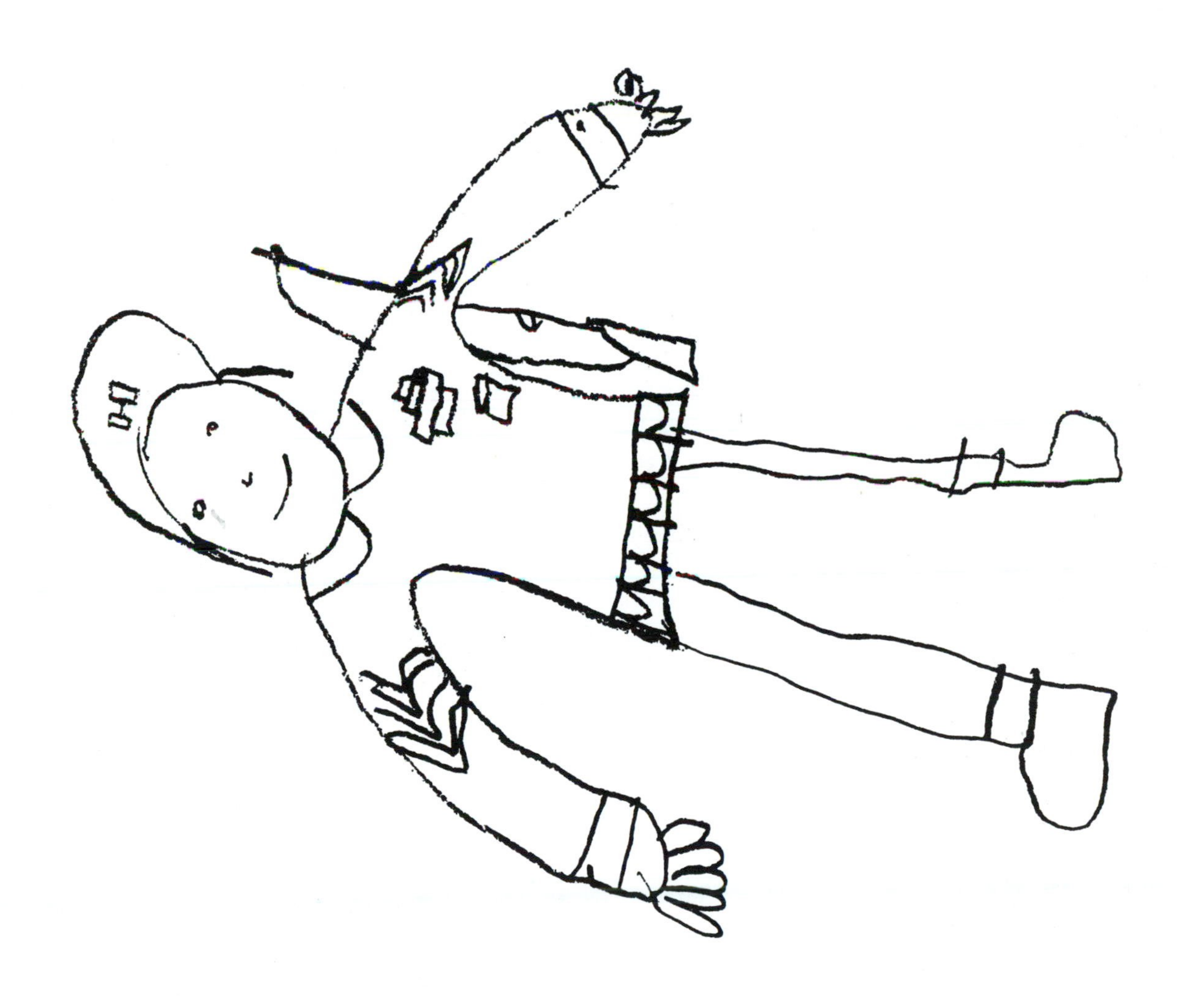

FIGURE 169

FIGURE 170

Drawing by an adopted boy of ten years. He presents clinical signs suggestive of minimal cerebral dysfunction. He is awkward, has difficulty with math, is rejected by his peers, and prefers younger children. He derives compensatory gratification from food, asks for 3-4 dessert servings, described as "a great eater". All members of the family are included in his drawing; significantly, they are dining. Rejection by peers is probably due to his poor ability in sports. Asked to draw a person, he drew a baseball player (wishful thinking).

FIGURE 171

Over-Protected At Home; Maladjusted At School. This drawing by an adopted boy of seven years 8 months shows him between his parents holding their hands. His adopting parents are over-protective, over-indulgent. The boy is cheerful and cooperative at home but aggressive and domineering at school, "awful in class" "a pest in class" "spitting on the gym floor" "disturbing the class". Capable of doing good school work. Average intelligence but immature concept of body image.

FIGURE 172

This drawing is by an adopted boy of six years 6 months. He has left himself out of the picture. He has been doing poorly at school, functioning below capacity. His lack of motivation was interpreted as related to anxiety over his status in the family. The drawing was shown to his adoptive parents, who were informed of the child's need for unqualified acceptance and praise. In the drawing on the following page, made when he was eight years 11 months, he has included himself, after his brother. He appeared more secure but he was doing only fairly well at school; his reading was poor.

FIGURE 173

Drawing of family at age eight years 11 months. He has now included himself. The figure below, done at the same session, shows how the individual figure is executed at a higher intellectual level than the group figures.

FIGURE 174

Stereotypy

The following group of drawings are by children whose measurable intelligence is in the average range but who are doing poorly at school and whose concept of the body image, as expressed in their figure drawings, is immature and stereotyped. The same figure is repeated in each case, regardless of the subject being represented. This writer has found this disparity in many adopted children though not confined to them by any means. Minimal variations, if they occur, are generally limited to size and hair length; the first to indicate the children, the second to depict sex. But in many drawings, not even these differences can be seen. Occasionally, the male figure can be identified by a hat; this is rarely seen on a female figure.

FIGURE 175

Drawing by a boy of ten years. IQ 92.

FIGURE 176

Adopted boy, age five years 8 months. Average intelligence. Has drawn self first. Search for status.

FIGURE 177

Drawing by girl, age nine years 6 months. Poor school work. Immature concept of body image. Under achiever. Has drawn self last.

FIGURE 178

Drawing by a girl, age six years 10 months. IQ 93. Stereotyped figures. Father has no arms.

FIGURE 179

Drawing by adopted boy of nine years 4 months. Poor school work. Average IQ but immature concept of body image.

18

OMISSION AND OVEREMPHASIS

These are devices by means of which children express feelings and attitudes in their drawings. In many instances the feelings thus expressed graphically are not verbalized by the child or acted out so that the drawing becomes a valuable clue to understanding the child's behavior and his difficulty.

The arms and hands are often accentuated by children who are either the victims or the dispensers of punishment. Conversely, the upper extremities are often omitted in the drawings by timid, nonreactive children. In one of the drawings that follow, it seems clear to the writer that the male figure represented by the ten year old boy, who is beaten by his father, is an adult male with large strong arms and hands.

It will be seen from the drawings that where the mother is the disciplinarian, it is she whose upper extremities are emphasized.

FIGURE 180

Transparencies. Limbs visible. Stereotyped figures. Age nine years. Average IQ. Poor school work.

FIGURE 181

This and the following drawing are by a girl of five years 7 months. Mother is the disciplinarian in the family. Note the rudimentary arms on the man and the strongly emphasized arms and hands of the female figure.

FIGURE 182

FIGURE 183

Drawing by a bright but emotionally immature boy of six years 11 months. Mother is the disciplinarian; father is easy going. Note who has the arms.

FIGURE 184

Drawing of family by a dyslexic boy of seven years 10 months. The figure without arms is his permissive father.

FIGURE 185

The arms as a symbol of aggression. Note accentuation of arms and hands. Drawn by a boy of ten years 8 months. Poorly motivated at school, functioning below capacity. Frequently beaten by authoritarian father. Wants to sleep with mother.

19

THE MENTALLY SUBNORMAL

The Goodenough Draw-a-Man test has found wide acceptance as a quick method of appraising the child's level of intellectual maturation. For a comprehensive treatment of the subject, the reader is referred to the classical work by Goodenough and to the more recent study by Harris.

In some respects the drawings by subnormal children are like those by younger normal children. But this statement is only partly true. The differences are not merely quantitative but qualitative as well. This is to be expected, for the drawing of the human figure is a complex gestalt involving integration of all the sensory, motor, and perceptual, as well as social experiences that are expressed in the action that leaves its record on paper. A child of eleven with a mental age of five is not the same as a child of five with a mental age of five. The IQ's are the same, but they do not represent the children from whom the IQ's were derived. The drawings of subnormal children resemble those by younger children in lack of individual details, in unrealistic body proportions, in lack of optical perspective. Qualitative differences, however, permit the differentiation from superficially similar drawings by the younger normal child. Among the differences is a lack of cohesion more clearly expressed by Kerschensteiner as Zusammenhangenlosigkeit, a deficiency in the relationship of body parts to each other. Another difference is in the presence of both primitive and mature features in the drawing of the mentally subnormal.

The Goodenough Draw-a-Man Test is probably as close as we have come to the ideal of a culture-free test of intelligence. Cross-cultural studies confirm the universal symbolism and stages that mark the child's developing concept of the body image. Comparison with the earliest available human figure drawings by young children, those collected by Corrado Ricci, reveals striking similarities though separated by a century. The basic schemata are practically identical; the differences are only in the incidentals. In Ricci's specimens, many of the men are depicted smoking a pipe or wearing stove-pipe hats, items not commonly added by today's children. Universal features in the drawings of young children express the basic unity of mankind, a unity that tends to become obscured and even shattered as cultural influences impose themselves and gradually pull the child away from one world into many segregated little worlds, often in hostile competition with one another. As expressions of the child's developing concept of the body image, figure drawings are especially revealing of intellectual development during the preschool years during which the child is still expressing his individuality albeit within the context of a common racial inheritance. It is during these years that he and consequently his drawings are least affected by a culture that will impose its own adult view upon his perceptions. The Goodenough Draw-a-Man test is most culture-free and, therefore, most valid, during the preschool years, while the child is still making a statement about himself. How else can one account for the steady decline in Goodenough IQ among the culturally disadvantaged as the effect of the cultural variable increases with age? In their study on Negro elementary school children, Kennedy and Lindner found the Goodenough mean IQ to be 99.3 at age five, declining to 83.6 by the time the children reached sixth grade.

A series of five drawings (Figures 186-190) of the human figure by a girl (Marie M N) of borderline IQ. The drawings were executed at intervals and show the evolution of human figure drawing in an intellectually limited child. Drawings were made at chronological ages six years 3 months, six years 10 months, seven years 4 months, eight years 1 month, and ten years 6 months. The mother bled from the uterus two days prior to delivery by Caesarean section.

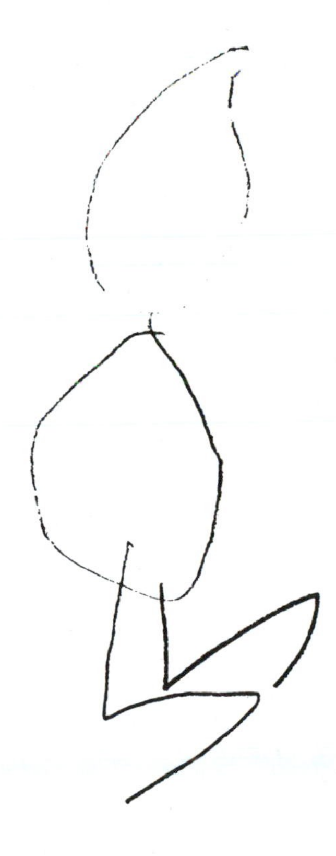

FIGURE 186

Marie M N; drawing of a man at chronological age six years 3 months.

FIGURE 187

Marie M N: drawing of a man at chronological age six years 10 months.

FIGURE 188

Marie M N: drawing of a man at chronological age seven years 4 months.

FIGURE 189

Marie M N: drawing of a man at chronological age eight years 1 month.

FIGURE 190

Marie M N: drawing of human figure at chronological age ten years 6 months.

FIGURE 191

Drawn by a boy. Chronological age: 11 years. Binet IQ: 69. Goodenough IQ: 57.

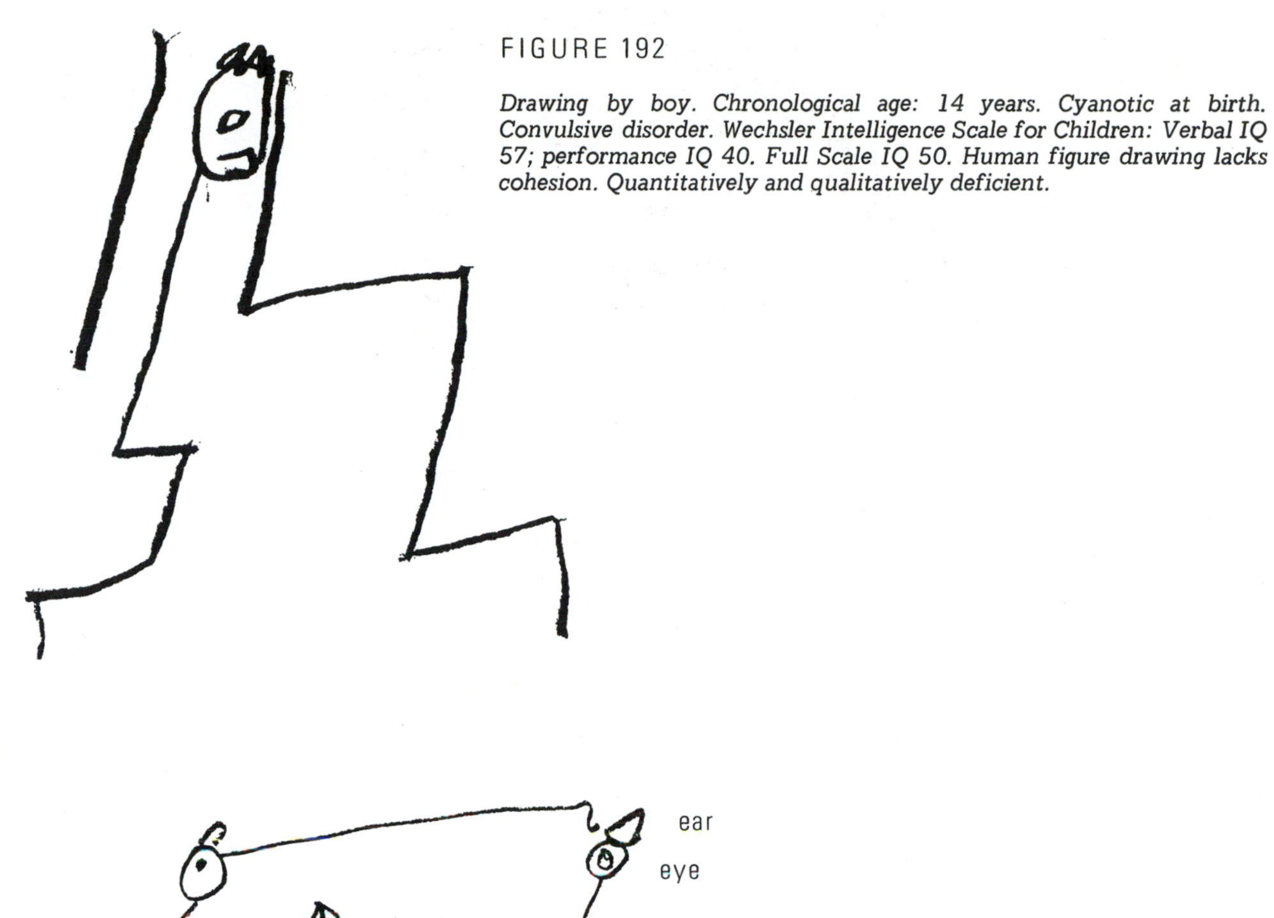

FIGURE 192

Drawing by boy. Chronological age: 14 years. Cyanotic at birth. Convulsive disorder. Wechsler Intelligence Scale for Children: Verbal IQ 57; performance IQ 40. Full Scale IQ 50. Human figure drawing lacks cohesion. Quantitatively and qualitatively deficient.

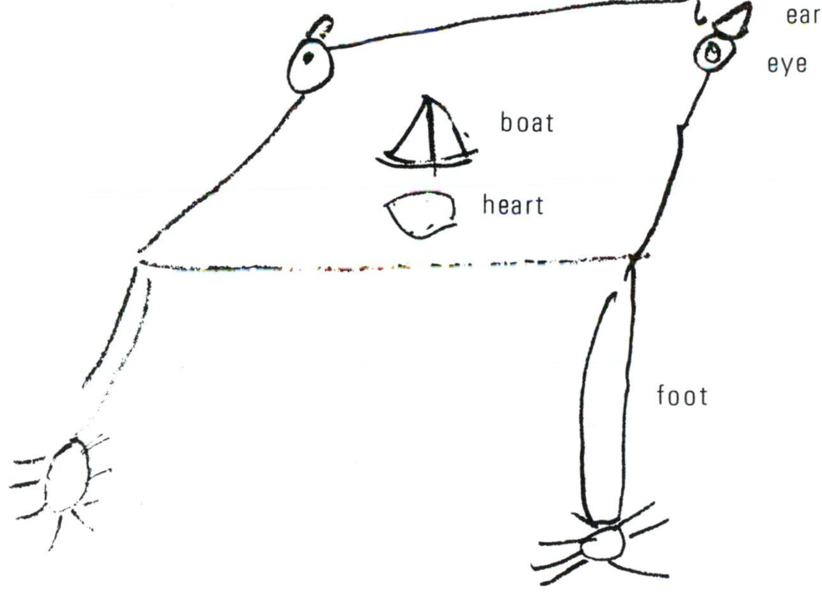

FIGURE 193

Drawing of a person by a mentally retarded girl. Chronological age: 14 years. Mental age: five years. Cleft palate. Cyanotic spells during neonatal period. Abnormal electro-encephalogram. The figure has no head. She identified: ears, eyes, heart, feet. Said the toes were spiders. Above the heart, she drew a boat. Note the deficiency in relationship of body parts and the presence of the heart, a mature feature, and the incongruous addition of the boat.

FIGURE 194

Drawing of a man by a girl of seven years 10 months. She has added the navel. IQ: 83.

FIGURE 195

Female. Chronological age fifteen years. Drawing of family. Figures are very similar, though mother and sisters can be distinguished by their longer hair and dresses. Stanford-Binet IQ: 63.

FIGURE 196

Down's Syndrome. Human figure: mental age: three years 9 months. Drawn by G. I. at chronological age six years 8 months.

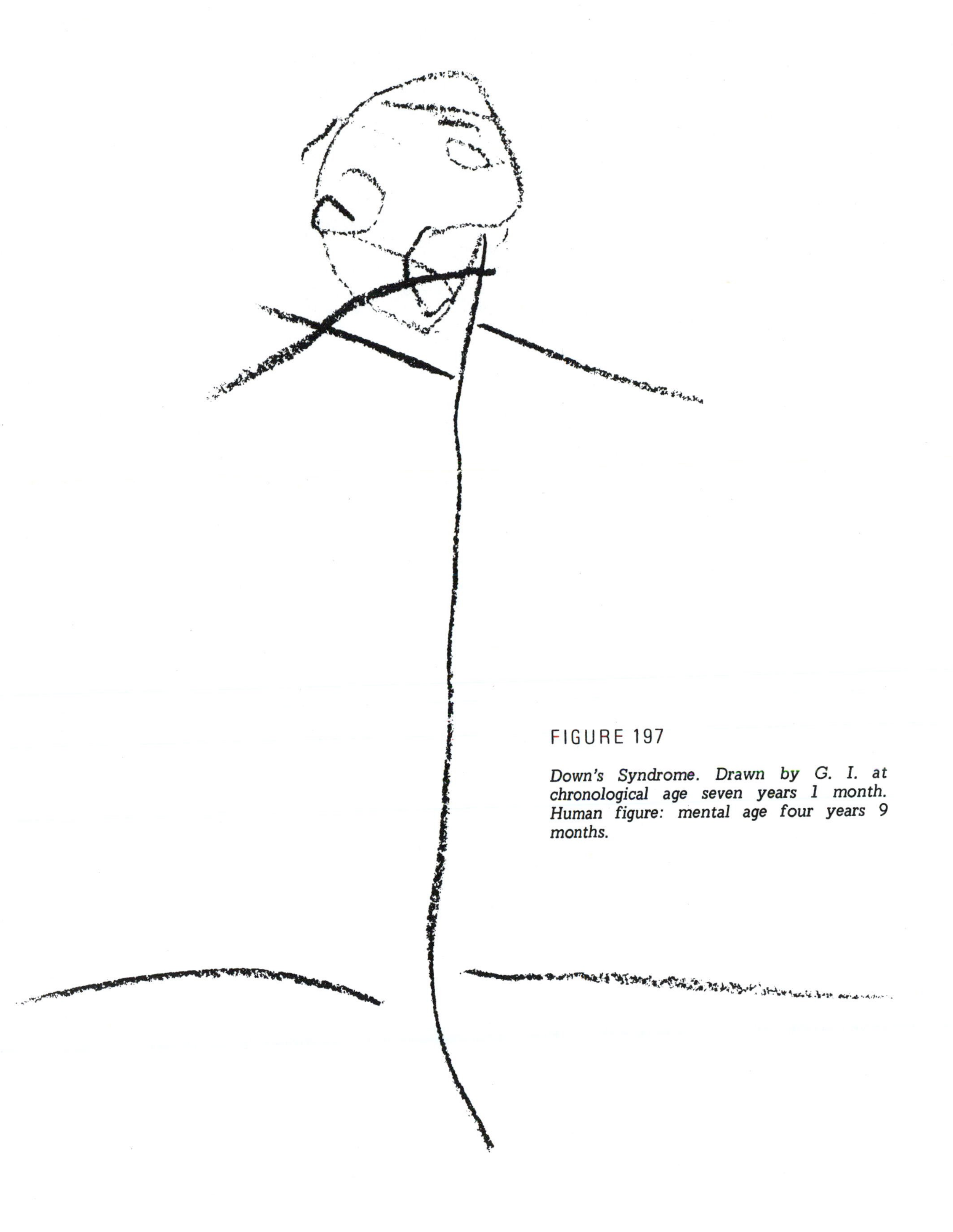

FIGURE 197

Down's Syndrome. Drawn by G. I. at chronological age seven years 1 month. Human figure: mental age four years 9 months.

FIGURE 198

Down's Syndrome. Drawing of the human figure by a girl of six years 10 months. The figure expresses a mental age of four years 6 months.

Down's Syndrome. The following series of six drawings (Figures 199-204) made at intervals show the evolution of human figure drawing in a Mongoloid boy (F. W.). Drawn at chronological age seven years 3 months, eight years, eight years 11 months, ten years 4 months, fourteen years 6 months, fifteen years 6 months. IQ below 50. Trainable. Living at home, attends special school.

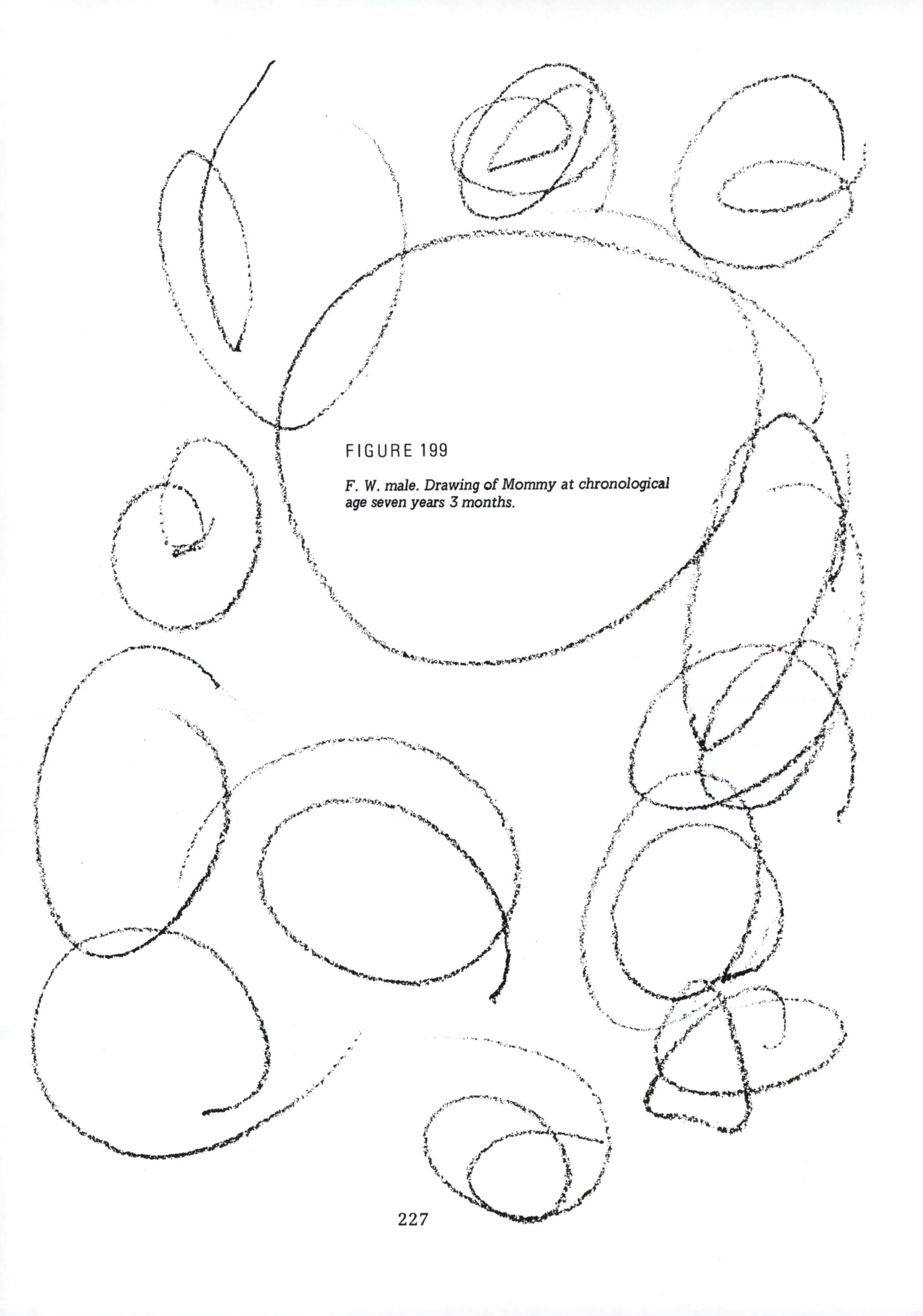

FIGURE 199

F. W. male. Drawing of Mommy at chronological age seven years 3 months.

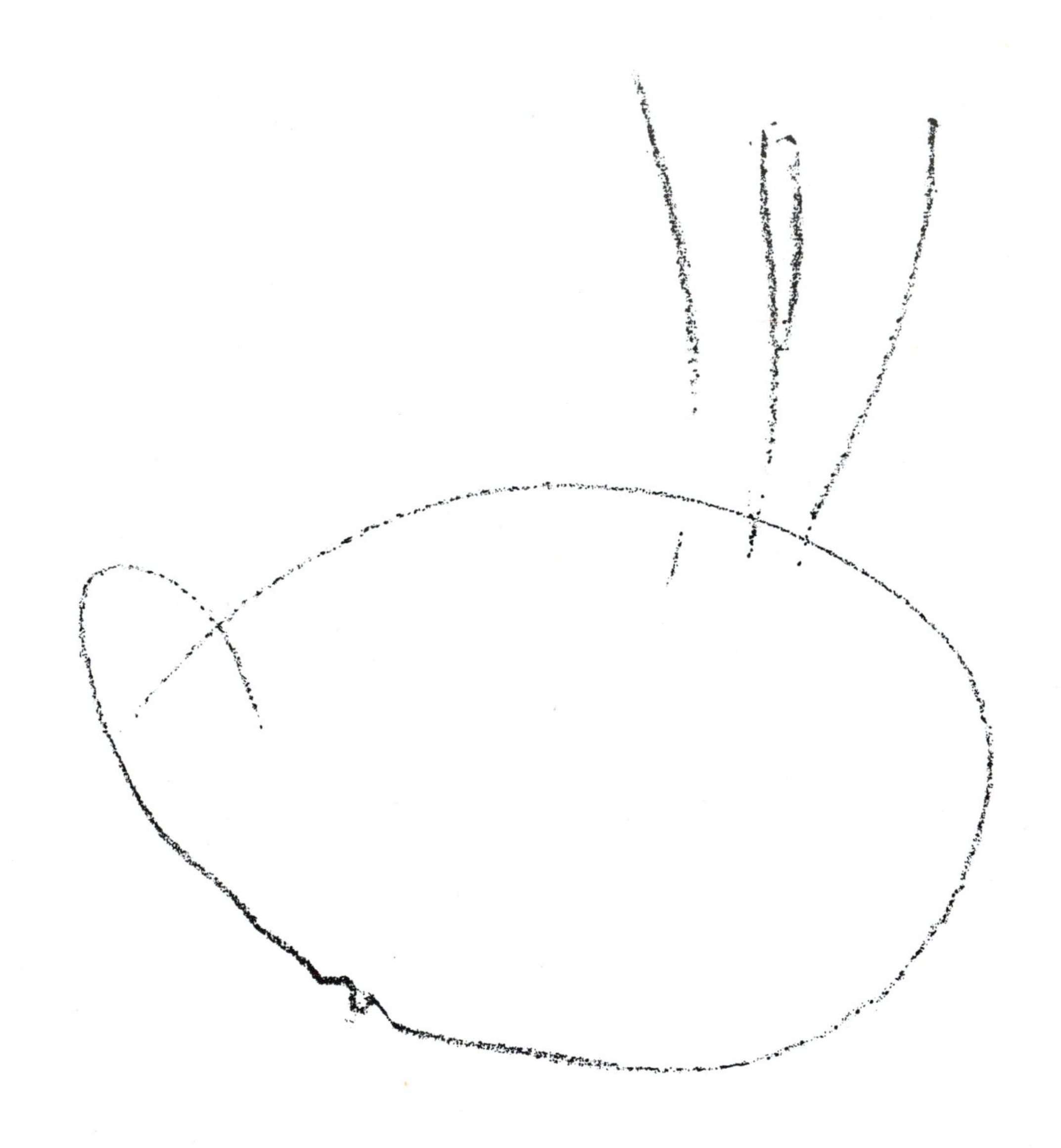

FIGURE 200

F. W. male. Drawing of a man at chronological age eight years. Figure has head, hair, and one ear.

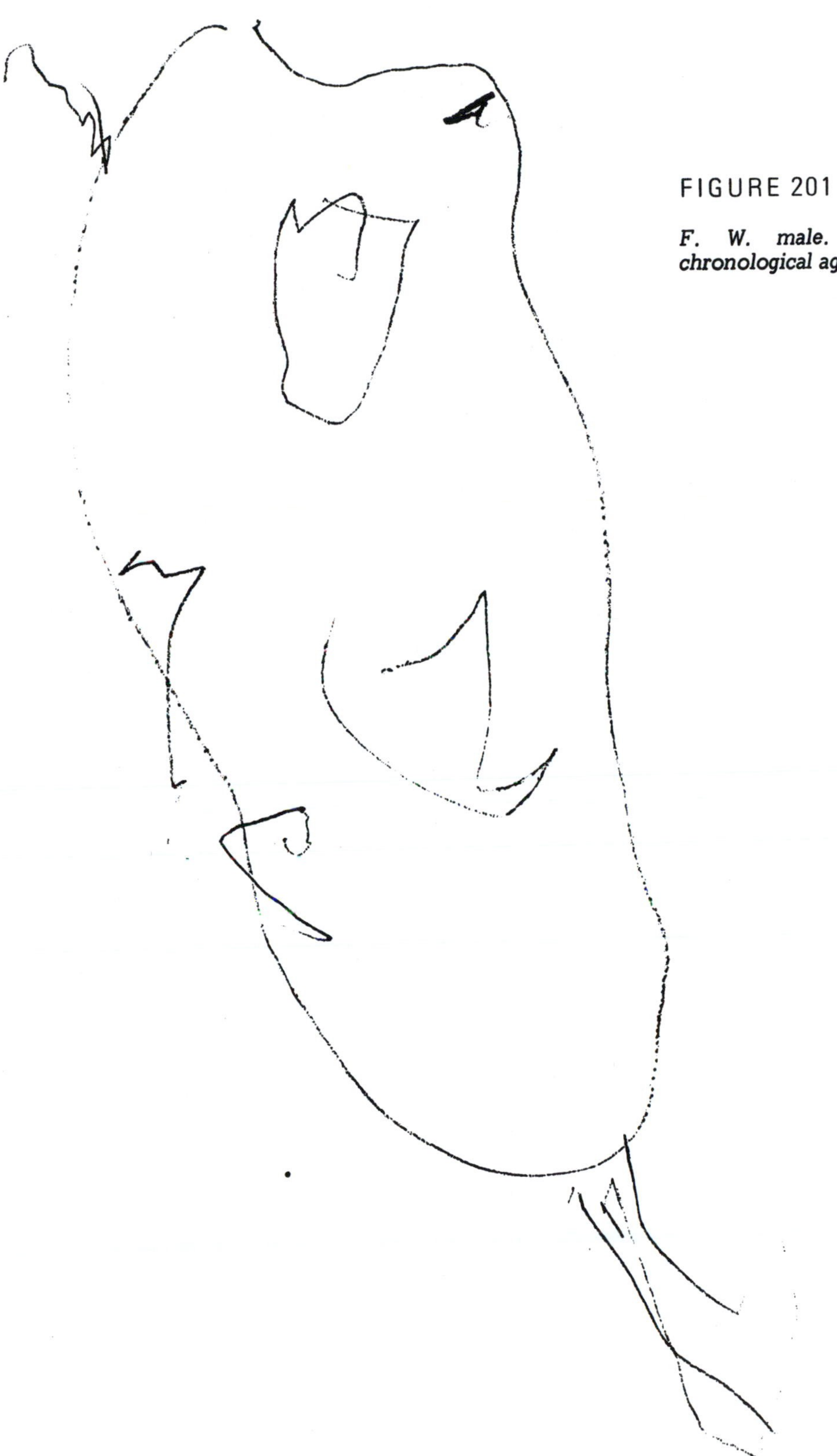

FIGURE 201

F. W. male. Drawing of a man at chronological age eight years 11 months.

FIGURE 202

F. W. male. Drawing of a man at chronological age ten years 4 months.

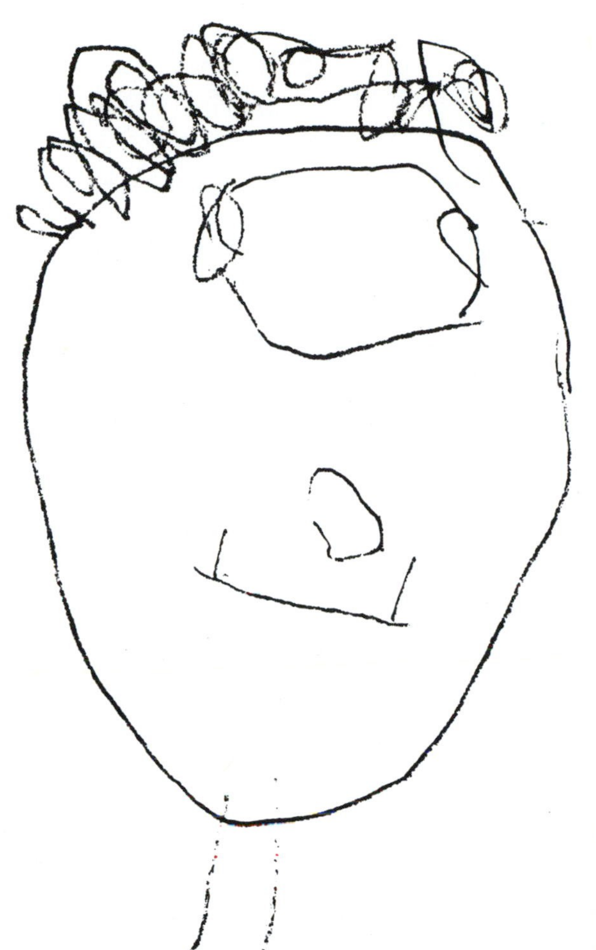

FIGURE 203

"If there is abnormal discrepancy between chronological age and developmental stage, the existence of mental retardation can be accepted as a certainty." V. Lowenfeld. F. W. Drawing of man at chronological age fourteen years 6 months.

FIGURE 204

F. W. male. Drawing of a man at chronological age sixteen years 6 months.

20

CEREBRAL PALSY

Cerebral palsy is a term used to designate a group of conditions having in common disorders of motor control originating in the brain, resulting from organic or metabolic abnormality of the developing brain. The distinction between cerebral palsy at one end and minimal cerebral dysfunction at the other is one of degree rather than of kind. The disorder will fit into the general classification of cerebral palsy when the over-riding difficulty is motor, though other impairments of cerebral function are usually associated with the predominant motor disorder. The association of intellectual, visual, and perceptual elements must be borne in mind in studying drawings by cerebral-palsied children lest we ascribe the inadequacies to the motor disability alone.

Drawings by children with cerebral dysfunction of organic or metabolic nature show perceptual impairment and disturbance of body concept. These difficulties are to be taken into account in treatment. The orthopedic problem is only one aspect of the disability. The more intelligent the child the more likely is he to have emotional problems stemming from his inadequacies. It has been noted that adjustment to disability is more difficult in those who are more nearly normal.

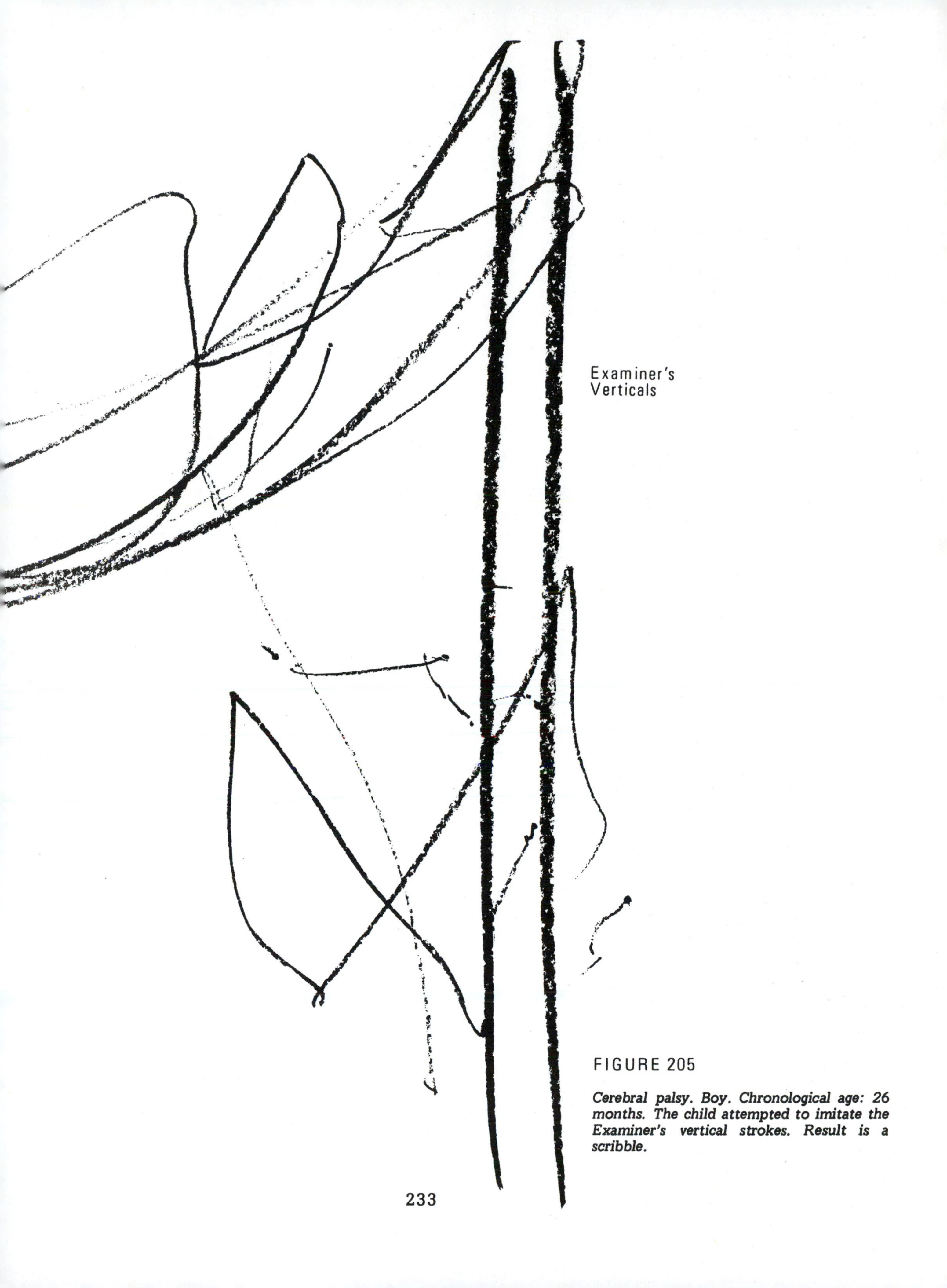

FIGURE 205

Cerebral palsy. Boy. Chronological age: 26 months. The child attempted to imitate the Examiner's vertical strokes. Result is a scribble.

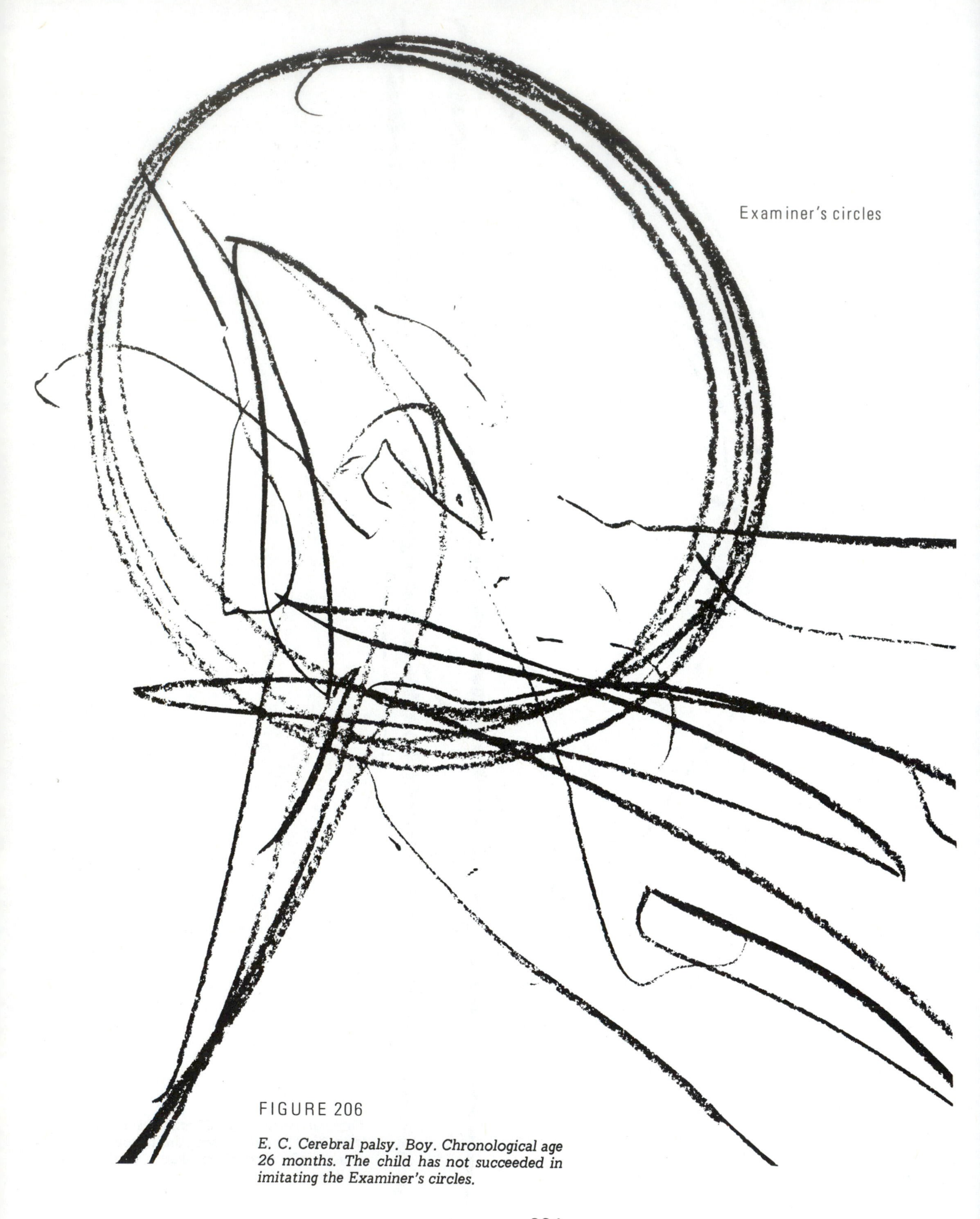

FIGURE 206

E. C. Cerebral palsy. Boy. Chronological age 26 months. The child has not succeeded in imitating the Examiner's circles.

Cerebral Palsy, female child N. J. The drawings that follow (Figures 207-214) are by a girl whose history is highly suggestive of brain damage due to lack of oxygen. She presented signs of fetal distress, the amniotic fluid was meconium-stained, she was cyanotic and required resuscitation, there were recurrent episodes of cyanosis during the first day of life. Her main disability is motor, but perceptual and body image difficulties are apparent from the drawings. These were made at age two years 4 months, three years 6 months, and five years. The series of drawings at roughly yearly intervals shows the slow improvement to the point where she is able to imitate a cross at age five (the norm is three years) while her drawing of the human figure is still unrecognizable and at an immature level of three years 6 months.

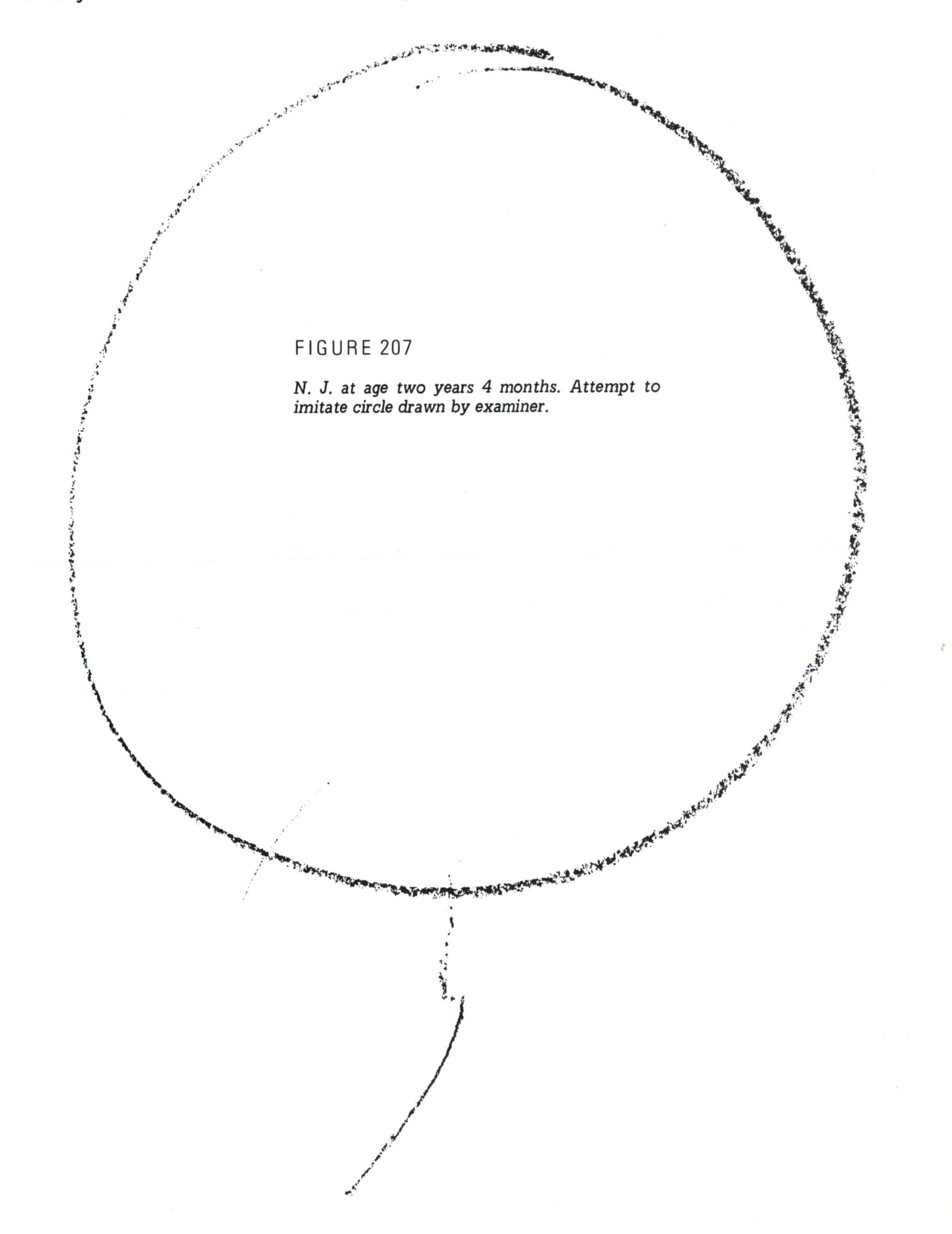

FIGURE 207

N. J. at age two years 4 months. Attempt to imitate circle drawn by examiner.

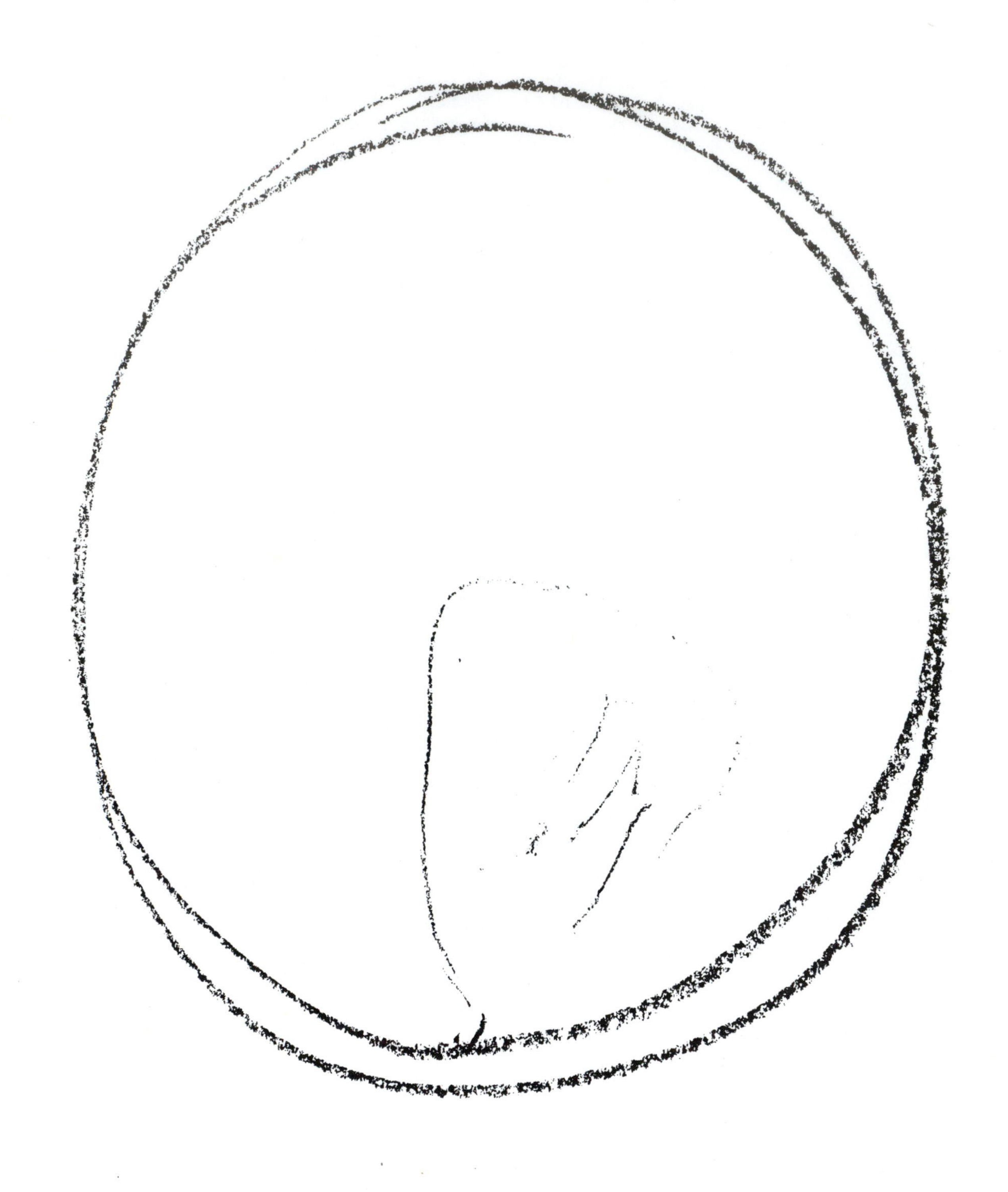

FIGURE 208

N. J. at age two years 4 months. Attempt to imitate Examiner's circle.

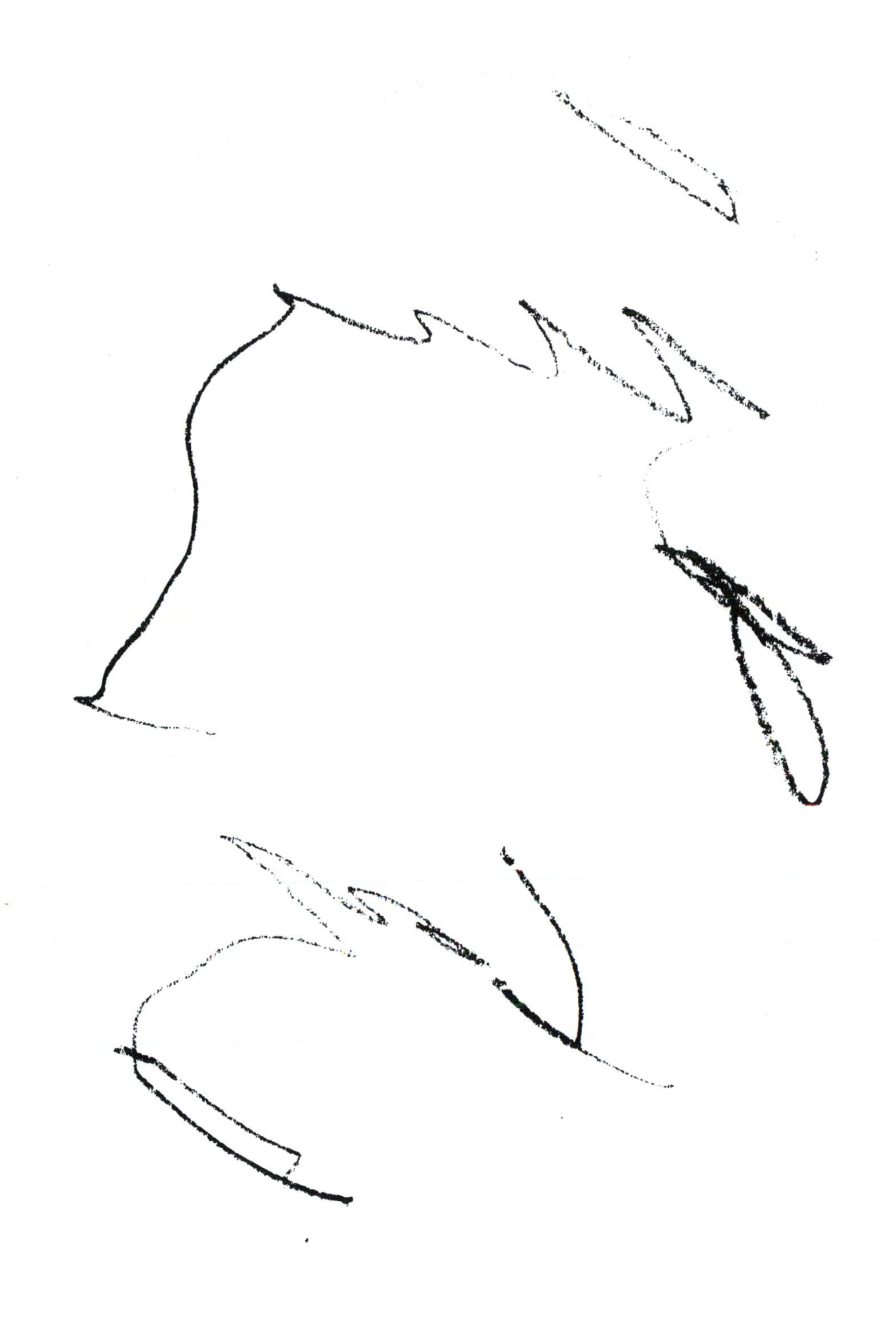

FIGURE 209

Spontaneous drawing by N. J. at chronological age three years 6 months.

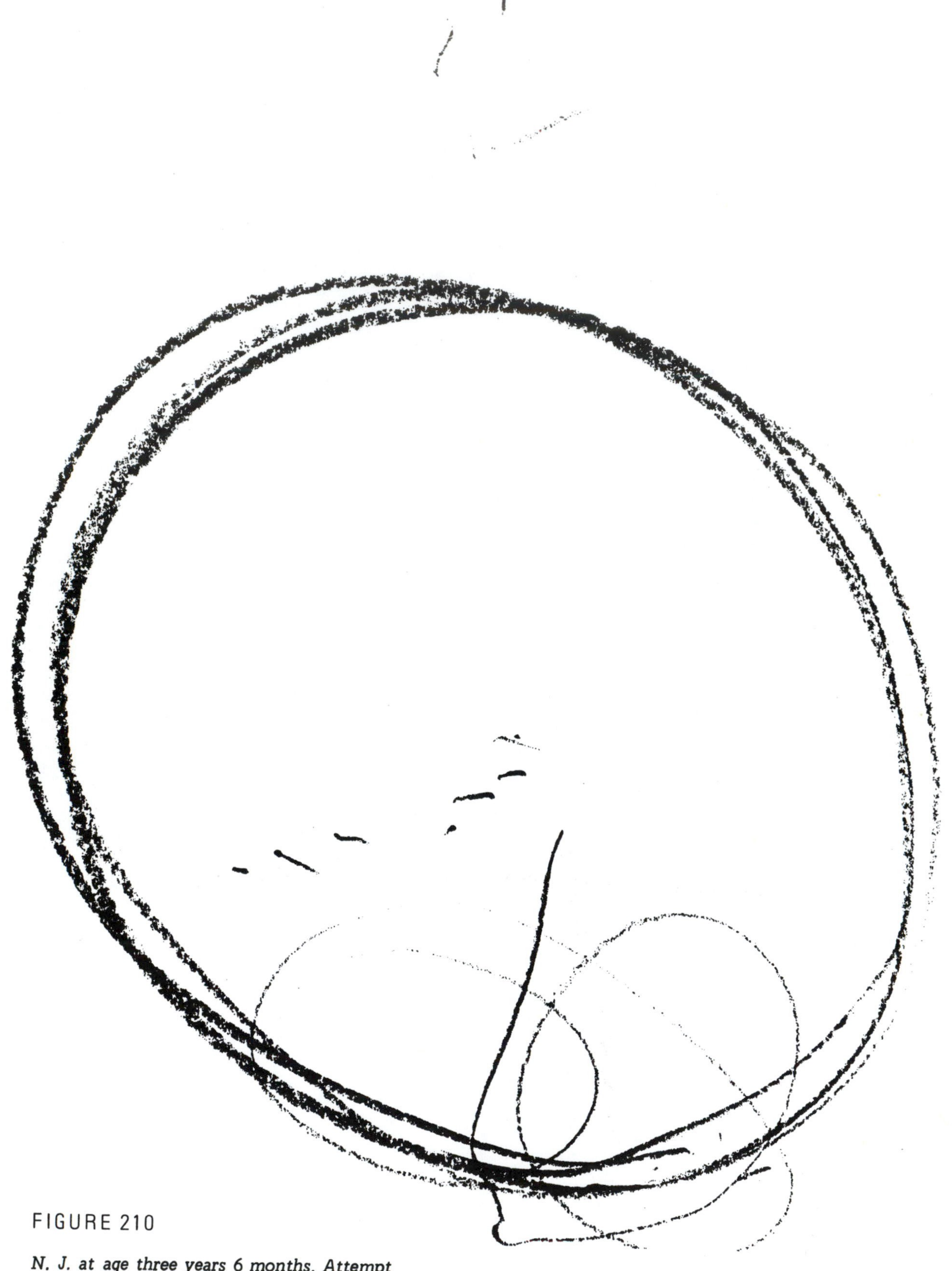

FIGURE 210

N. J. at age three years 6 months. Attempt to imitate Examiner's circle.

FIGURE 211

N. J. at age three years 6 months. Attempt to imitate Examiner's cross.

FIGURE 212

N. J.: Drawing of a person at age five. She is functioning adaptively at the four year level but her concept of the body image as revealed by her drawings is not on a level with her other intellectual responses.

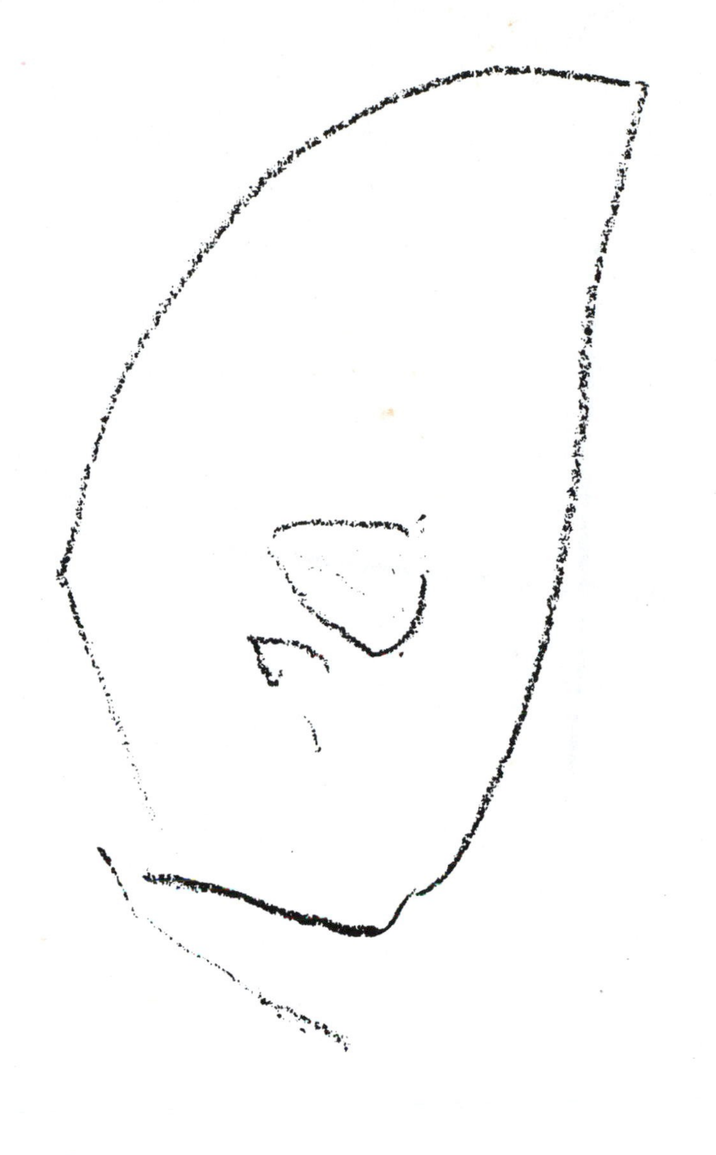

FIGURE 213

Drawing of "Mommy" by N. J. at age five years. The body concept is poorly organized. The child said she was making head, nose, ear, and eyes..

Drawing of "Daddy".

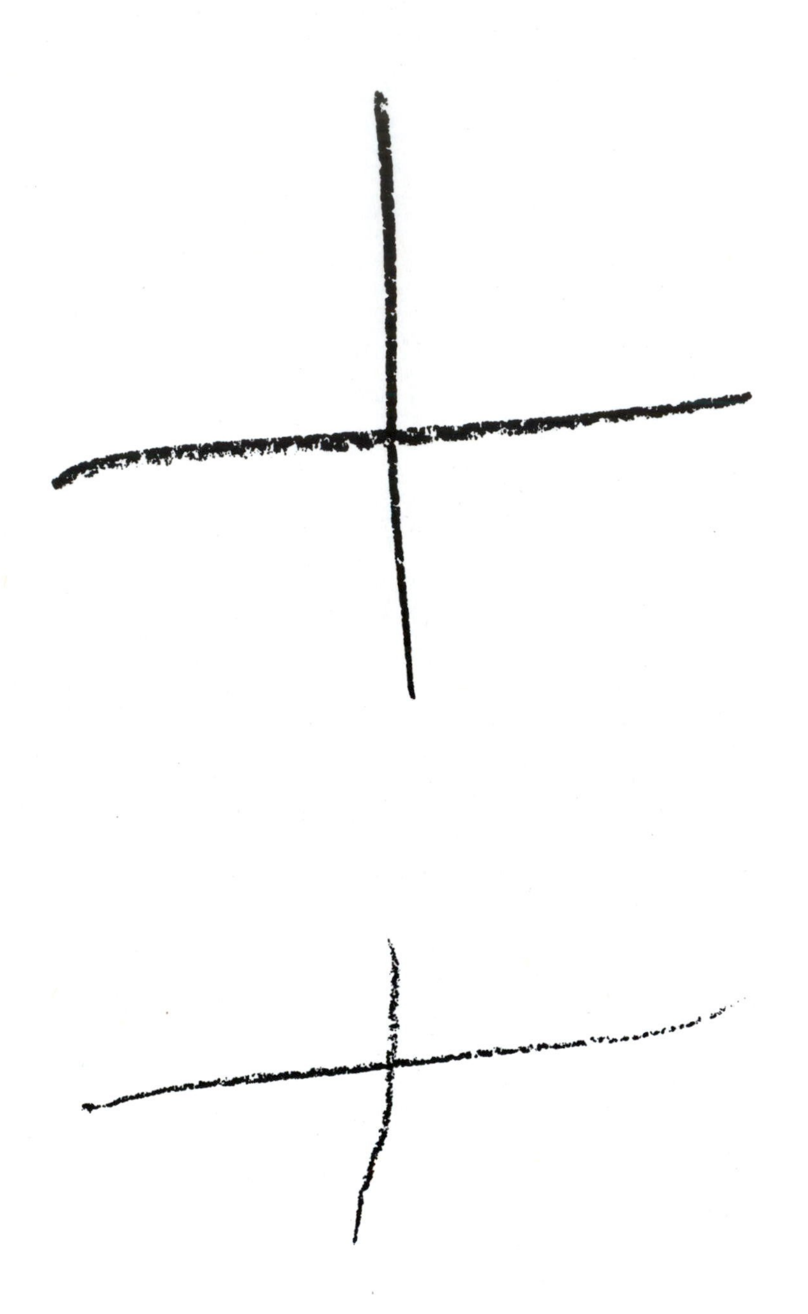

FIGURE 214

N. J. At age five years. She is now able to imitate a cross. Second try.

H. N. Cerebral palsy. Girl of five years 6 months. Left hemiplegia. Right hand used for drawings. Immature, barely recognizable drawing of a man. Distorted copies of circle. Inability to copy cross. Distorted, rotated imitation of cross. (Figures 215-218)

FIGURE 215

H. N. Cerebral Palsy. Left hemiplegia. Girl age five years 6 months. Uterine spotting throughout pregnancy. Drawing of a man. All drawings by right hand.

FIGURE 216

H. N. Syndrome of Cerebral Dysfunction: Cerebral Palsy, Left Hemiplegia: chronological age: five years 6 months. Girl. Premature. "Spotting" throughout pregnancy. Seizures during first day of life. Copies of circle.

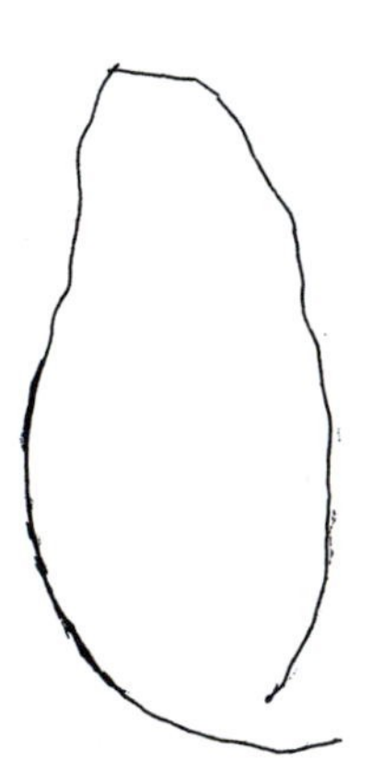

FIGURE 217

H. N. Copy of cross.

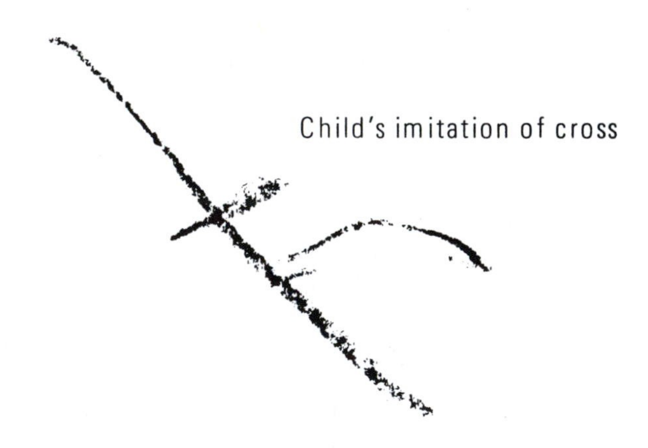

FIGURE 218

H. N. Imitation of cross.

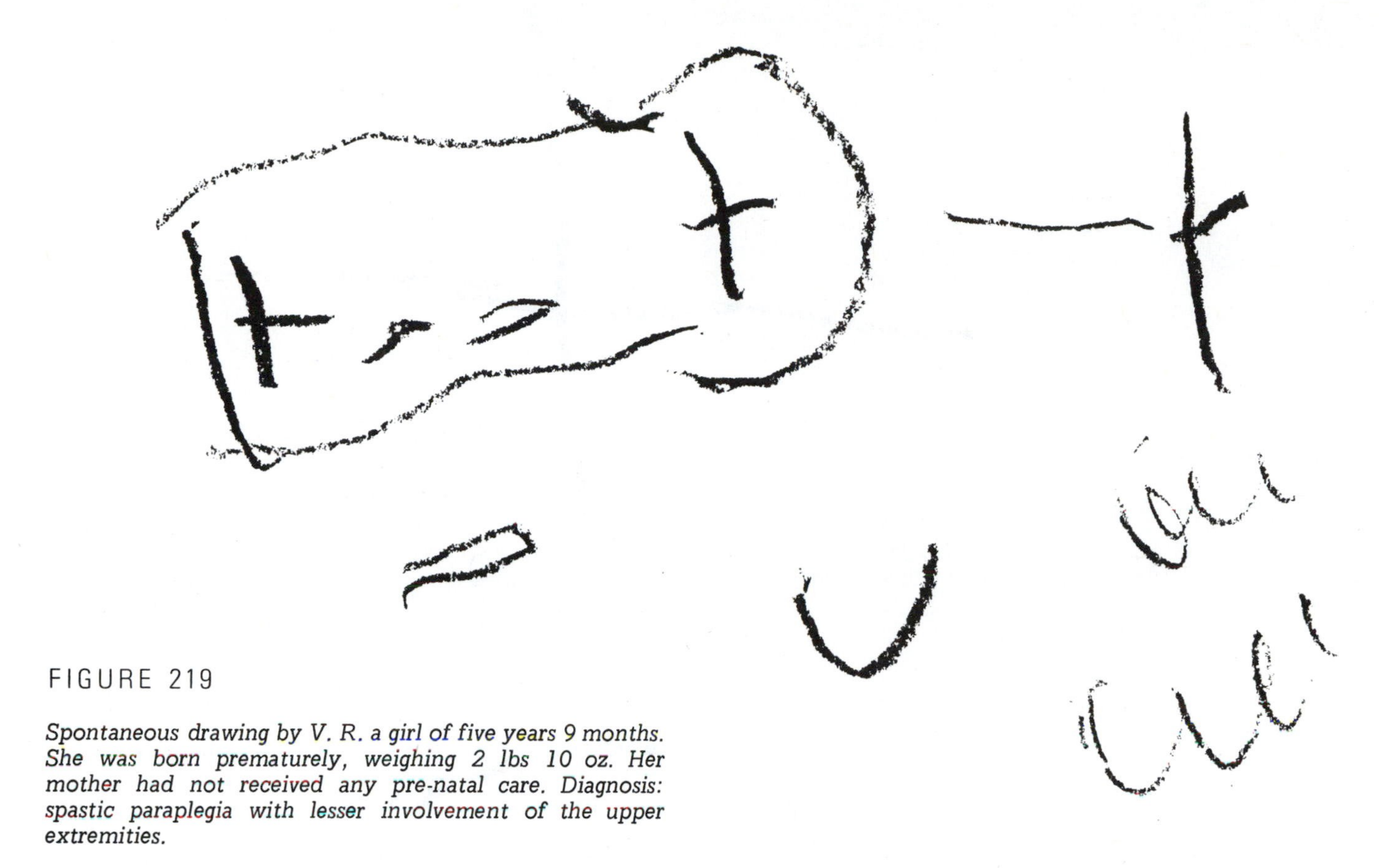

FIGURE 219

Spontaneous drawing by V. R. a girl of five years 9 months. She was born prematurely, weighing 2 lbs 10 oz. Her mother had not received any pre-natal care. Diagnosis: spastic paraplegia with lesser involvement of the upper extremities.

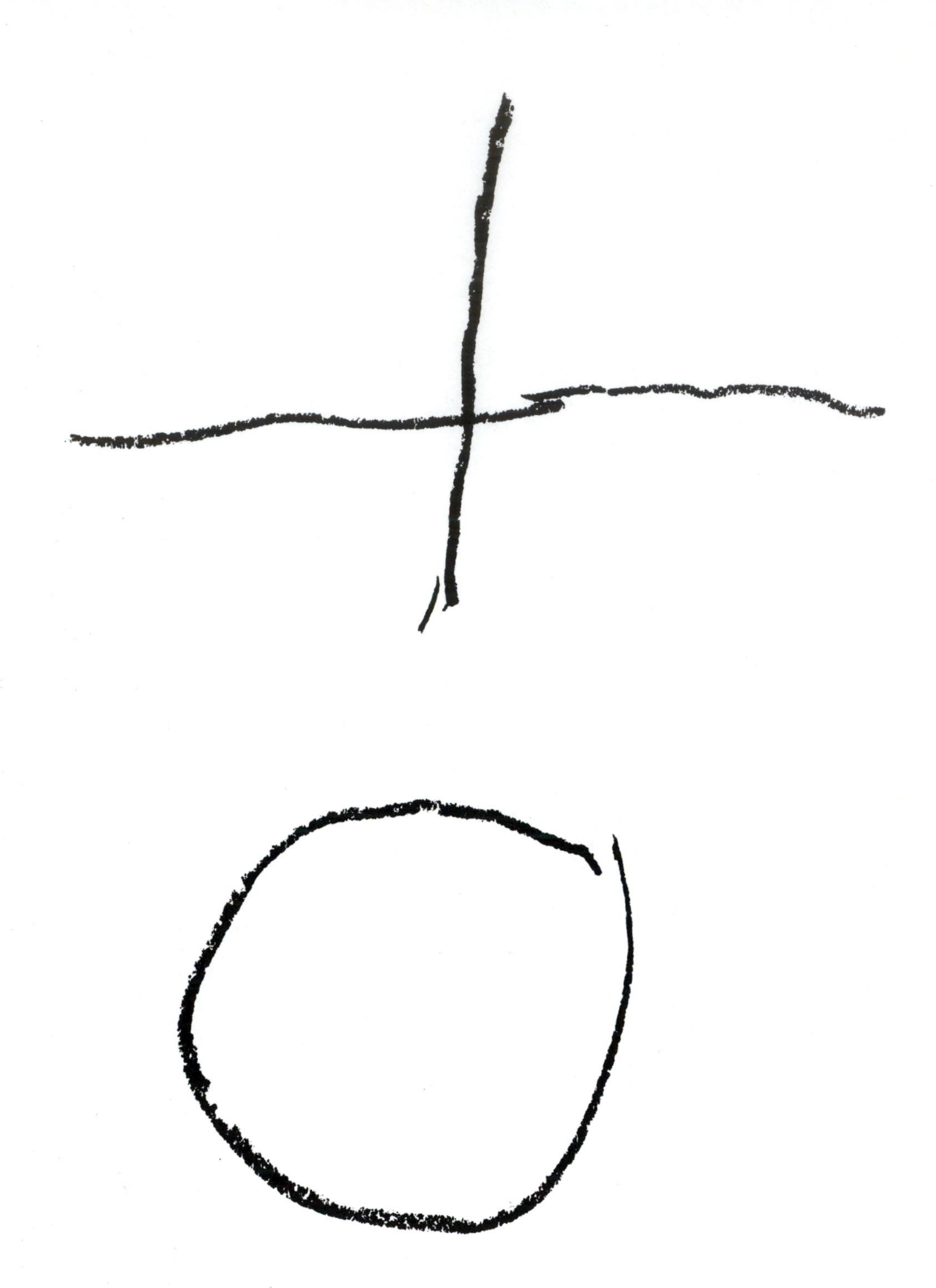

FIGURE 220

Copy of cross and circle by V. R. Cerebral palsy. Age five years 9 months. Note the distortion. Spastic paraplegia with some involvement of upper extremities.

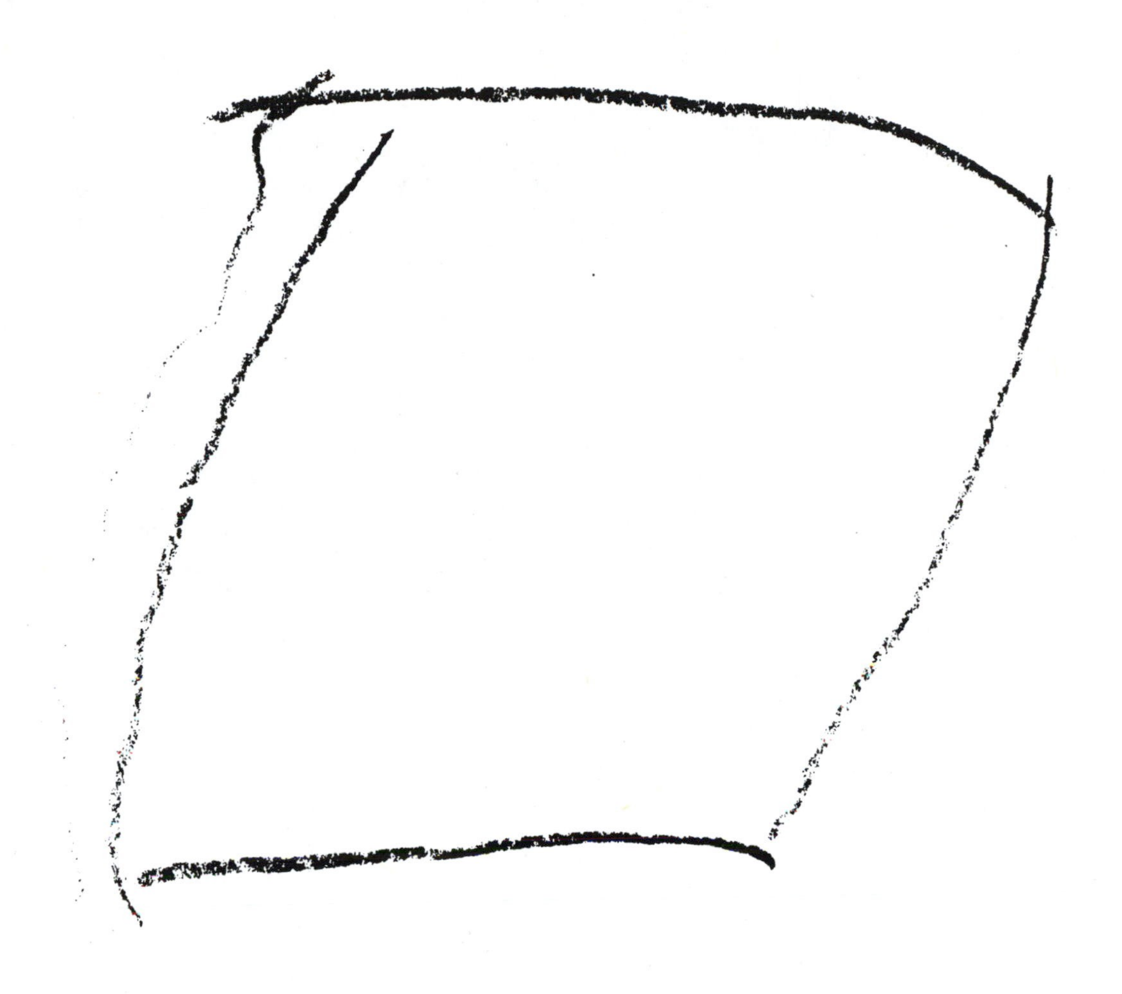

FIGURE 221

Copy of a square.

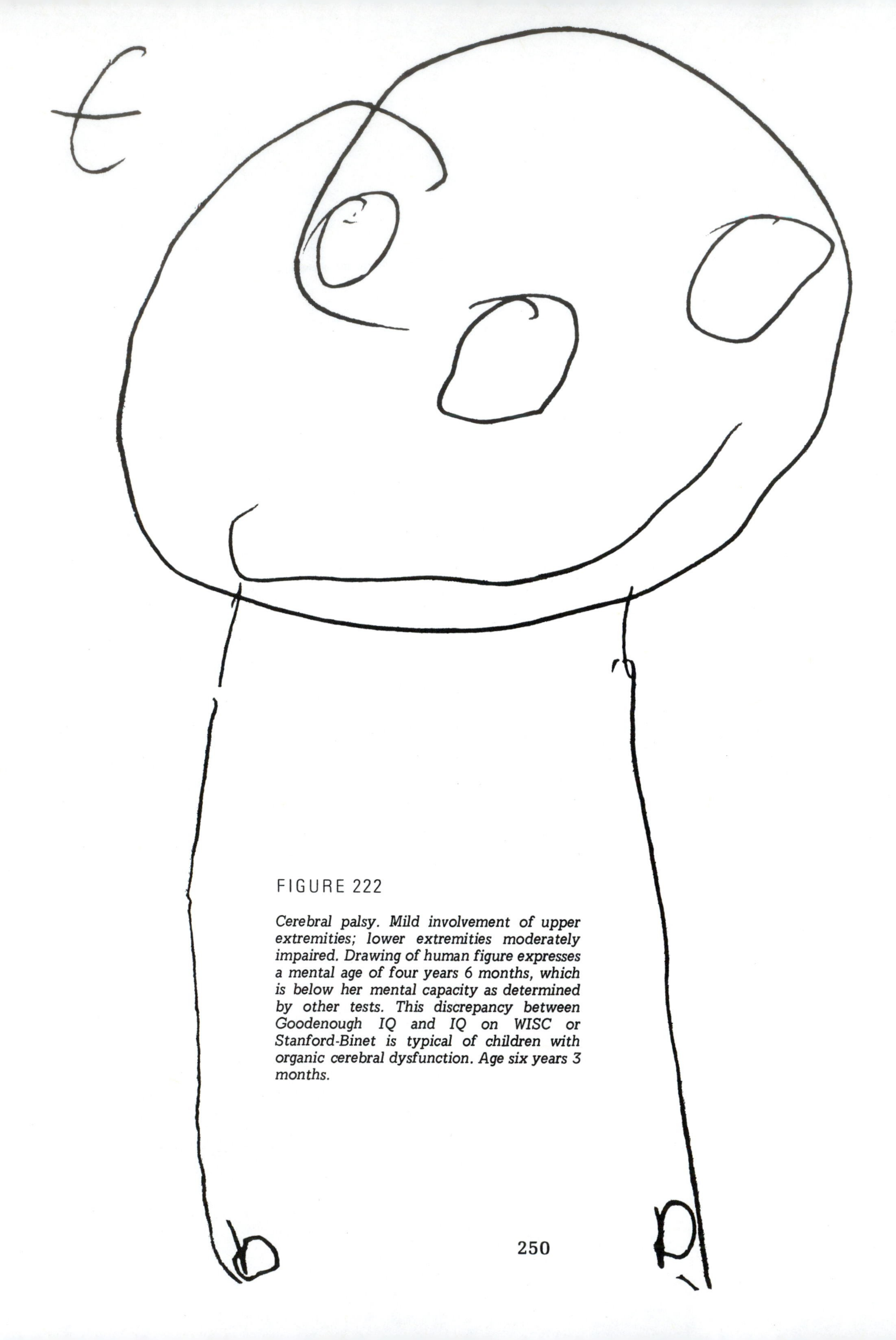

FIGURE 222

Cerebral palsy. Mild involvement of upper extremities; lower extremities moderately impaired. Drawing of human figure expresses a mental age of four years 6 months, which is below her mental capacity as determined by other tests. This discrepancy between Goodenough IQ and IQ on WISC or Stanford-Binet is typical of children with organic cerebral dysfunction. Age six years 3 months.

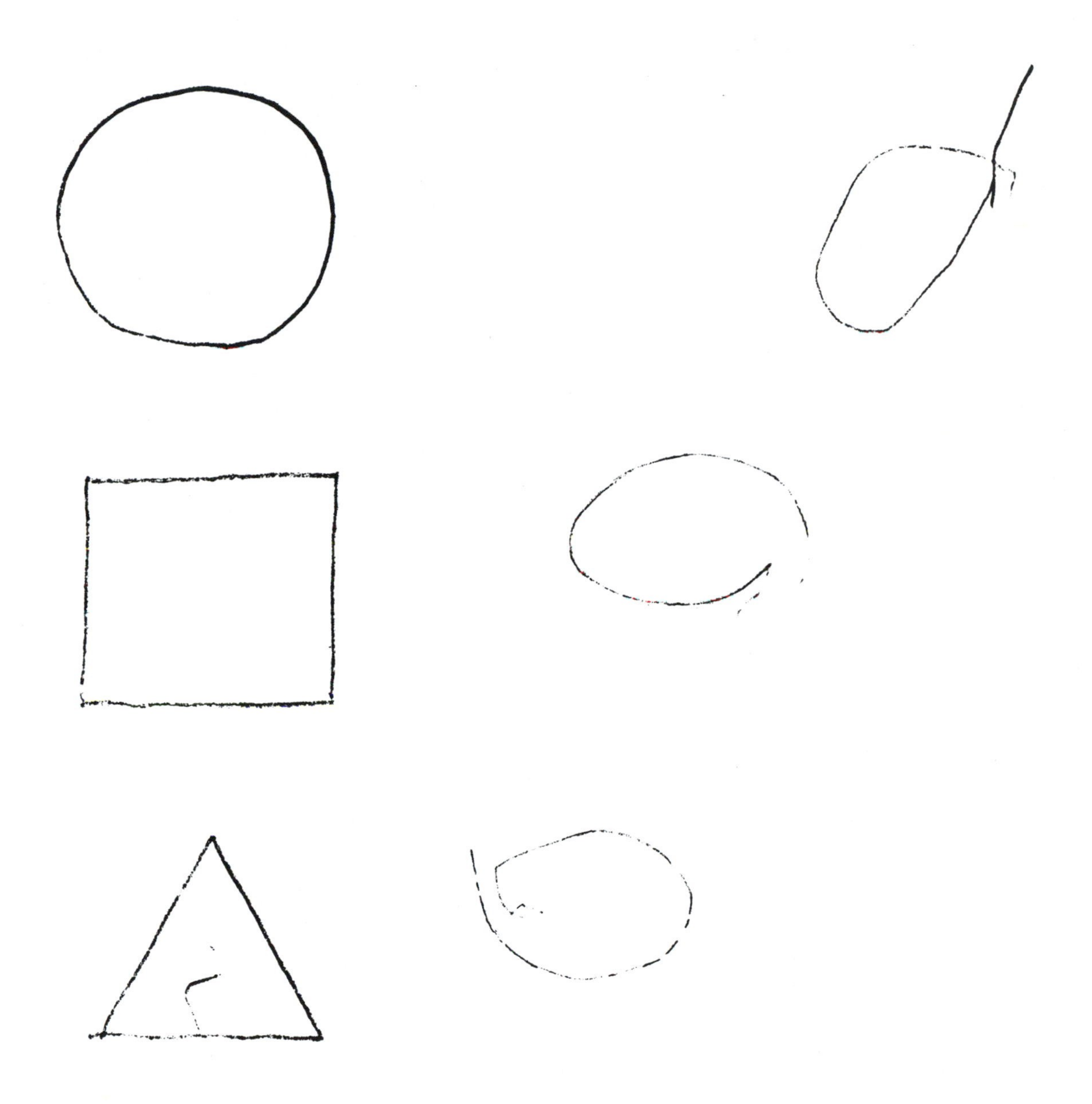

FIGURE 223

Cerebral palsy, right hemiplegia. Seizure disorder. C. D. boy. Chronological age seven years. Attempts to copy Examiner's circle, square and triangle. Drawings by child were made with his left hand.

21

SYNDROMES OF CEREBRAL DYSFUNCTION

The Disruptive Child

An organic nature for the behavior disorder may be suggested by a history of potentially damaging factors operating during the prenatal, circumnatal, or even postnatal development of the brain. Evidences of neurological deficit, occurrence of seizures, disorders of motion or equilibrium would strongly support a diagnosis of organicity. In the category of presumptive evidence for structural or physico-chemical determinants of the behavior disorder are grouped those minor impairments that rise to the level of major disorders when they impede the child's adaptation at school and interfere with his application of an otherwise normal intelligence. These presumptive signs comprise a variety of motor, sensory, and perceptual difficulties which, while not constituting a disability in themselves, give rise to disorders of behavior, thinking, and perception that render the child incapable of adjustment and profitable attendance in regular class.

Apparently, the male is more vulnerable to cerebral damage as well as to most other pathological influences and accordingly, boys make up the vast majority of disruptive children designated as minimally brain-damaged.

Since the focus of this opus is on drawings, other aspects of the problem will be considered only as they find expression in the drawings themselves.

Impulsivity, lack of inhibition: the child scribbles vigorously all over the paper, in a disorganized manner.

Disparity between immature concept of body image and mental age as determined by other tests.

Gross and fine motor awkwardness: inability to stay within lines in tracing.

Perceptual Difficulties: impaired ability to reproduce geometric forms, not due to incoordination or visual disorder. The child has difficulty in perceiving a pattern. Attempts to copy geometric forms result in figures that are distorted, rotated, disorganized. The child may draw the component parts of a pattern but may be unable to organize them in meaningful relationship.

Failure to establish laterality is manifested by shifting the crayon from one hand to the other.

Difficulty in learning to print letters: the child may engage in what is obviously an attempt at "writing" but none of the graphics will be recognizable. This difficulty is related to his inability to perceive patterns. How can one learn to read or write unless one is able to recognize symbols, unless one can differentiate *d* from *p* from *b* from *q;* Dyslexia and dysgraphia are sure to follow.

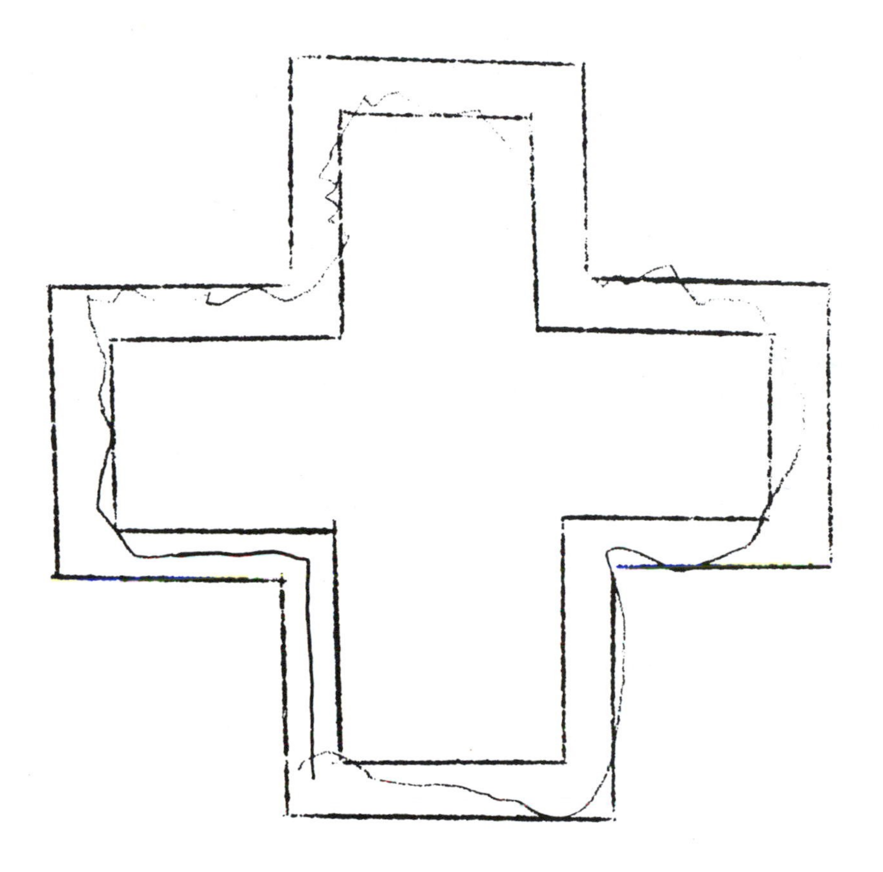

FIGURE 224

D. S. age four years 9 months. Inability to stay within the lines in tracing cross. This task can be performed satisfactorily by most children at age four years 6 months.

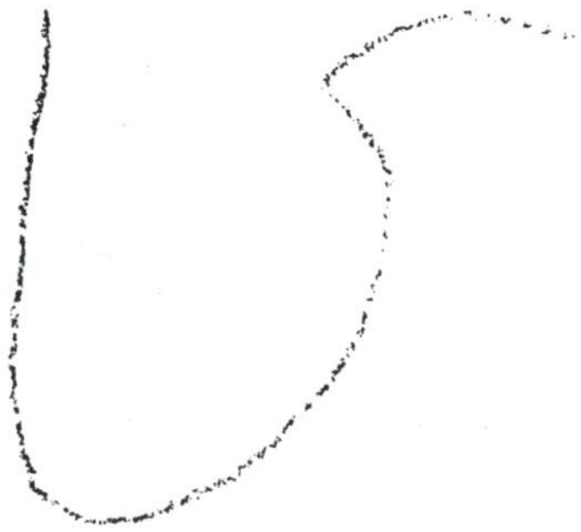

FIGURE 225

Copy of square by D. S. at age four years 9 months. The square can be copied well by most children at four years 6 months.

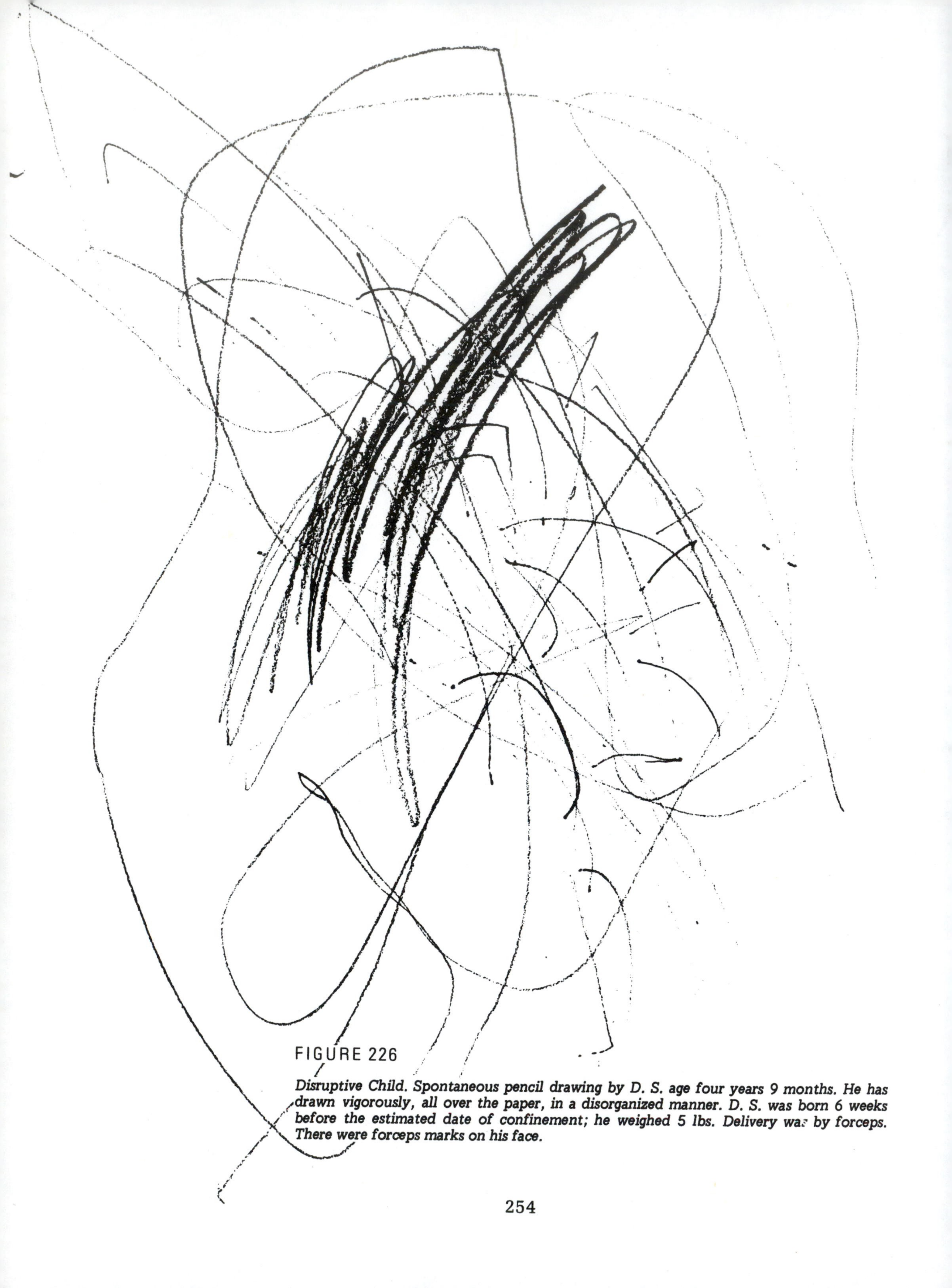

FIGURE 226

Disruptive Child. Spontaneous pencil drawing by D. S. age four years 9 months. He has drawn vigorously, all over the paper, in a disorganized manner. D. S. was born 6 weeks before the estimated date of confinement; he weighed 5 lbs. Delivery was by forceps. There were forceps marks on his face.

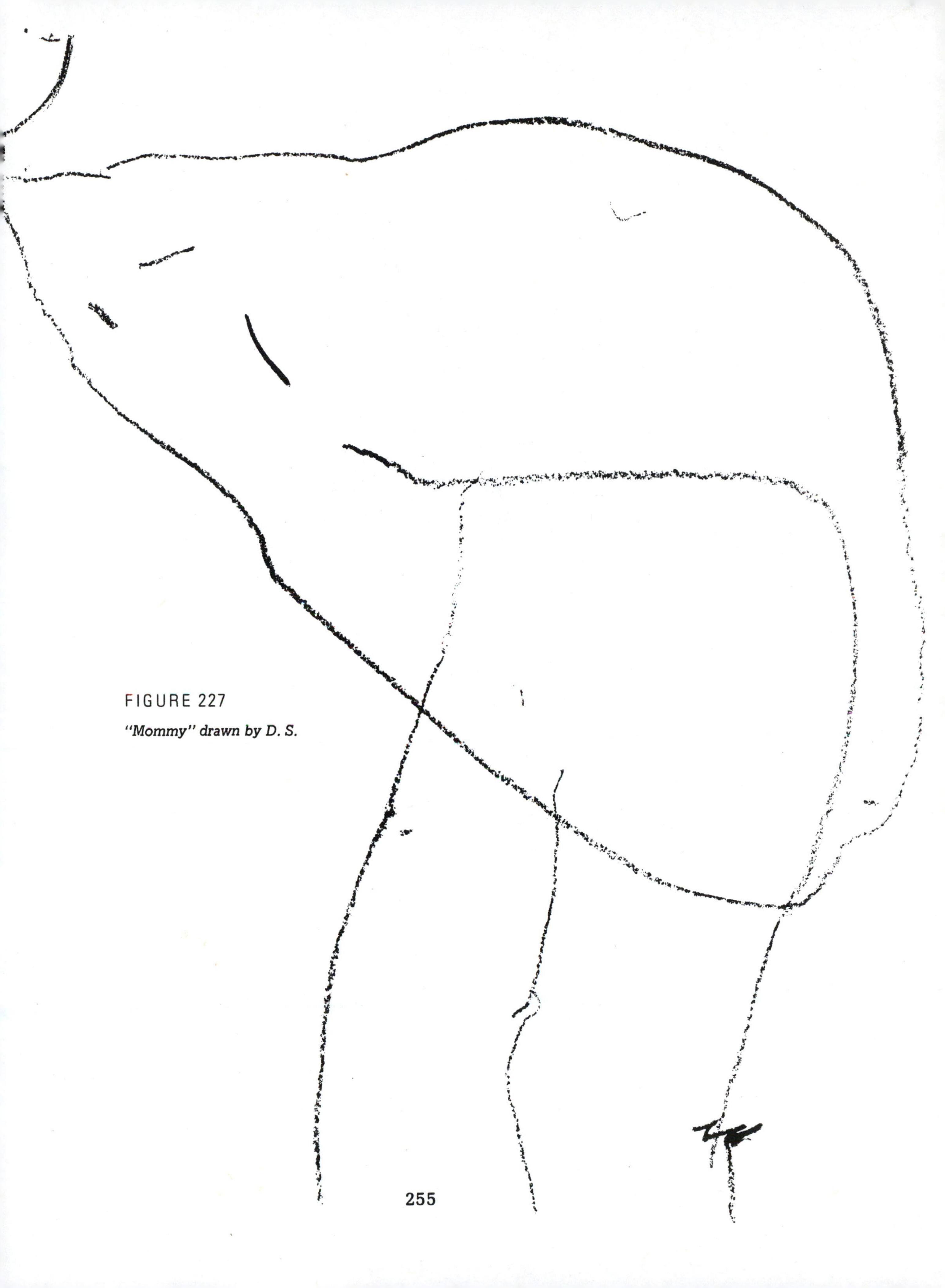

FIGURE 227

"Mommy" drawn by D. S.

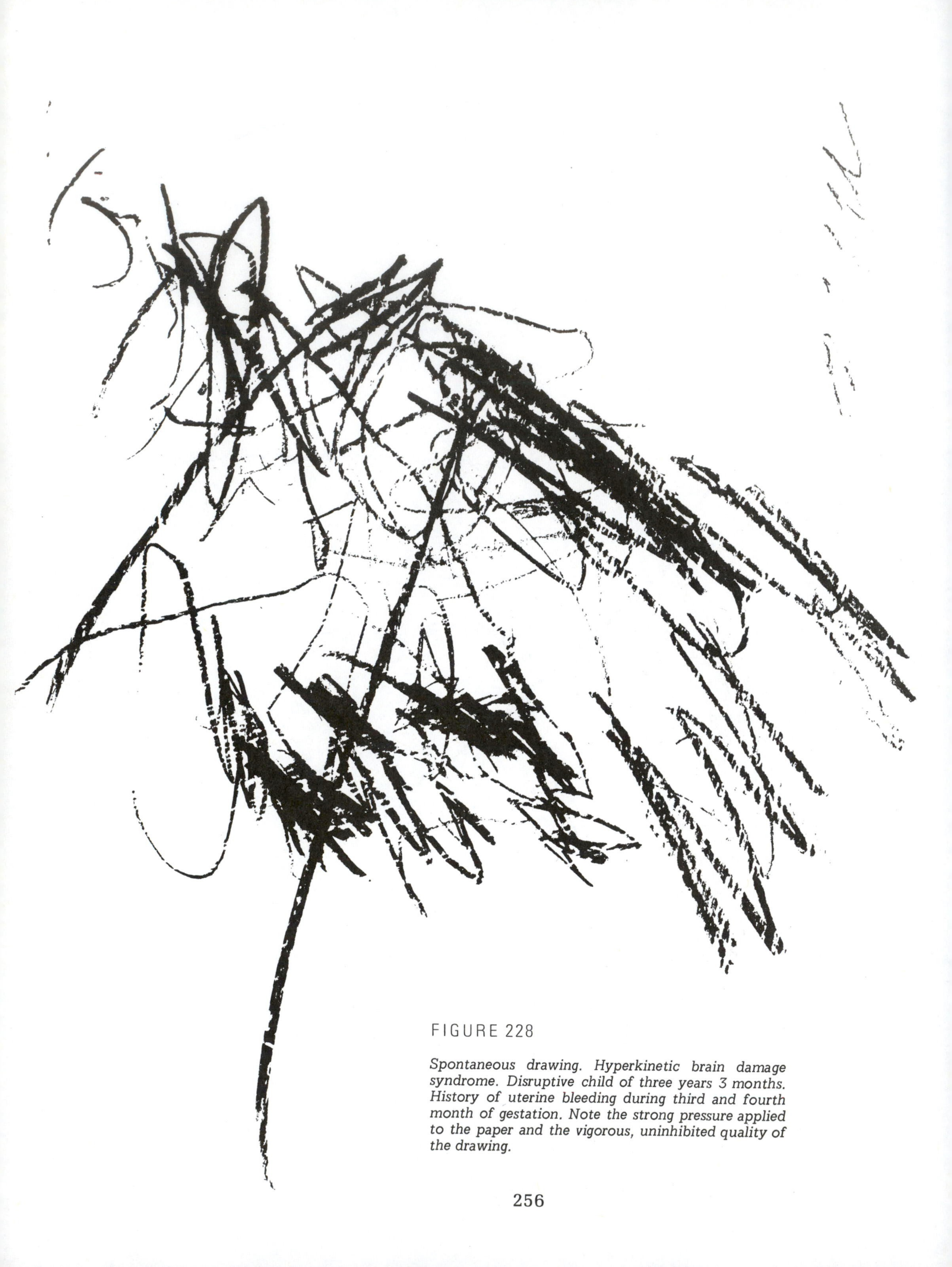

FIGURE 228

Spontaneous drawing. Hyperkinetic brain damage syndrome. Disruptive child of three years 3 months. History of uterine bleeding during third and fourth month of gestation. Note the strong pressure applied to the paper and the vigorous, uninhibited quality of the drawing.

FIGURE 229

Spontaneous drawing. Hyperkinetic brain damage syndrome. Responds to sound. No speech. Uninhibited, disruptive, affectionate towards mother. Boy. Age three years 3 months. History of uterine bleeding during 3rd-4th month of gestation. Vigorous scribble. Lumber crayon held in fist. Strong pressure applied to paper.

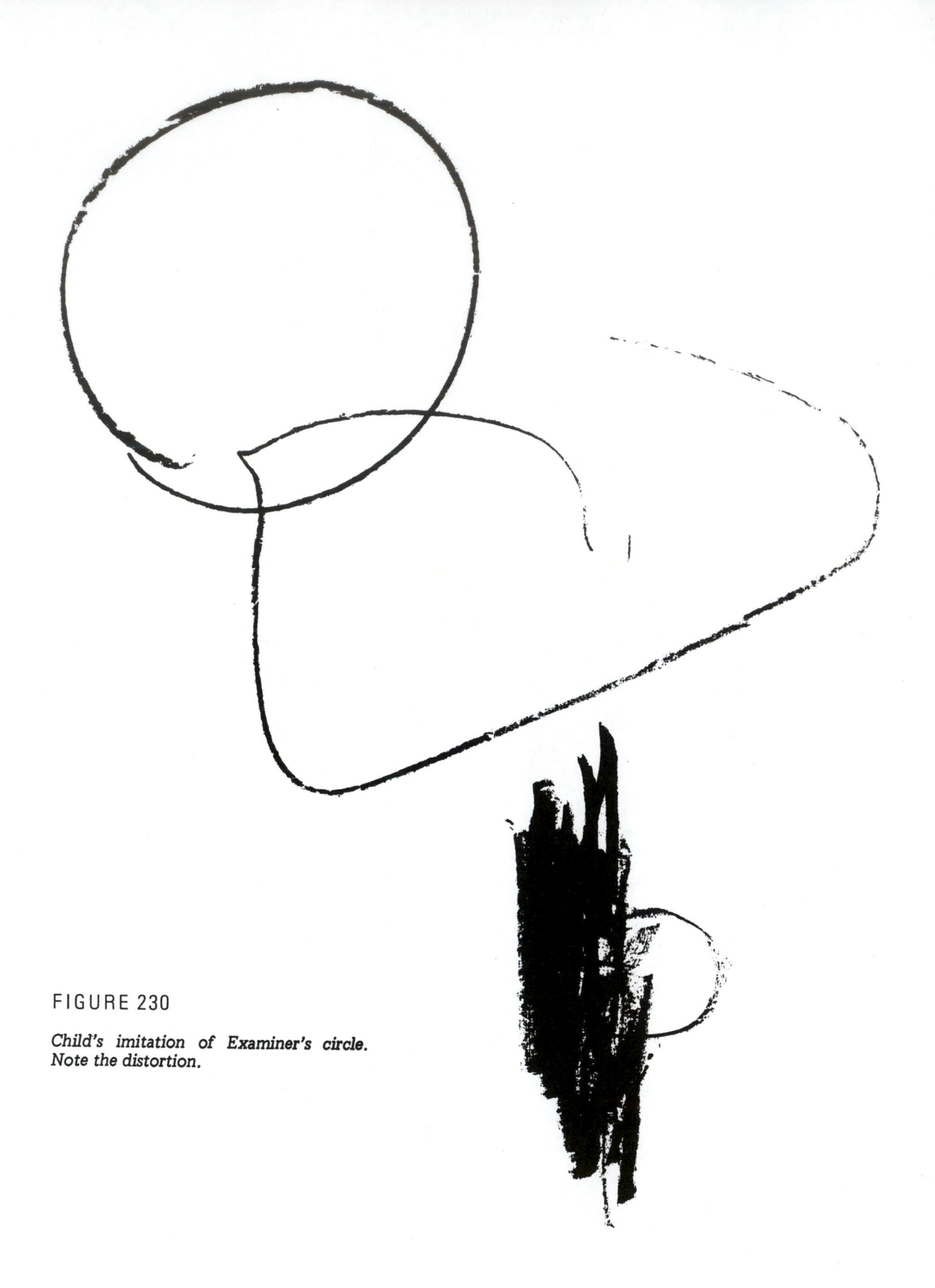

FIGURE 230

Child's imitation of Examiner's circle. Note the distortion.

FIGURE 231

First attempt to imitate Examiner's cross. The child has scribbled over the Examiner's cross.

FIGURE 232

Second attempt to imitate cross drawn by Examiner.

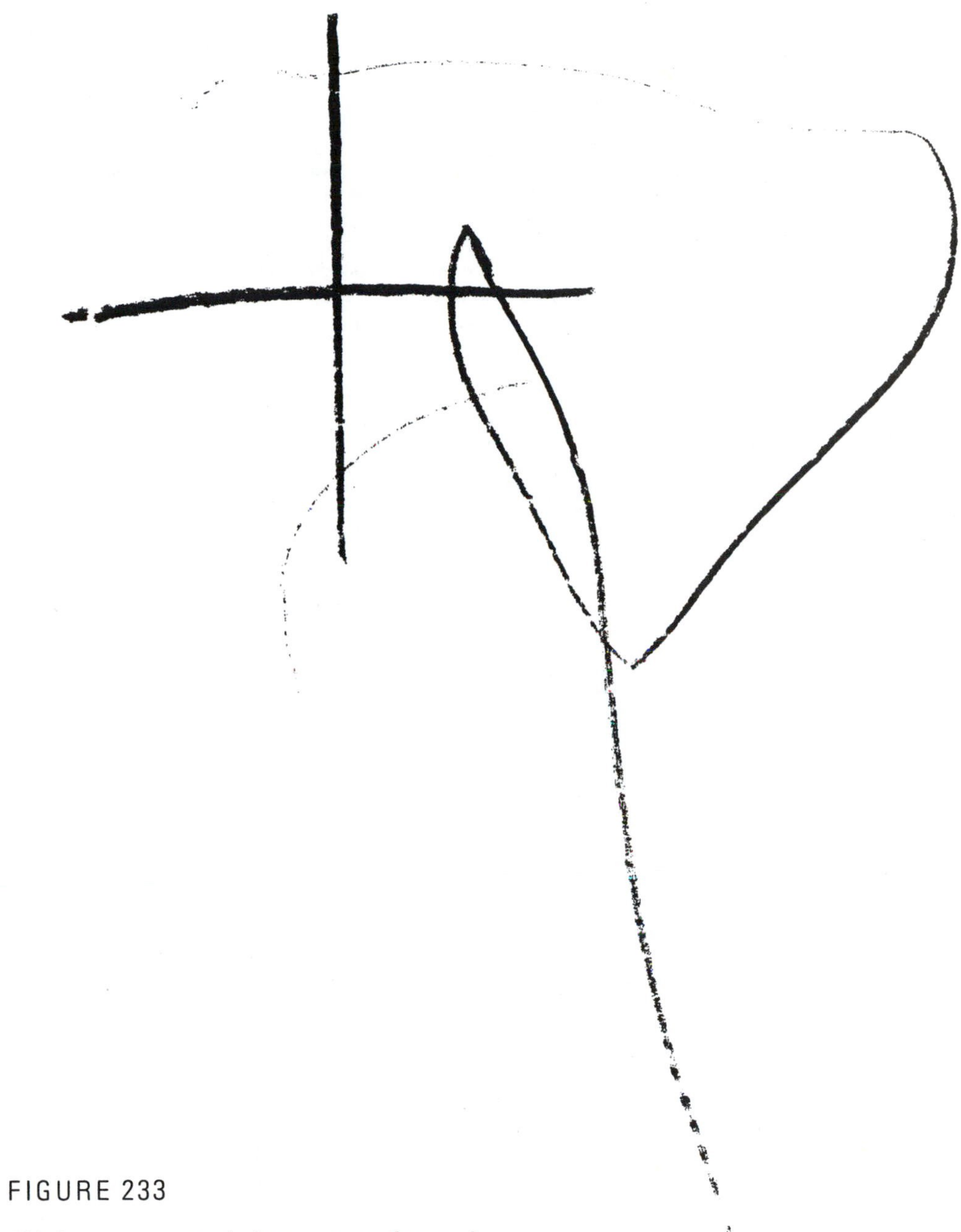

FIGURE 233

Third attempt to imitate cross drawn by Examiner.

Hyperkinetic Brain Damage Syndrome. J. I. boy. Age five years 6 months and also at age six years 9 months.

Disruptive. Low frustration threshold. Short attention span. Diffuse brain damage resulted from a head injury sustained at age 18 months. The child was unconscious for 10 minutes followed by vomiting. Not mentally retarded. Fine motor coordination fair. Speech well developed but indistinct.

The first set of drawings (Figures 234-236) made when he was five years 6 months show his inability to draw anything that even suggests a man; ability to imitate a vertical and a horizontal; but inability to even imitate a cross though able to draw its component parts. He could not perceive the cross as a pattern.

In his drawings made at age six years 9 months (Figures 237-241), he draws a recognizable man but at an immature level. The figure has no body. It yields a mental age of four years 9 months (Goodenough scoring). He tries to print his name but letters are poorly made. He copies a cross using 3 strokes to do so. Presented with a picture of a square, he makes a circle and makes a similar circular figure when presented with a picture of a triangle.

He has been unable to learn to read at all. Special education and perceptual training are recommended.

FIGURE 234

J. I. boy. Age five years 6 months. Drawing of a man: unrecognizable.

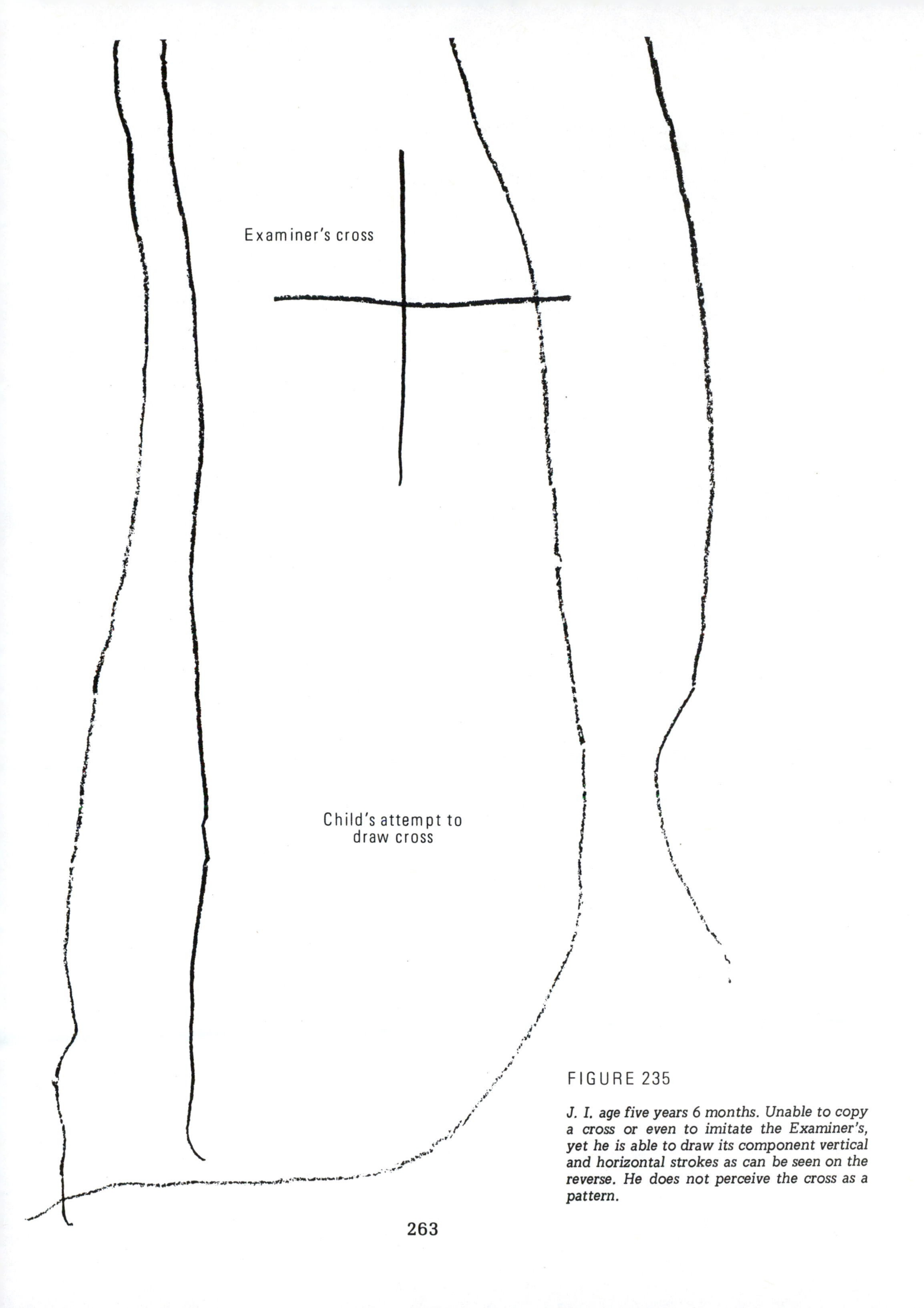

FIGURE 235

J. I. age five years 6 months. Unable to copy a cross or even to imitate the Examiner's, yet he is able to draw its component vertical and horizontal strokes as can be seen on the reverse. He does not perceive the cross as a pattern.

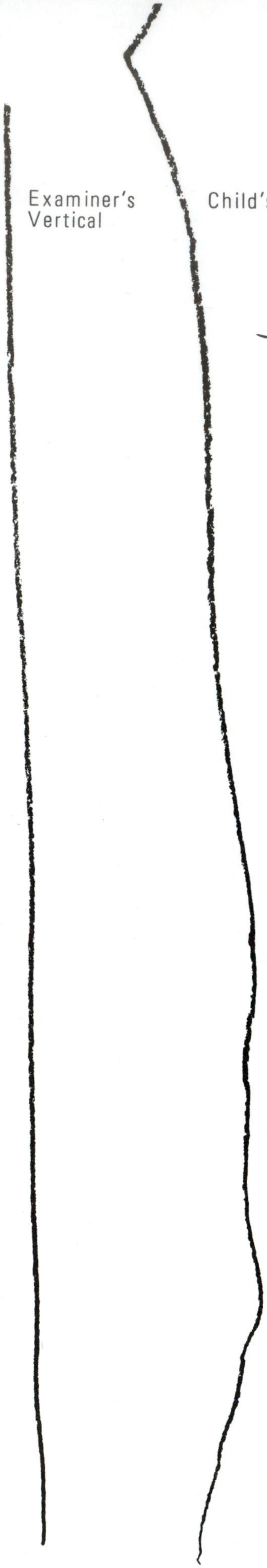

Examiner's
Vertical

Child's vertical

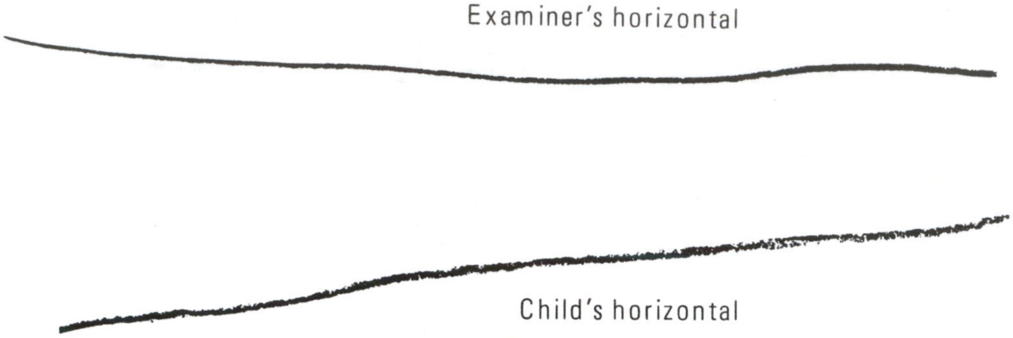

Examiner's horizontal

Child's horizontal

FIGURE 236

Able to draw vertical and horizontal strokes but unable to relate them into a new figure, a cross.

FIGURE 237

J. I. age six years 9 months. Immature concept of body image.

FIGURE 238

J. I. age six years 9 months. Attempt to print name.

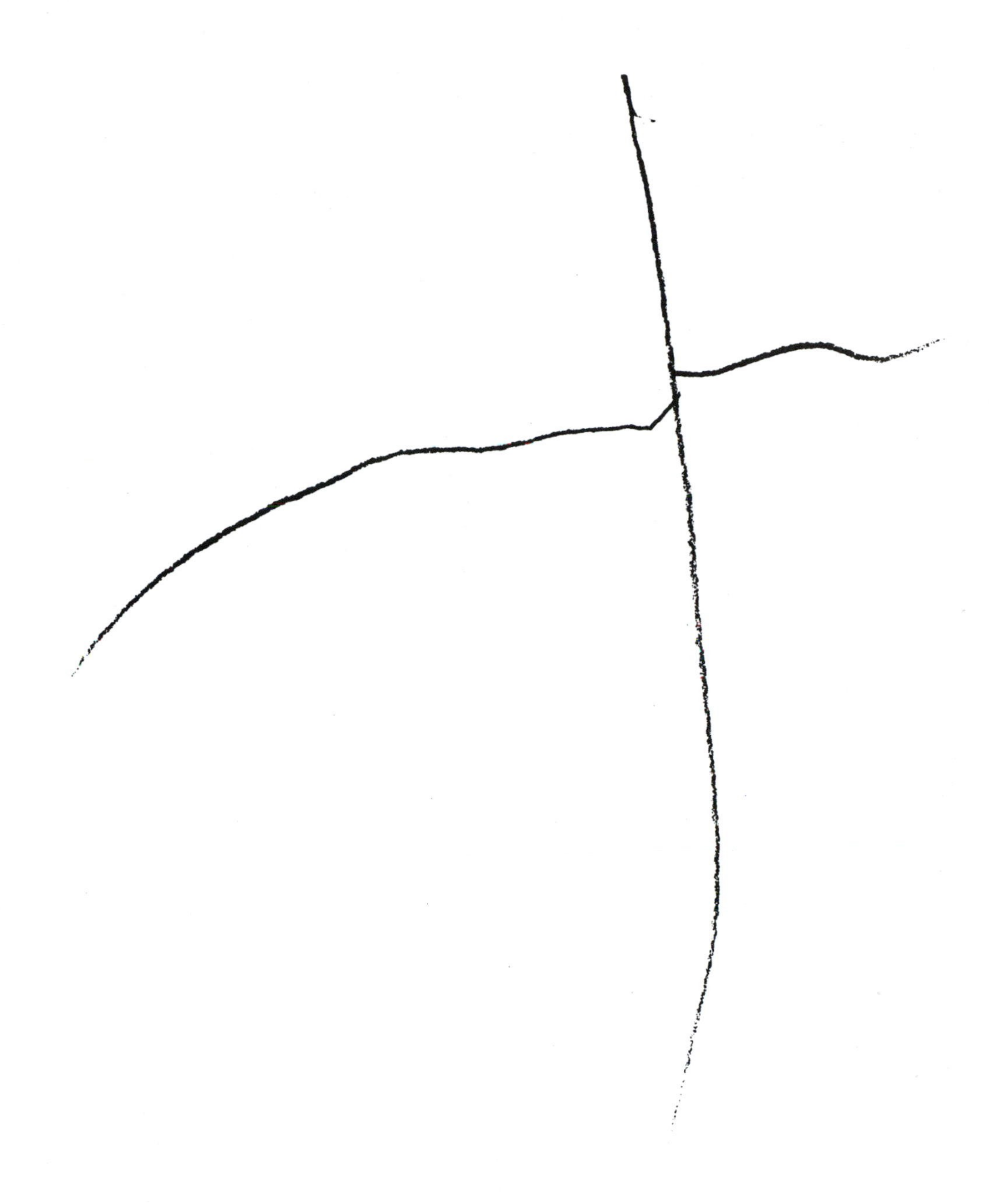

FIGURE 239

J. I. age six years 9 months. Copy of cross. Note 3 strokes.

FIGURE 240

J. I. age six years 9 months. Copy of square.

FIGURE 241

J. I. age six years 9 months. Copy of triangle.

FIGURE 242

E. T. Hyperkinetic brain damage syndrome in an adopted boy. Age: six years 2 months. Mother had no prenatal care. Delivery was by mid-forceps at term. Birth weight was low: five lbs.

The shading in this figure drawing is considered an expression of anxiety. He is extremely jealous of a younger adopted sibling. Normal intelligence. WISC: verbal IQ 110, performance IQ 98. Crossed dominance: left-handed, right-eyed.

FIGURE 243

E. T. Drawing of family. Age: six years 2 months. Extremely jealous of younger adopted sibling (baby). Note that mother is holding baby and that she is turned away from him.

FIGURE 244

E. T. drawing of man at age seven years 9 months. He crossed over it and started jumping up and down saying he made a mistake.

FIGURE 245

E. T. Figure drawing at age seven years 9 months. Note the fierce expression. Teacher thinks the boy is mad at the world.

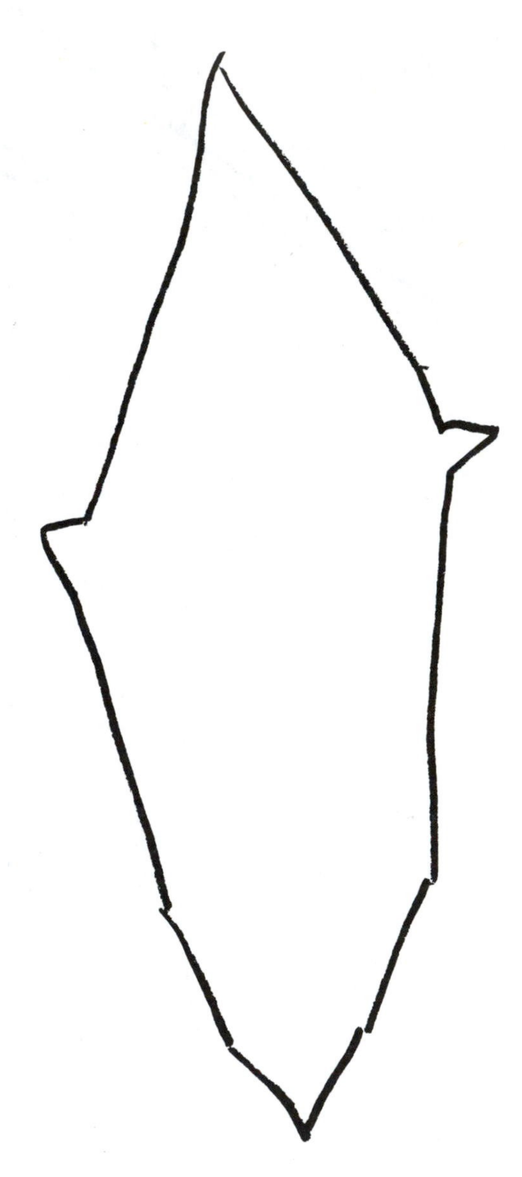

FIGURE 246

E. T. Copy of diamond at age seven years 9 months. Note the "ears".

FIGURE 247

E. T. Boy. Chronological age: seven years 8 months. Attempt to copy Bender Figure A. Most children of six can make a satisfactory copy.

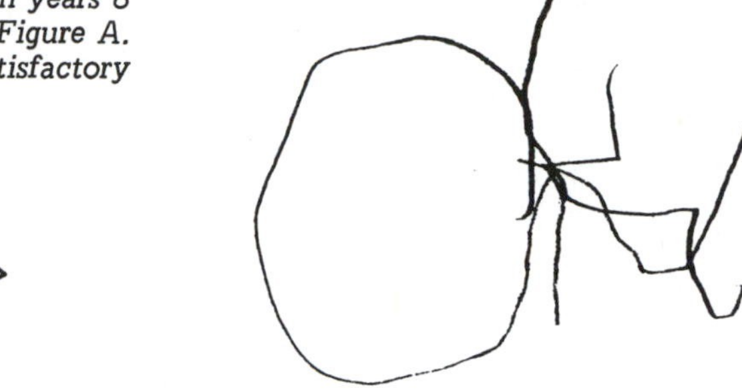

J. N. age seven years. Adopted. Presenting problem: extremely restless at school; provocative; poor school work in first grade. Neurological: no signs of deficit. Rapid alternating movements fair. Gait awkward. Intelligence: IQ 107 on the Revised Stanford-Binet Form M-L. Laterality: crossed dominance; right-handed but left-eyed. Psychologist reports poorly copied Bender figures. Figure drawing: reveals immature concept of body image at variance with child's IQ on Stanford-Binet, the figure drawing yields a mental age of five years 9 months (Goodenough test). Copy of geometric forms: unsatisfactory copy of diamond; other figures poorly drawn. Impression: minimal cerebral dysfunction. Etiology: obscure.

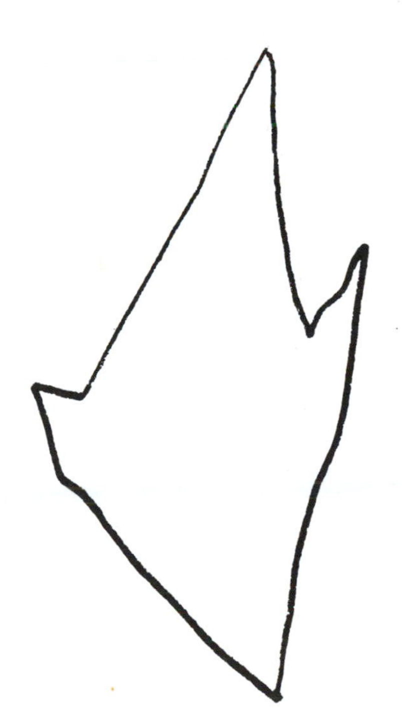

FIGURE 248

Copy of diamond. Note the "ears". The norm for copying a diamond is seven years.

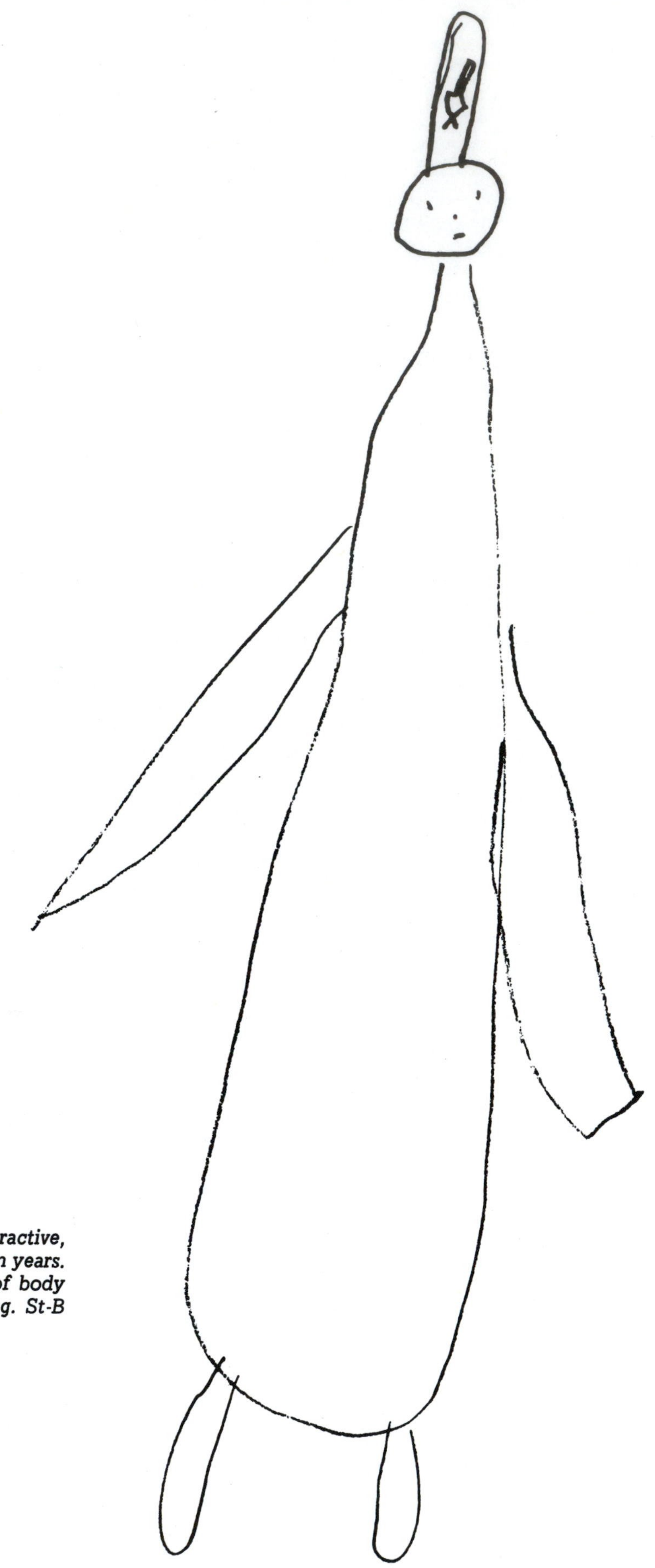

FIGURE 249

Minimal cerebral dysfunction. Hyperactive, poor adjustment at school. Age: seven years. Disparity between IQ and concept of body image as expressed in figure drawing. St-B IQ: 107. Goodenough IQ: 81.

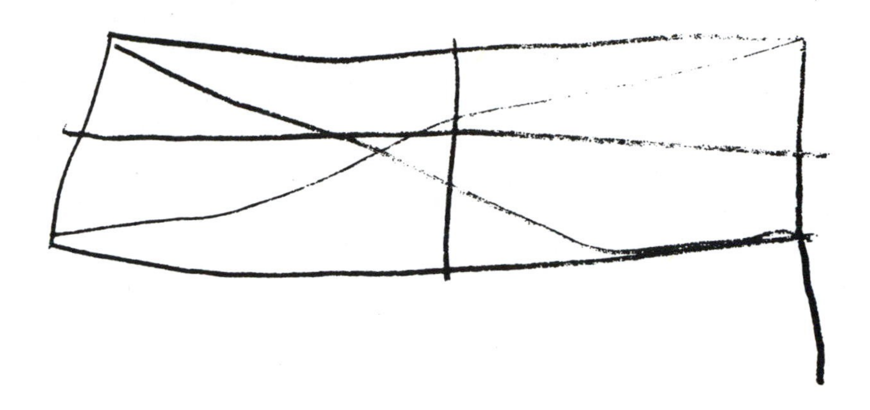

FIGURE 250

Copy of rectangle with diagonals. Most children can copy the figure well at age five years 6 months.

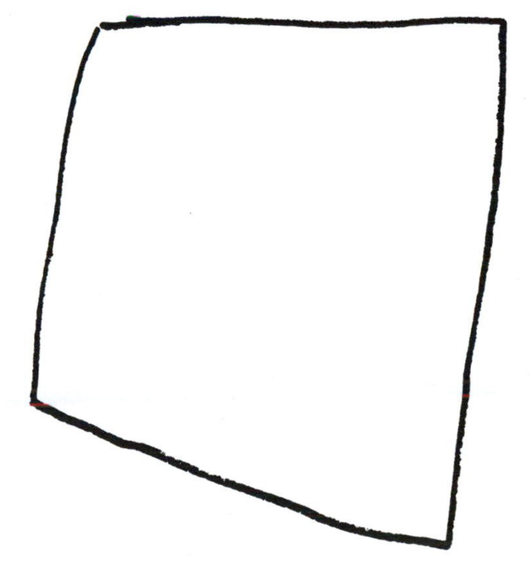

FIGURE 251

Copy of square. The norm for copying the square is four years 6 months.

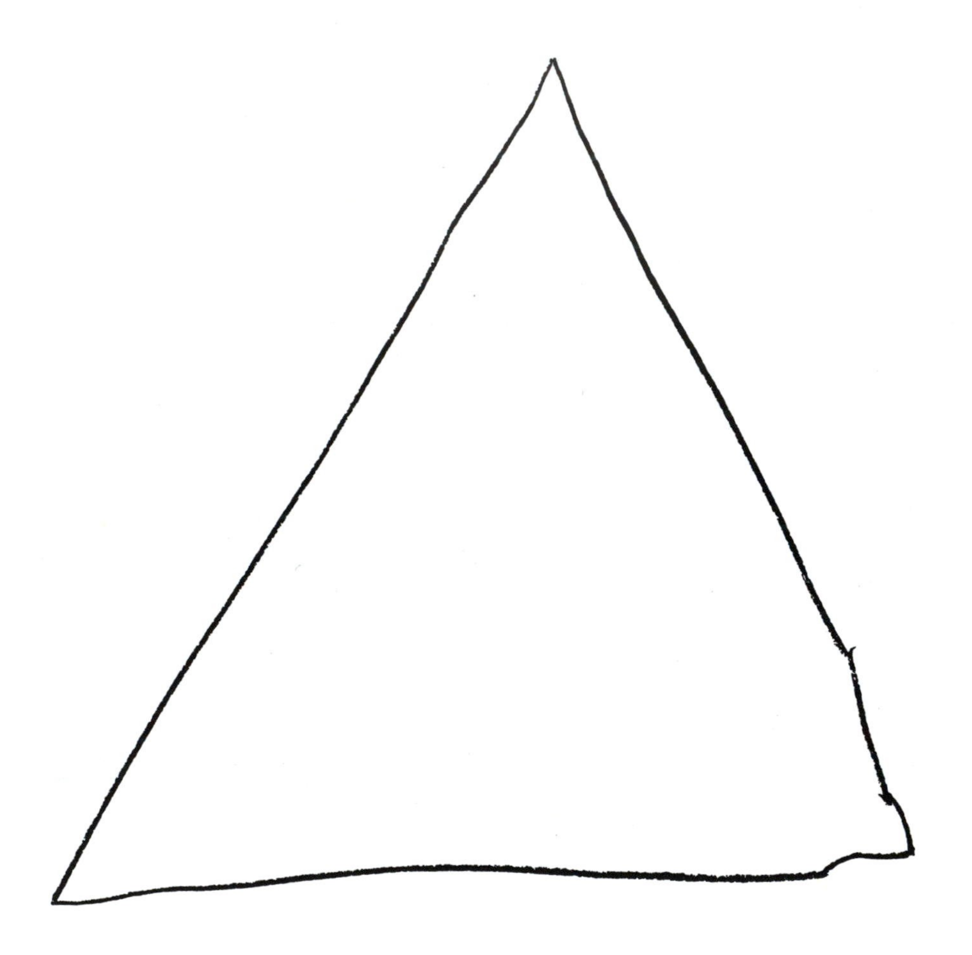

FIGURE 252

Copy of triangle. The norm for this figure is five years.

J. T. Two drawings by a seven-year-old boy with a history of meningitis at age 6 months.

The first is his drawing of a man and is at a level significantly lower than one would expect of a child of his intelligence. This disparity illustrates the immature concept of the body image that is typical of children with organic cerebral dysfunction.

The second drawing is his copy of a diamond. This difficulty in reproducing geometric forms at age level expectations and mental age expectations is likewise typical of children with minimal cerebral dysfunction as well as of children with clear-cut evidence of brain damage.

FIGURE 253

J. T. Disparity between Goodenough score and mental age. Immature concept of body image in a boy of seven years 5 months with a history of meningitis at age 6 months. Average intelligence. Perceptual impairment evident in his attempt to copy a diamond *(see next page).*

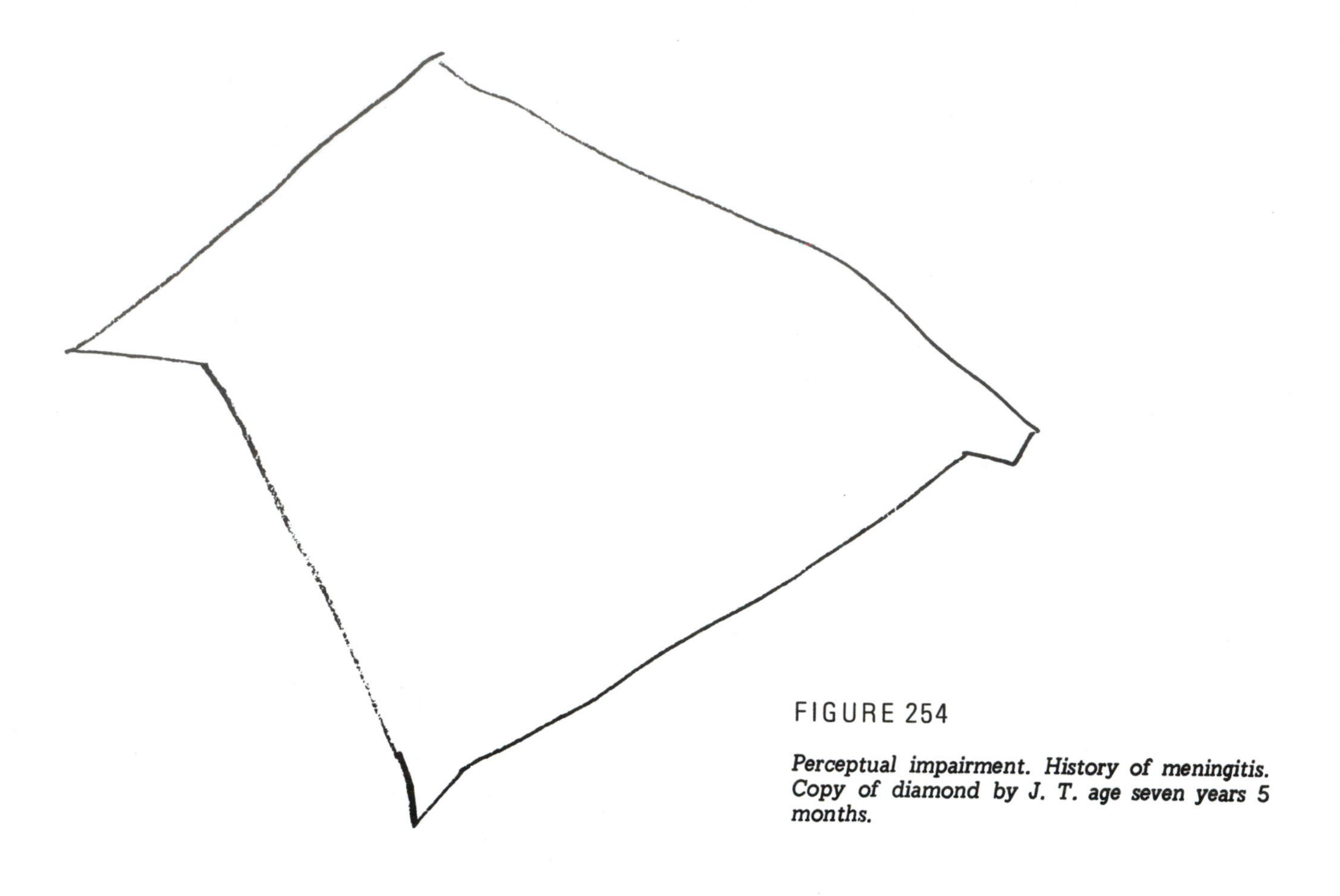

FIGURE 254

Perceptual impairment. History of meningitis. Copy of diamond by J. T. age seven years 5 months.

FIGURE 255

Immature perception of body image in a boy of nine years 6 months. Dyslexia. Disruptive at school. Disparity between low score on Goodenough Draw-a-man test (mental age eight years 3 months) and high average to superior performance on Stanford-Binet and WISC.

FIGURE 256

Minimal Cerebral Dysfunction, J. N., boy. Age eight years 6 months. Crossed dominance; immature concept body image; perceptual impairment; inability to copy diamond (note typical "ears" on the diamond); short attention span. Disruptive at school. History of uterine bleeding during pregnancy.

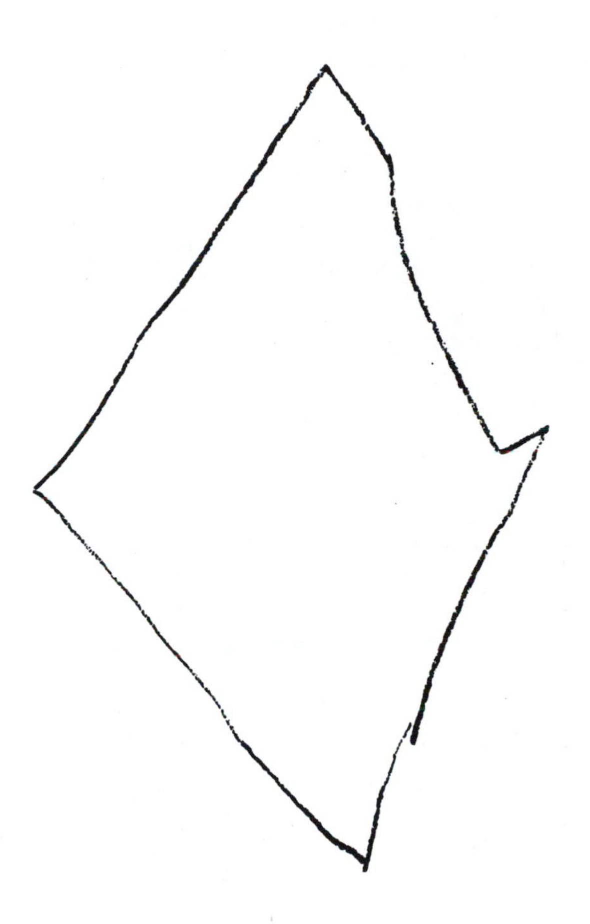

FIGURE 257

Typical copy of diamond in perceptual impairment, boy of eight years 6 months.

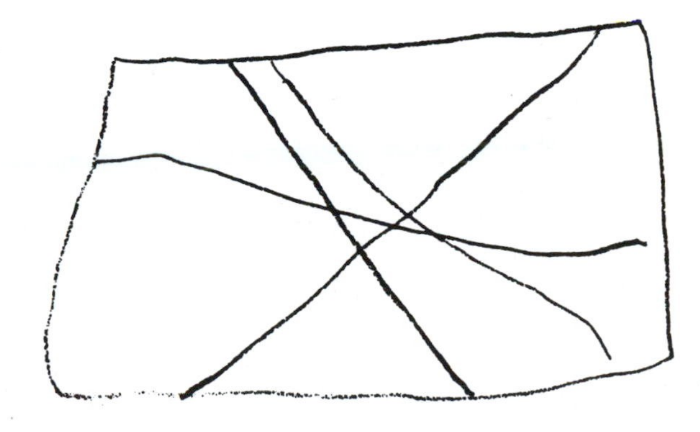

FIGURE 258

22

COMMUNICATION DISORDERS: SENSORI-NEURAL HEARING LOSS

The inability to speak or to develop language may stem from a variety of causes operating singly or in combination. Clarity of diagnosis and early case-finding are at the base of effective treatment. Hearing loss, receptive or expressive aphasia, emotional disorder may be responsible for the child's failure to communicate verbally. Differential diagnosis is often difficult and requires the combined skills of a multidisciplinary staff composed of pediatrician, otologist, audiometrist, psychologist, social worker, special educator, in some cases a child psychiatrist, and above all a coordinator to integrate the specialists' findings and plan an appropriate program.

In the three categories of communication disorders mentioned above, that is, those resulting from hearing loss, cerebral dysfunction, or emotional disorder, drawings are often valuable aids in supporting or in formulating a diagnostic impression. Diagnosis is particularly difficult when, as is often the case, a combination of factors are complicating and obscuring the basic deficit. A disorder of language originally traceable to hearing loss may be aggravated by an emotional overlay due in turn to parental rejection or lack of understanding.

Sensori-Neural Hearing Loss

This term is used to designate impairment of hearing when the site of the lesion is in the cochlea or in the auditory nerve before it enters the brain stem. Hence, it is also called 8th nerve deafness. In uncomplicated cases, the brain is structurally intact. One would, therefore, not expect to find impaired perception as is typically the case where the disorder is central—in the brain itself. Experimental findings, however, indicate that impaired perception is frequently found in deaf children, even where there is no evidence of organic cerebral involvement. Myklebust and Brutten were able to demonstrate a marked inferiority in the ability of deaf children to reproduce marble patterns and in figure–ground tests. This should not be surprising if one considers the interrelatedness of the senses. "No receptor operates in isolation" (Hartmann). The functional unity of the entire sensorium has been stressed by the Gestalt School of psychology as well as by Gesell who speaks of the "interweaving" of vision with the other sensory modalities, of hearing as a "specialized form of touch which makes the organism aware of vibrations of distant origin." An intimate relationship is demonstrable, both structurally and functionally, between the visual and auditory systems; neurological connections exist at both cortical and subcortical levels. Furthermore, the unit of the senses is integrated into a greater unity that comprises the motor function: movements of eyes and fingers enhance vision and touch respectively. In normal children, all sensory and motor activities contribute to form perceptions and concepts of the outside world of persons and things. Luisa T. was not lovely to look at, she was short and quite heavy; but when she sang, she was "divine." Obviously, the deaf person's perception of Luisa differed from that of the listener who could appreciate the most attractive of her generous dimensions. Logically, then, the impairment of one of the two distance receptors will tend to affect perception in a negative sense. And since perception affects thinking, it follows that perceptual impairment may hamper the child's mental functioning. In this instance, logic and the facts seem to be in agreement, in that deaf children tend to exhibit difficulty in their ability to abstract; their thinking continues to be in concrete terms long after normal children have attained the higher level of thought.

In what way do the drawings of deaf children reflect the impairment of perception noted by Myklebust and Brutten and mentioned in the preceding paragraph? So far as the present writer has been able to determine from a study of drawings produced by preschool children attending a special school, the lack of the auditory component in perceptual patterning does not affect the child's ability to reproduce a circle, a cross, a triangle, or a square; nor does it impede his ability to draw the human figure at a level consonant with his chronological and mental age. Not unless the brain, too, is either structurally or metabolically contributing to the disorder. If this interpretation is correct, drawings by children with communication disorders may be validly used as criteria in differentiating peripheral from central disorders. Where the brain is intact, the drawings will fail to show the distortions and deficiencies typically present in the drawings of children with known cerebral involvement. Nor will the drawings of the human figure by the child with a sensori-neural hearing loss show the discrepancy between Goodenough and mental age typical of children with central language disorder.

FIGURE 259

Sensori-Neural Hearing Loss. No perceptual impairment. The geometric figures are drawn at expected levels of competence for her chronological age. She has made satisfactory copies of the cross, square, and triangle. She is only six years 6 months of age. The average age for copying the diamond is seven. The figure drawing yields a mental age of six, which is in the range of average. Drawing of a person is readily recognizable and at the expected level for the child's chronological age. In this case the communication disorder is the result of damage to the cochlea; the brain is not involved, cerebral functions are not impaired.

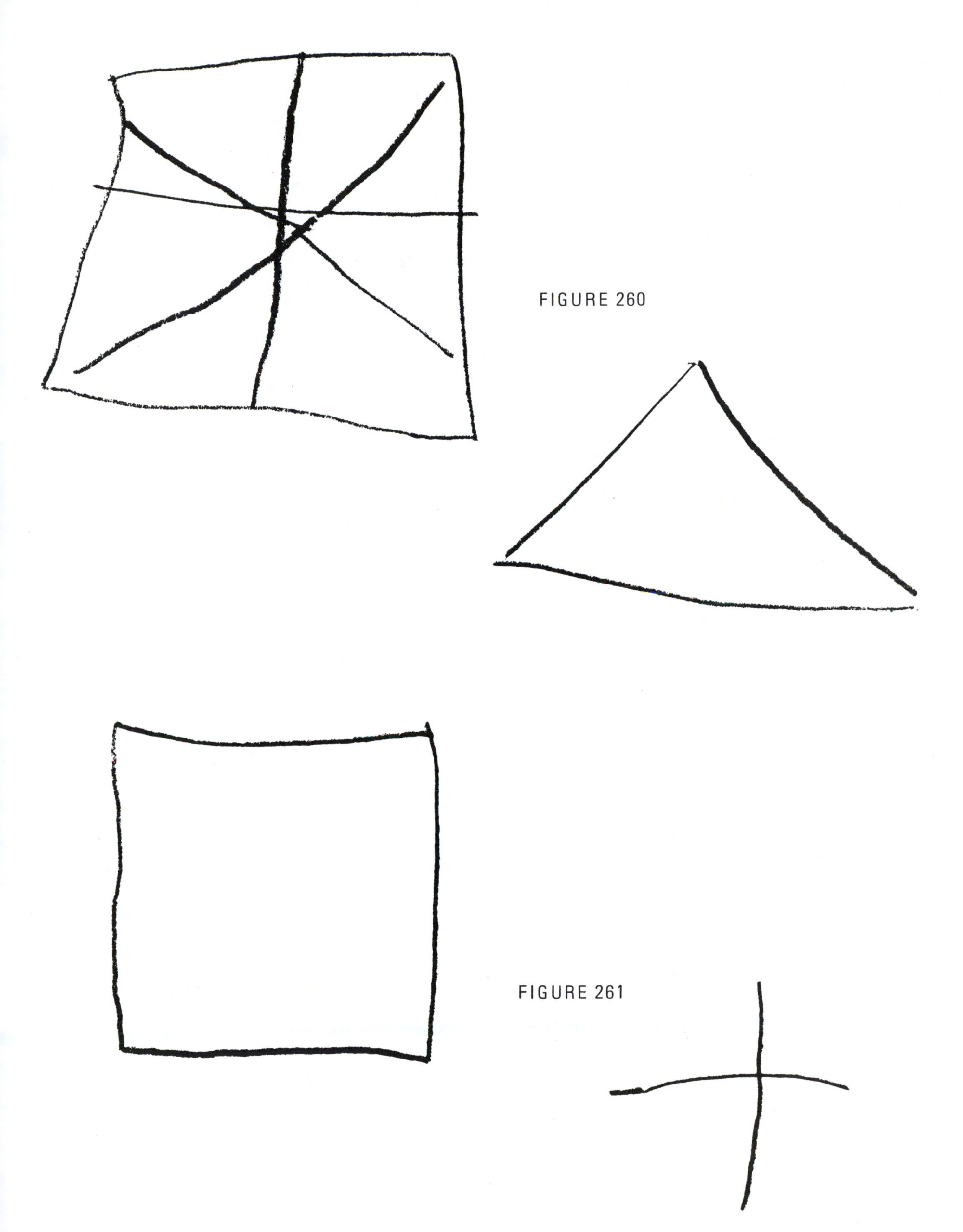

FIGURE 260

FIGURE 261

FIGURE 262

Sensori-neural hearing loss. No signs of perceptual impairment. Chronological age: six years 6 months. Goodenough mental age: six years 6 months. No disparity between figure drawing and other functioning. On the next page are the child's copies of the Examiner's geometric forms.

FIGURE 263

The following set of drawings were made by children attending a school for the deaf. They were all in the same class, but each drawing was done individually so that there could be no copying. The age range was from eight years 6 months to eleven years 8 months. WISC performance IQ's ranged from 80 to 135.

The viewer will note that in nine of the fifteen drawings the man has no ears. Most of the six with ears have them insignificantly small as compared with the attention given the eyes. These children are all highly alert visually. Many of the figures are precisely clothed: belts, buckles, turtle-neck, ties, creases in trousers. Most of the men are smiling.

FIGURE 264

G. K. age eight years 6 months, male, WISC IQ: 126. Severe hearing loss. No ears.

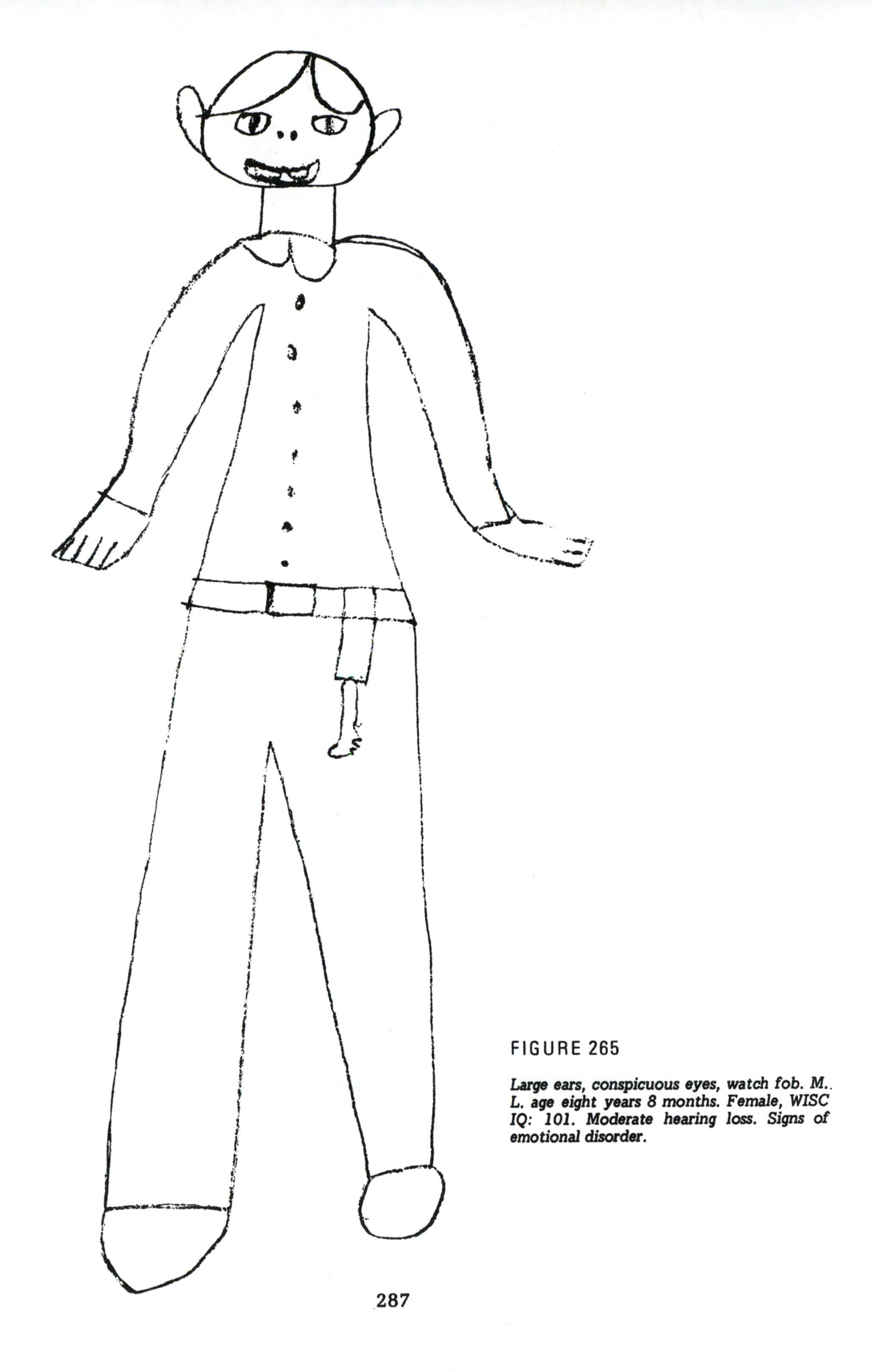

FIGURE 265

Large ears, conspicuous eyes, watch fob. M.. L. age eight years 8 months. Female, WISC IQ: 101. Moderate hearing loss. Signs of emotional disorder.

FIGURE 266

J. B. age eight years 8 months. Male, WISC IQ: 90. Severe hearing loss and emotional problem.

FIGURE 267

C. D. age eight years 9 months. Male. No ears, no mouth. WISC IQ: 103. Severe hearing loss and indications of organicity.

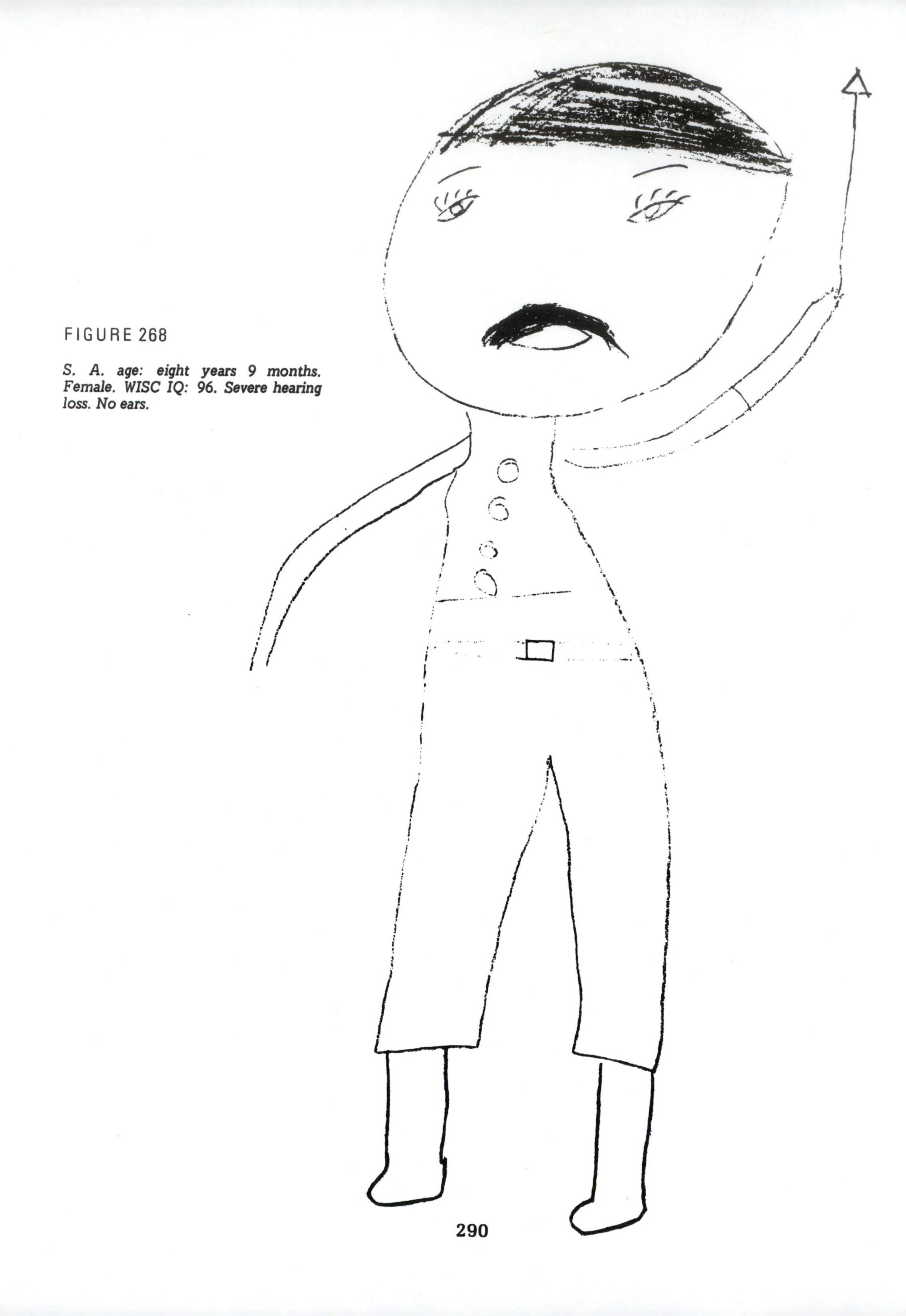

FIGURE 268

S. A. age: eight years 9 months. Female. WISC IQ: 96. Severe hearing loss. No ears.

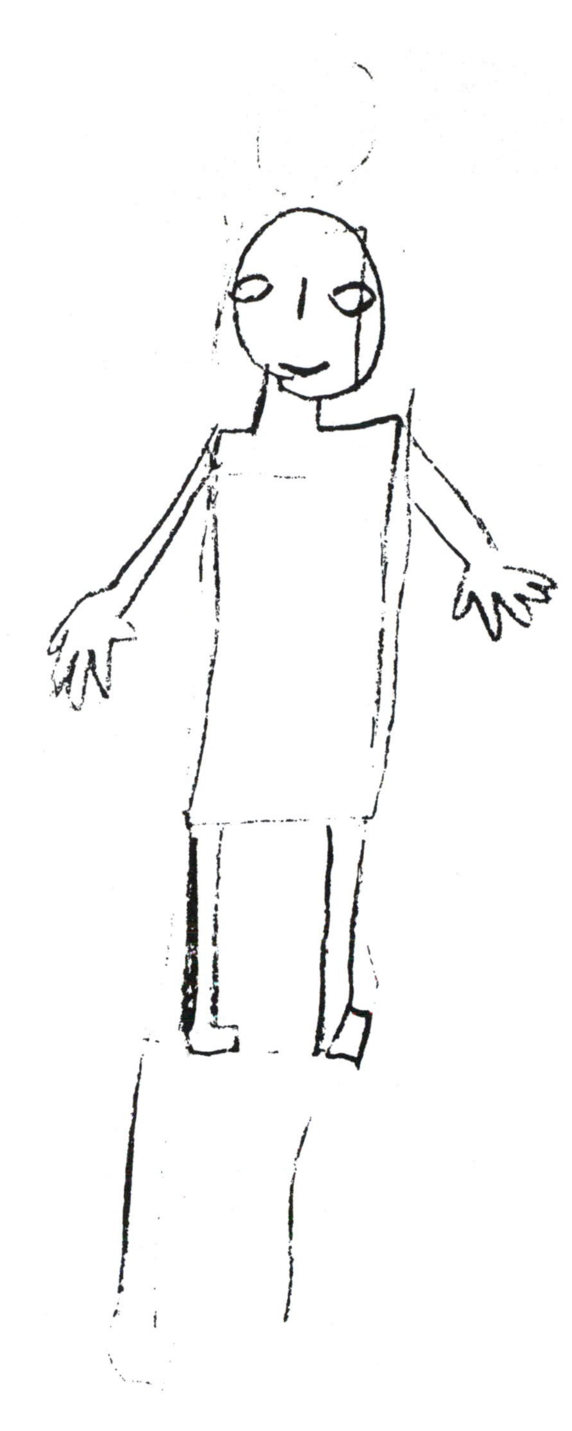

FIGURE 269

A. H. age nine years 3 months, female, WISC IQ: 90. No ears. Moderately severe hearing loss and receptive language disorder.

FIGURE 270

M. R. age nine years 3 months, female, WISC IQ: 83. Hearing loss and central impairment. No ears.

FIGURE 271

J. P. age nine years 4 months. Female, WISC IQ: 121. Audiogram indicates severe hearing loss but her speech suggests good deal of residual hearing. Small ears.

FIGURE 272

S. M. age nine years 4 months, female, WISC IQ: 97. Moderately severe hearing loss and emotional problem. No ears.

FIGURE 273

J. B. age nine years 10 months. Male. WISC IQ: 135. Severe hearing loss. Ears present.

FIGURE 274

M. C. age 10 years 4 months. Female, WISC IQ: 124. Severe hearing loss. Small ears.

FIGURE 275

K. M. age 10 years 6 months. Male, WISC IQ: 100. Severe hearing loss and possible expressive disorder. No ears.

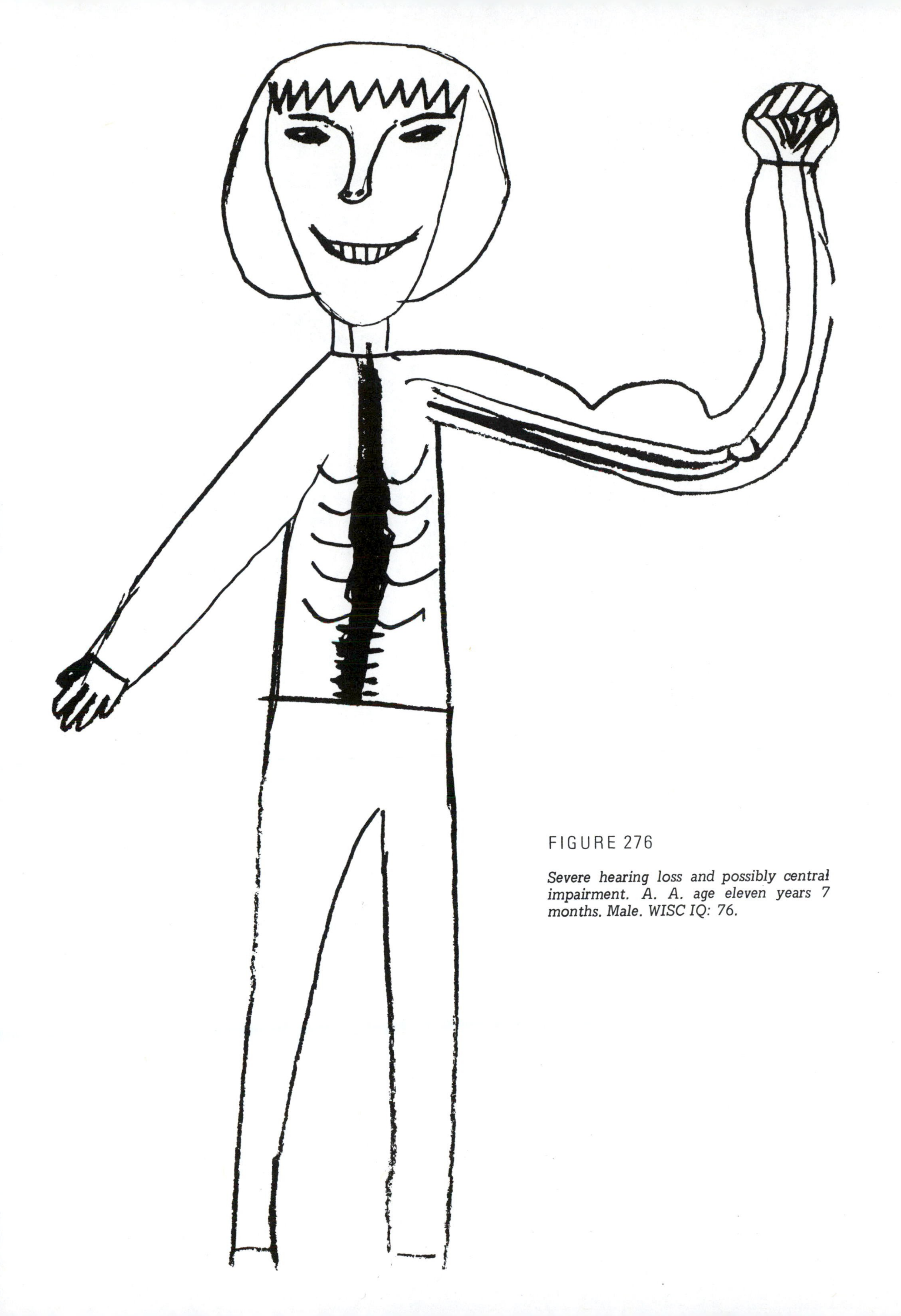

FIGURE 276

Severe hearing loss and possibly central impairment. A. A. age eleven years 7 months. Male. WISC IQ: 76.

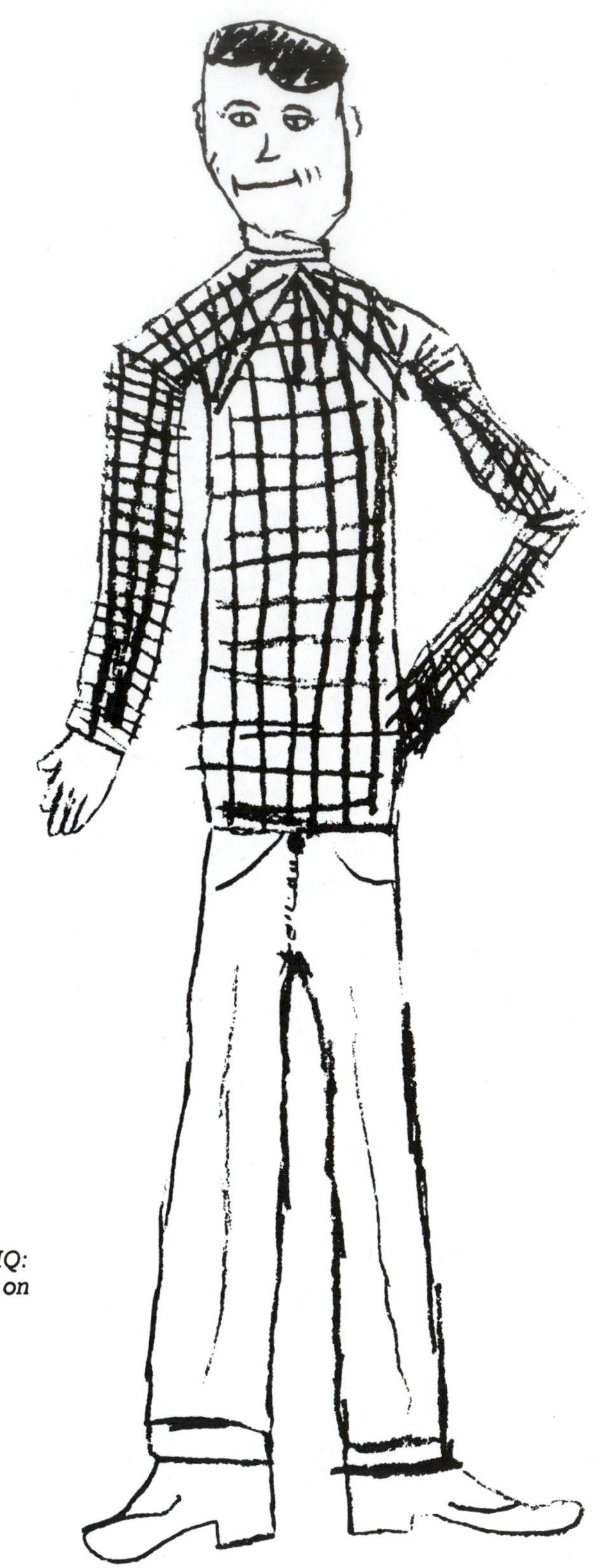

FIGURE 277

L. N. age 11 years 8 months, Male, WISC IQ: 128. Severe hearing loss. Small ears. Zipper on trousers.

FIGURE 278

F. C. age 11 years 11 months, Male, WISC IQ: 80. Severe hearing loss and poor coordination.

23

COMMUNICATION DISORDERS

Central Language Disorders

Under this heading are grouped a variety of communication disorders affecting the ability to comprehend or decode the spoken language symbols (receptive aphasia) and/or the ability to encode or to use the symbols though they are heard and even understood. These developmental aphasias are congenital and are presumably due to lesions in the temporal cortex. Audiometric findings are inconsistent, the parent reports equivocal responses to sound. Careful examination will rule out deafness, psychosis, mental retardation, and environmental deprivation, so that often by exclusion the clinician is left with developmental aphasia as the remaining explanation for failure to speak. The central nature of the disorder is indicated by the presence in many children of associated impairments of perception and impulse control typically observed in children with organic cerebral dysfunction. Of particular interest are the defects noted in the drawings: difficulty in reproducing geometric forms and discrepancy between the immature human figure drawing and the intellectual level as determined by standard IQ tests, such as the WISC, Stanford-Binet, and Merrill-Palmer.

FIGURE 279

J. S. a boy of seven years 3 months. Communication Disorder: developmental aphasia (or receptive aphasia or dysacusis, etc.); normal hearing; markedly delayed speech development. Not mentally retarded or emotionally withdrawn. Immature concept of body image. Perceptual impairment. Fair gross and fine motor coordination. Unable to tie shoe laces. Concrete thinking. Drawing of a person is at an immature level but readily recognizable. No sex differences are indicated in this drawing of a man and that of a lady on the reverse.

FIGURE 280

FIGURE 281

J. S. copy of a circle. All copies of geometric figures are distorted. Visual-motor impairment.

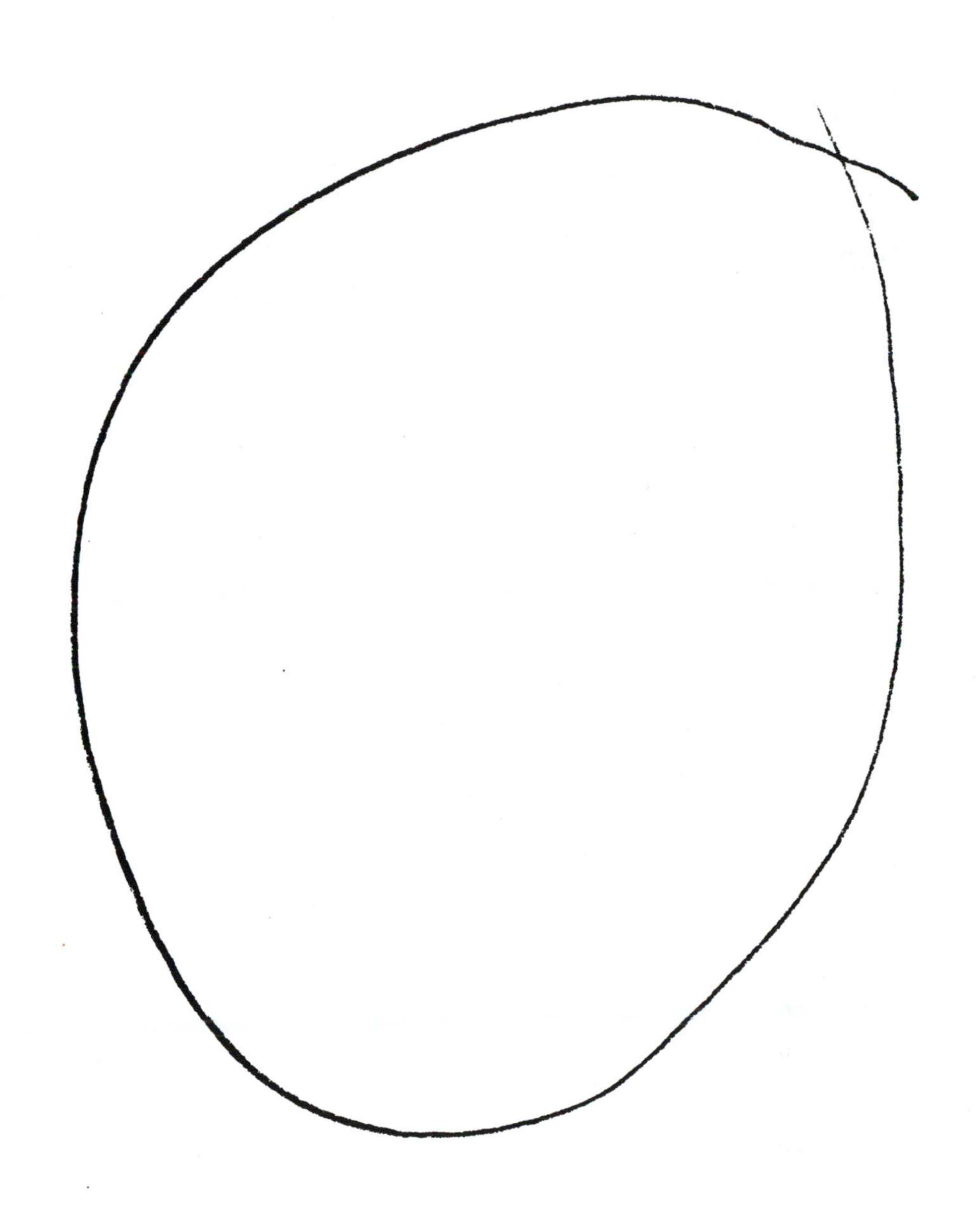

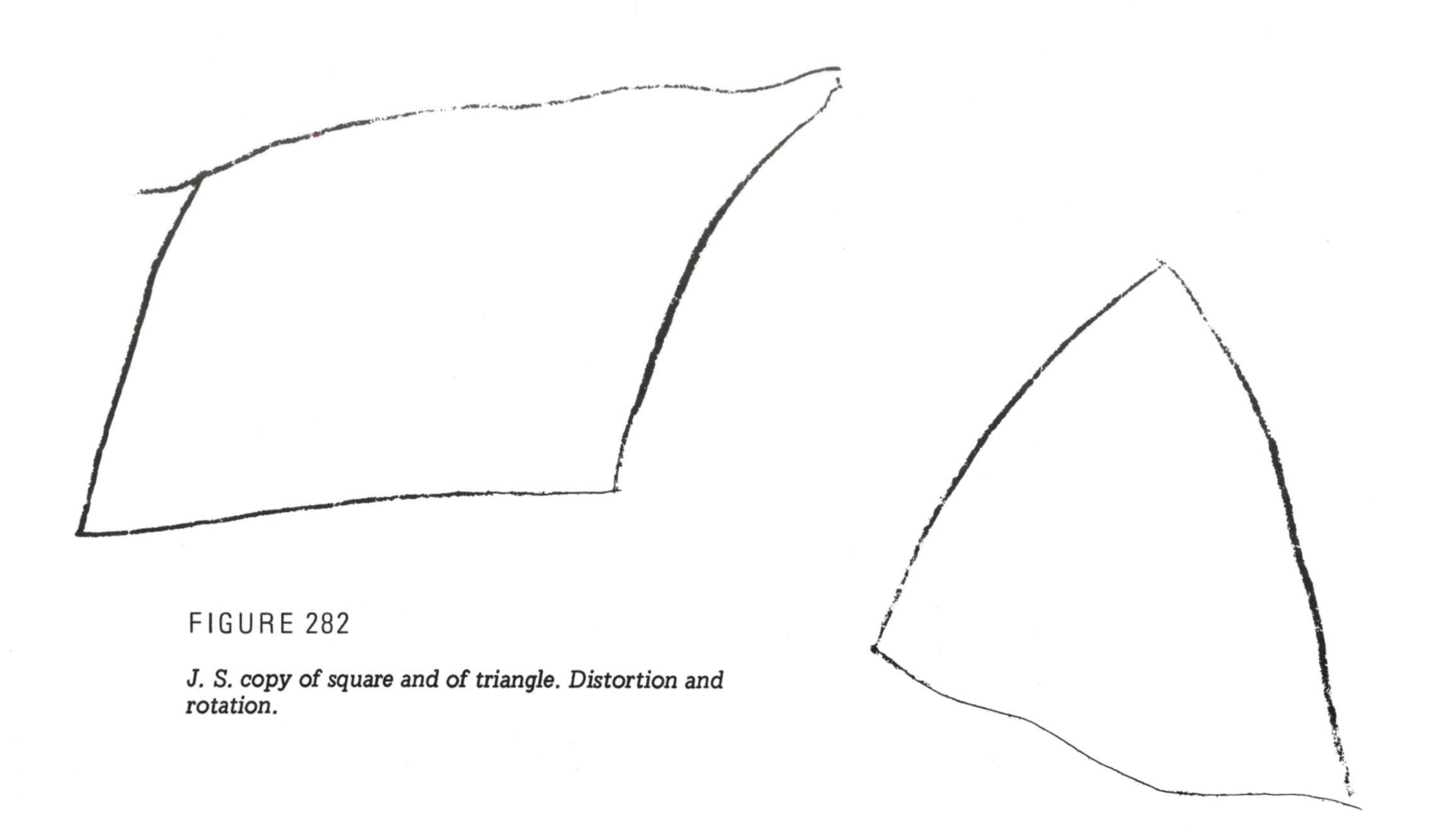

FIGURE 282

J. S. copy of square and of triangle. Distortion and rotation.

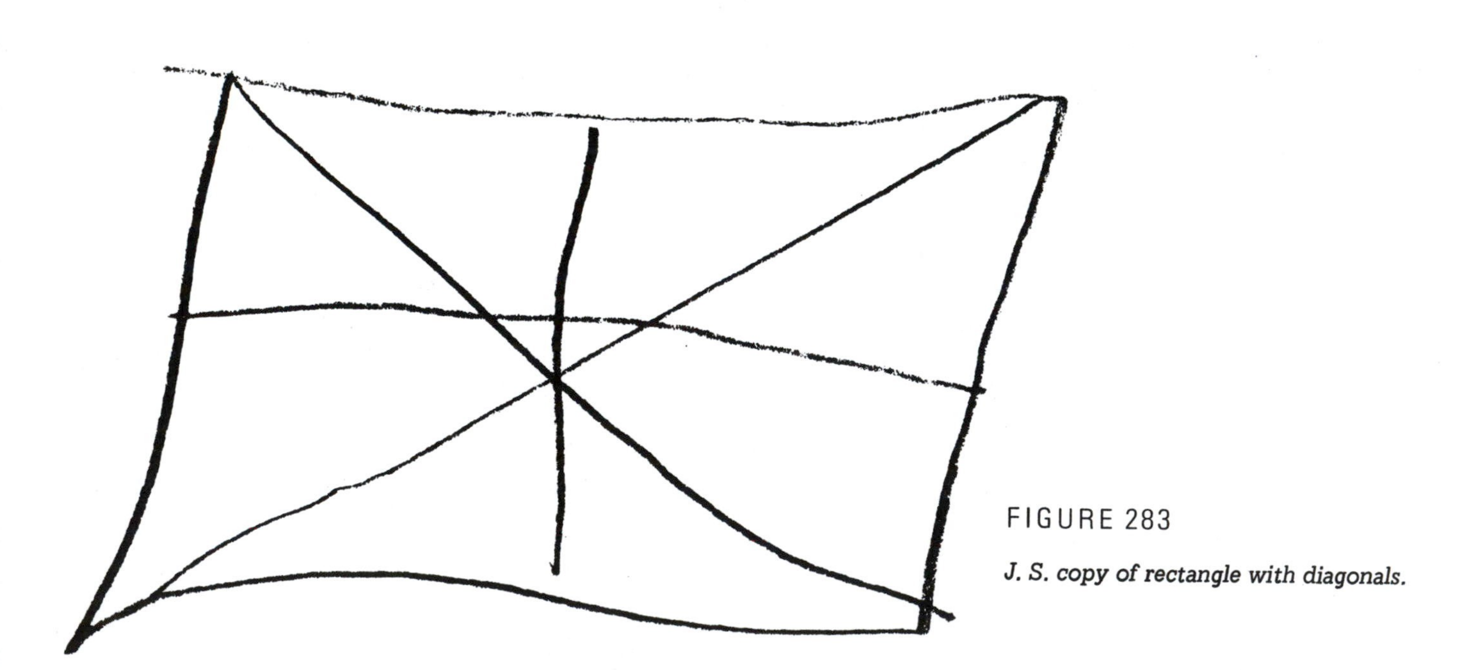

FIGURE 283

J. S. copy of rectangle with diagonals.

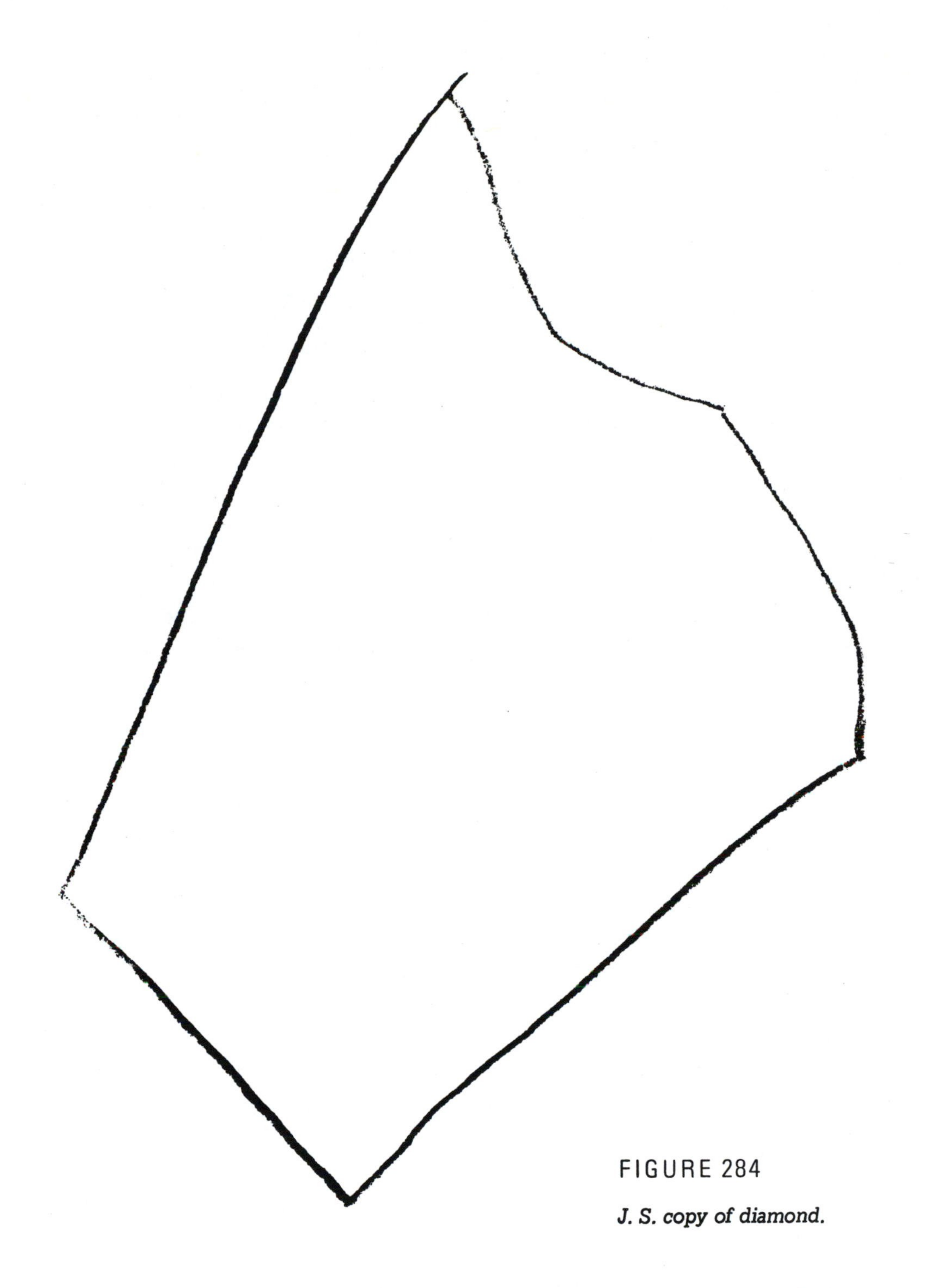

FIGURE 284

J. S. copy of diamond.

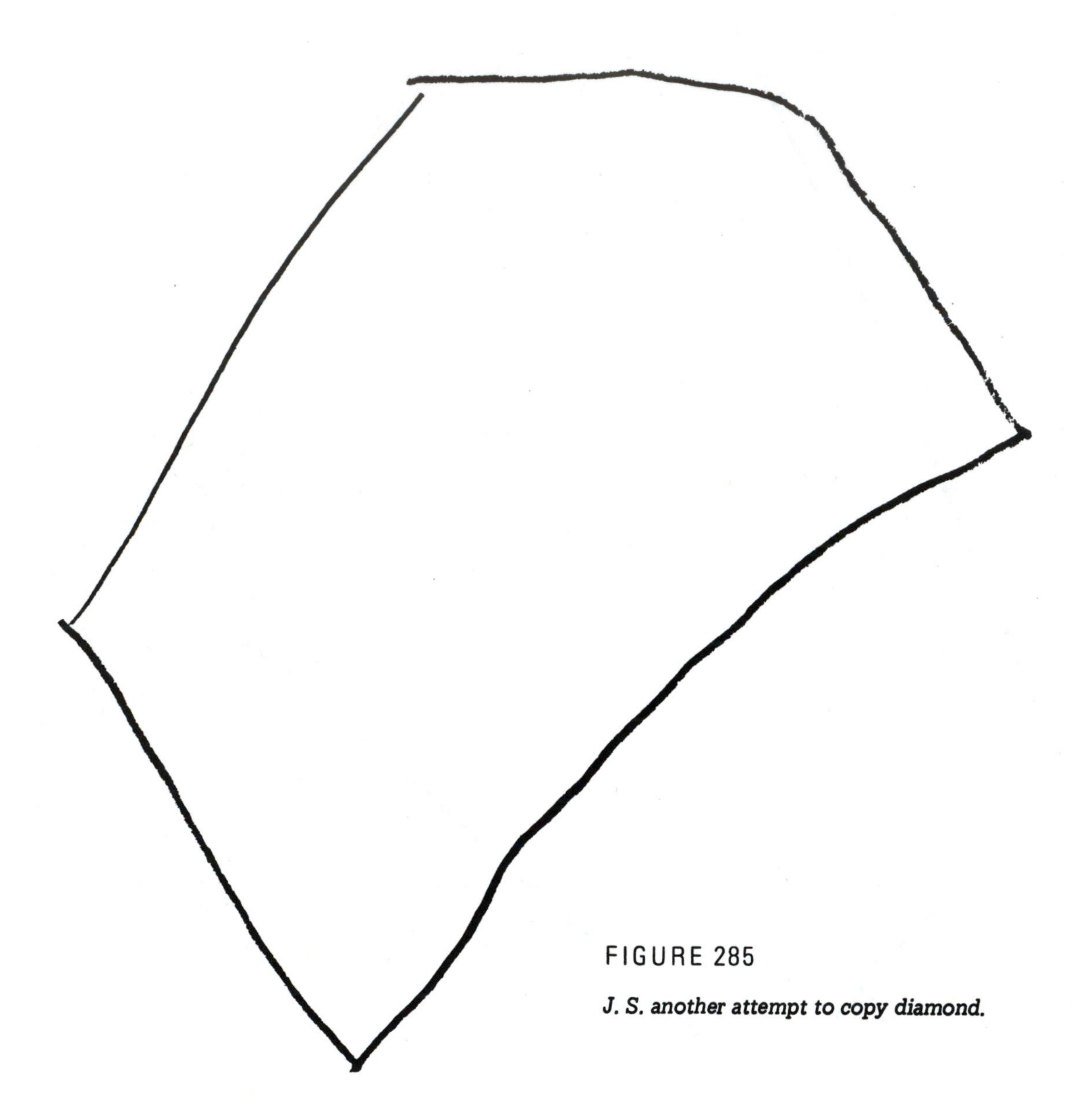

FIGURE 285

J. S. another attempt to copy diamond.

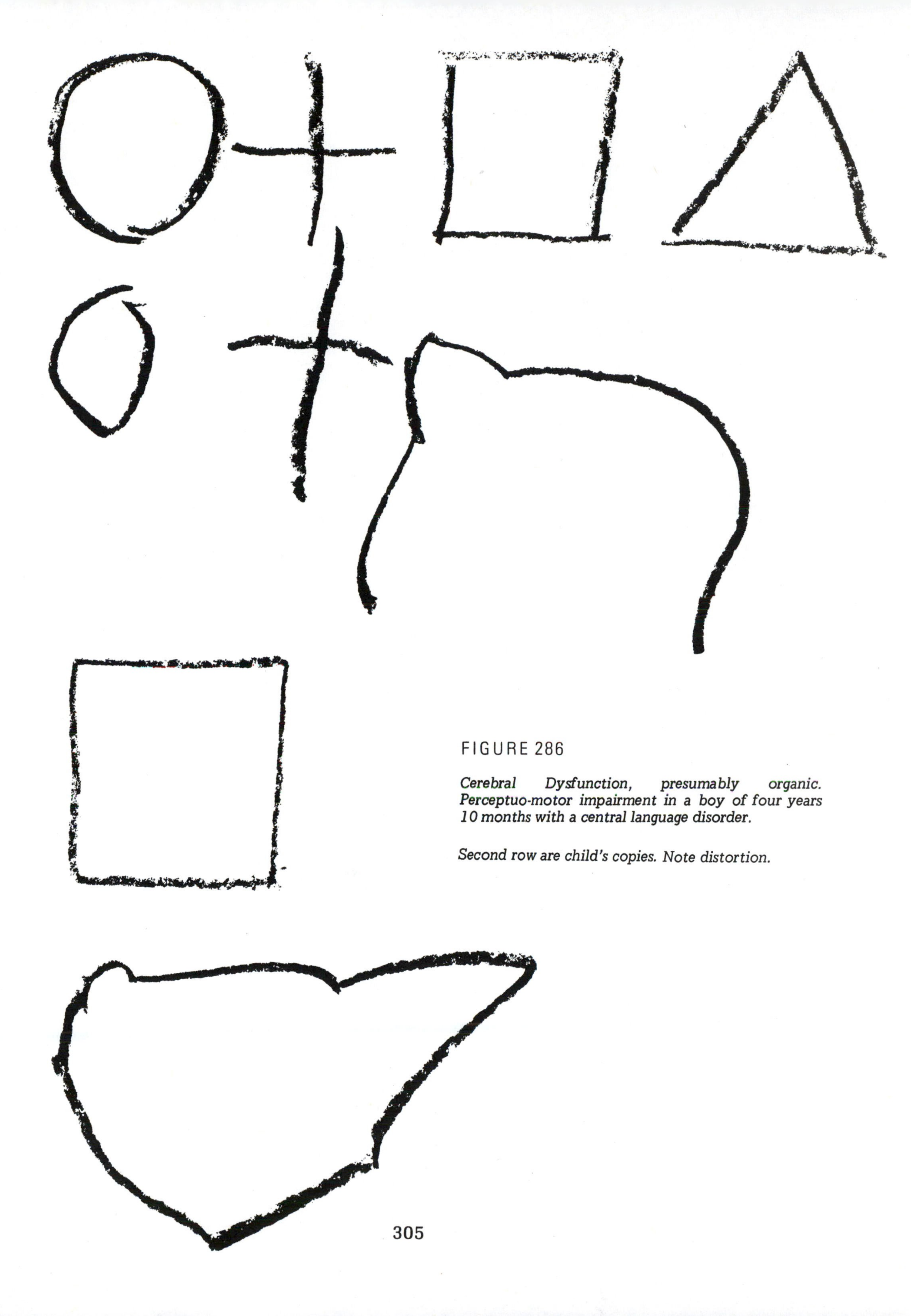

FIGURE 286

Cerebral Dysfunction, presumably organic. Perceptuo-motor impairment in a boy of four years 10 months with a central language disorder.

Second row are child's copies. Note distortion.

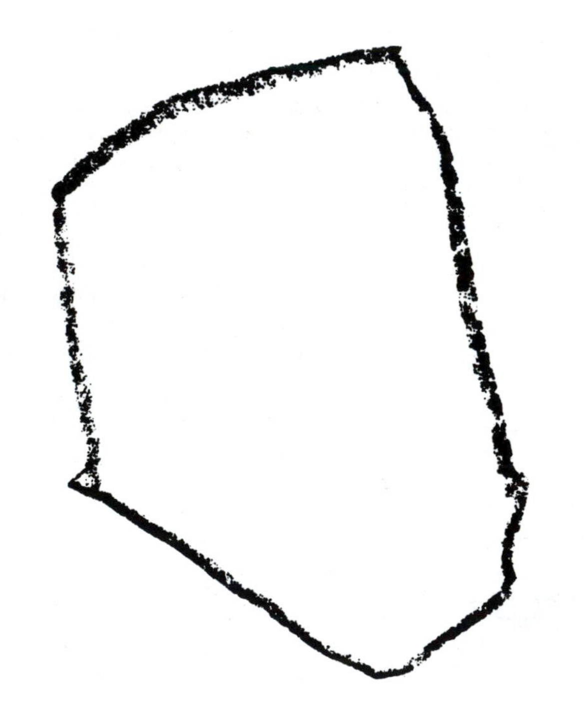

FIGURE 287

J. M. Dp. Age three years 6 months. The following series of 8 drawings (Figures 288-295) are by a girl of three years 6 months. Presenting problem: no speech. Communicates by gesture, facial expression, and unintelligible vowel sounds. The child's mother contracted rubella during the first trimester of pregnancy. The child is sociable, highly active, impulsive. She ignores sound. Audiometry has yielded variable results with responses varying from 45 db to 75 db in the speech range of frequencies. Psychological testing with selected items from the Stanford-Binet and with non-verbal items from the Cattell Scale indicate intelligence to be in the low range of average but with difficulty in perceptuo-motor functioning. Gross motor activity is unimpaired but awkward. A tendency to perseverate is evident especially in her repeated, self-corrected error in the 3-hold formboard situation and in the drawing tests.

1. Spontaneous drawing is vigorous, kinesthetic, uninhibited. Strong pressure was used as is evident from the type of strokes.
2. Copy circle: she is unable to copy, instead she makes a series of scribbles, mostly diagonal but some with a curve.
3. Imitate circle: when the Examiner demonstrates how the circle is made, she imitates the movement but continues the activity (PERSEVERATION), making a series of circles.
4. The Examiner demonstrates a cross: the child responds by continuing the previous activity, the result being a three-quarter circle with a horizontal across the circumference (PERSEVERATION continues).
5. Again, the Examiner demonstrates a cross: this time the response is part arc, part more or less straight lines (PERSEVERATION is waning).
6. Now the Examiner demonstrates the component parts of the cross and draws first a vertical, to which the child responds by imitating the general direction of stroke.
7. The Examiner then demonstrates a horizontal and the child imitates.
8. But when the Examiner returns to demonstrating a cross, the child, unable to perceive the gestalt, responds by making a scribble. Though able to perceive its component parts, the child is unable to perceive the new pattern. The whole is greater than the sum of its parts.

Impression: perceptuo-motor impairment indicating organic cerebral dysfunction. The communication disorder is considered to be of mixed type, with damage to the peripheral receptor (sensori-neural hearing loss) but also with central (cerebral) damage. The peripheral hearing loss alone does not account for the utter lack of speech and failure to benefit from several months of auditory training program. The variability of results on audiometric testing is a frequent finding in central language disorders. Etiology: the rubella virus could very well have damaged the cochlea as well as the cerebral decoding system.

FIGURE 288

J. M. Dp. Chronological age three years 6 months. Spontaneous drawing. A vigorous scribble. She is still drawing kinesthetically at an age when she should be attempting representation.

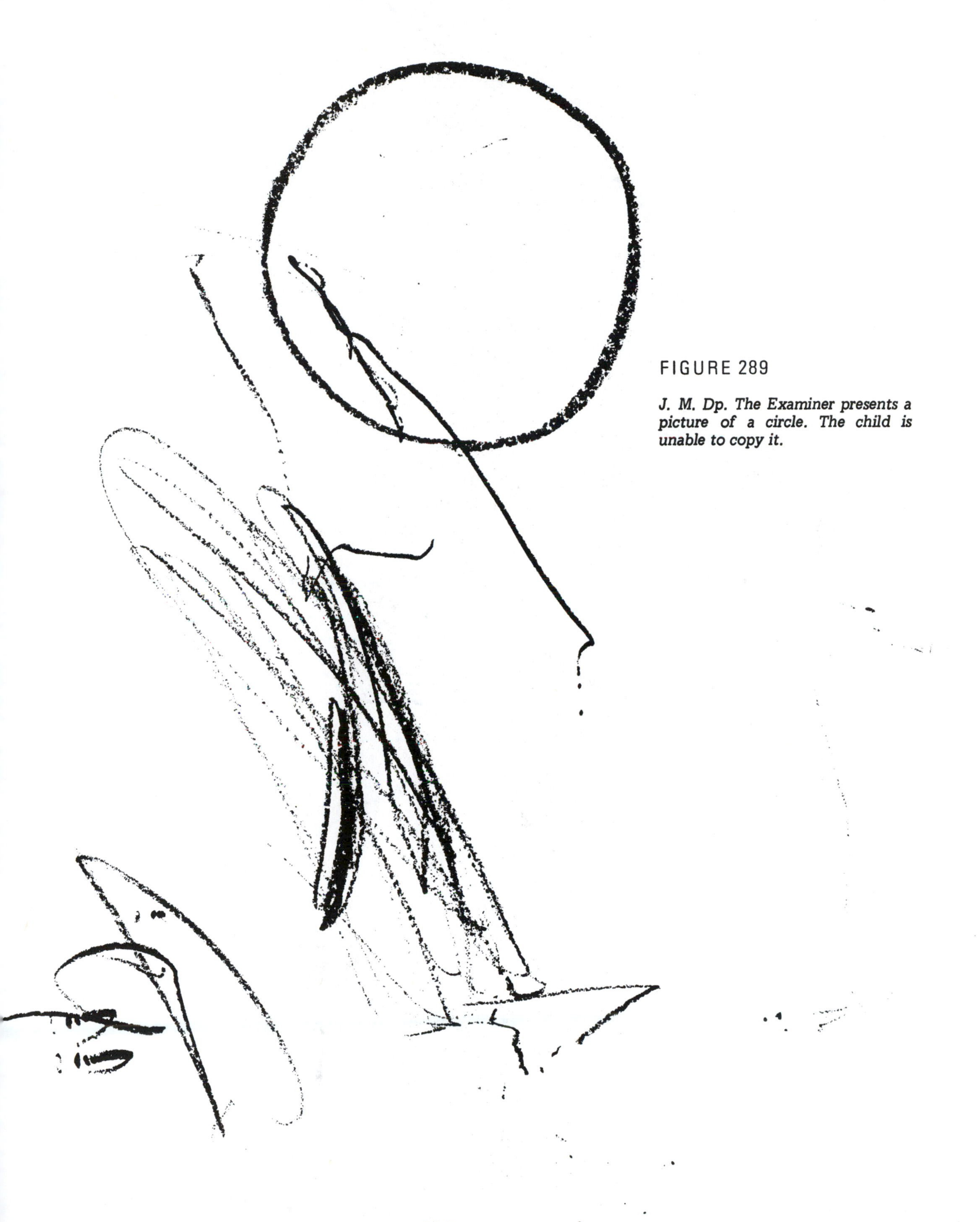

FIGURE 289

J. M. Dp. The Examiner presents a picture of a circle. The child is unable to copy it.

FIGURE 290

J. M. Dp. The Examiner demonstrates a circle. She imitates it but continues the drawing so that many circles are made (PERSEVERATION).

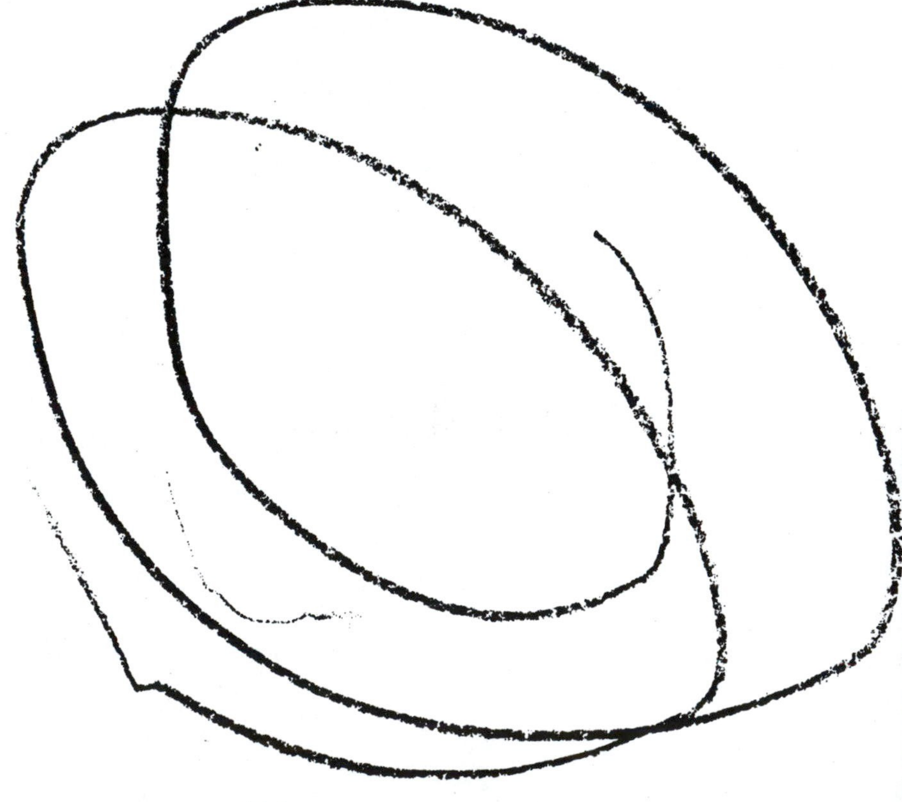

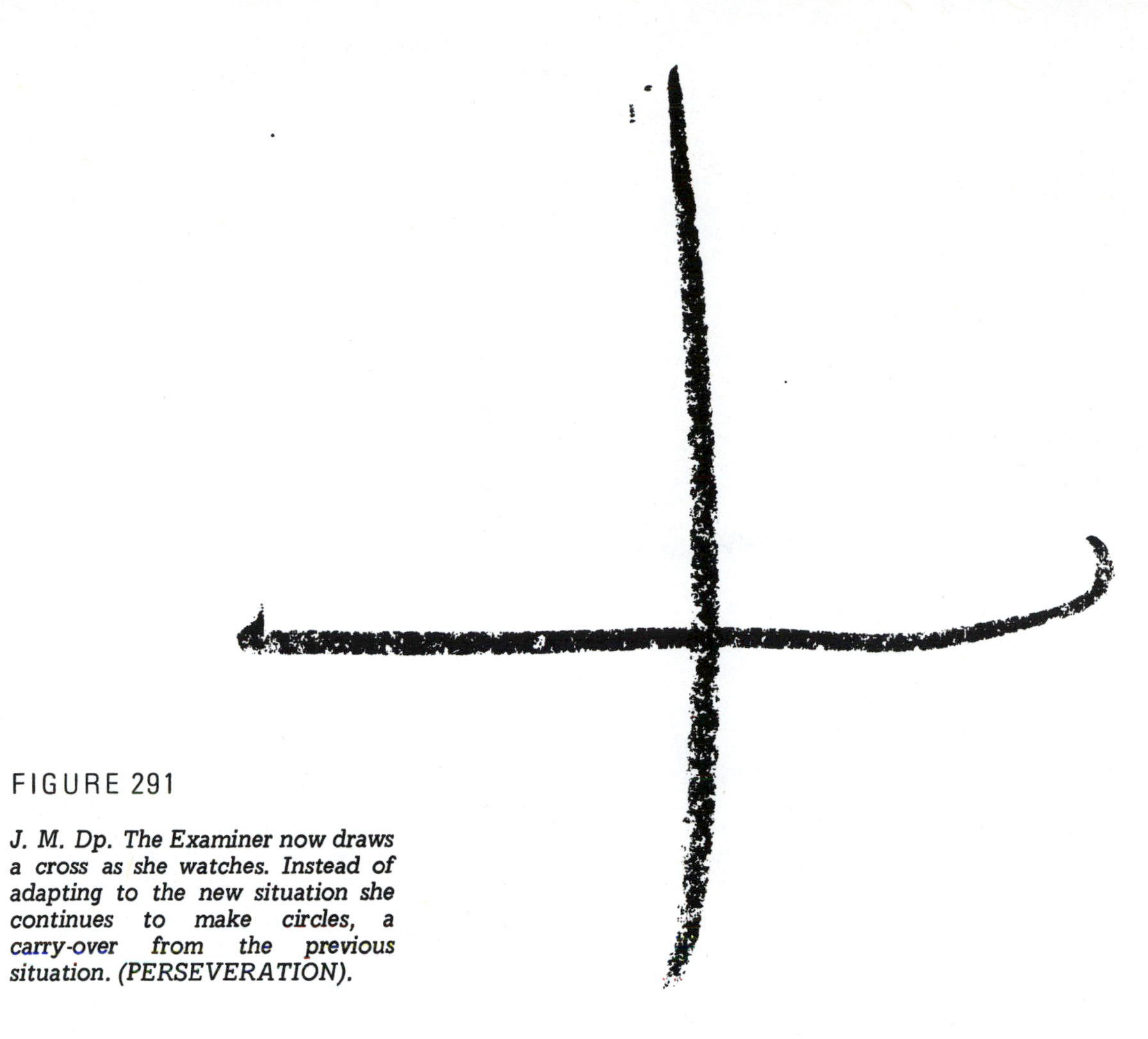

FIGURE 291

J. M. Dp. The Examiner now draws a cross as she watches. Instead of adapting to the new situation she continues to make circles, a carry-over from the previous situation. (PERSEVERATION).

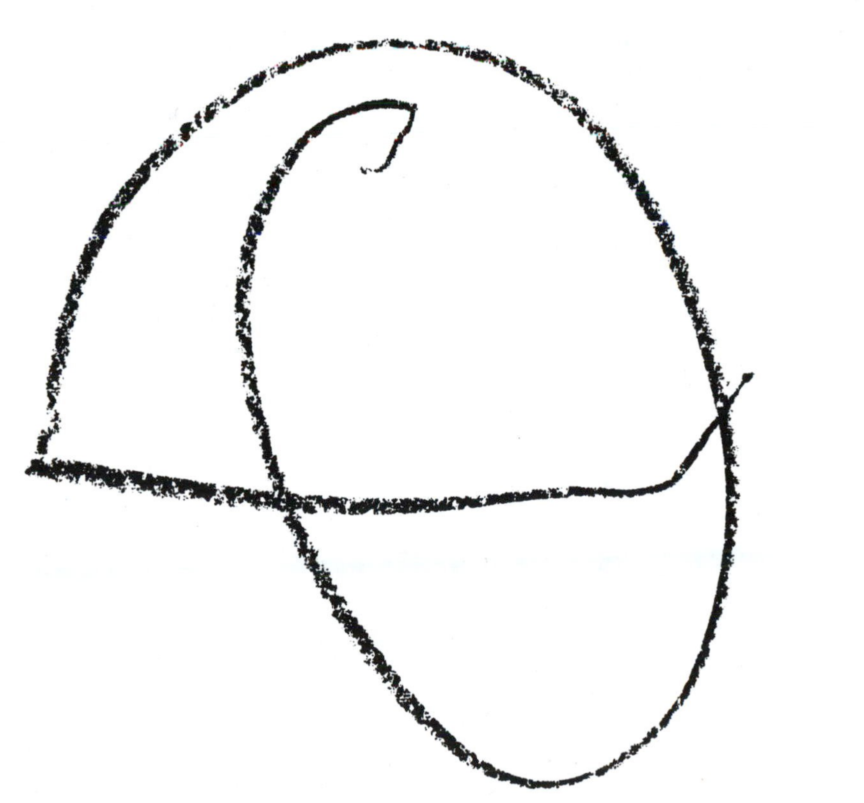

FIGURE 292

J. M. Dp. The Examiner demonstrates a second cross. Again she responds with circular strokes though this time they are less clearly defined. She is still perseverating but to a lesser degree.

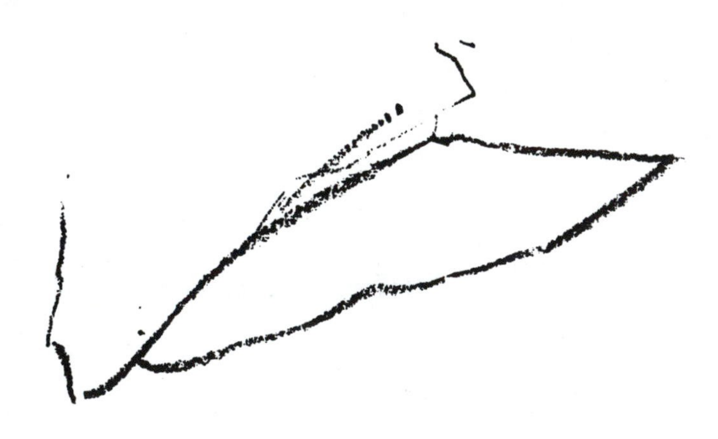

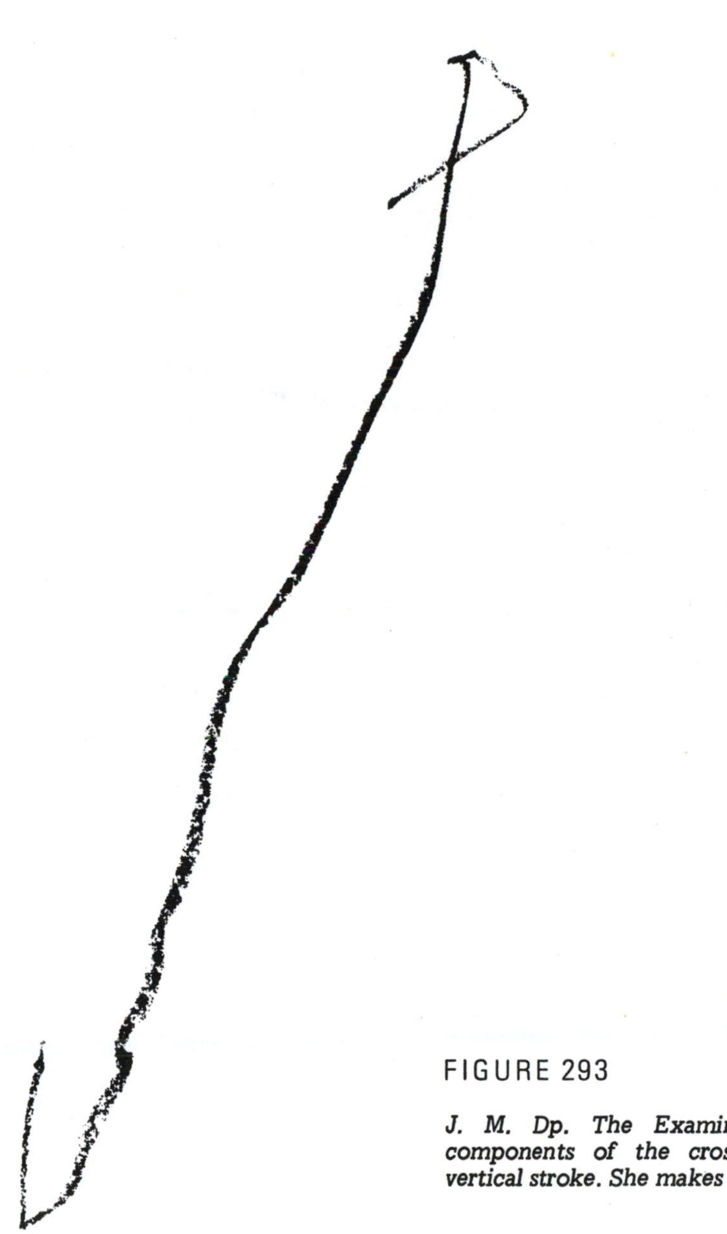

FIGURE 293

J. M. Dp. The Examiner now draws the components of the cross, beginning with a vertical stroke. She makes a fair imitation.

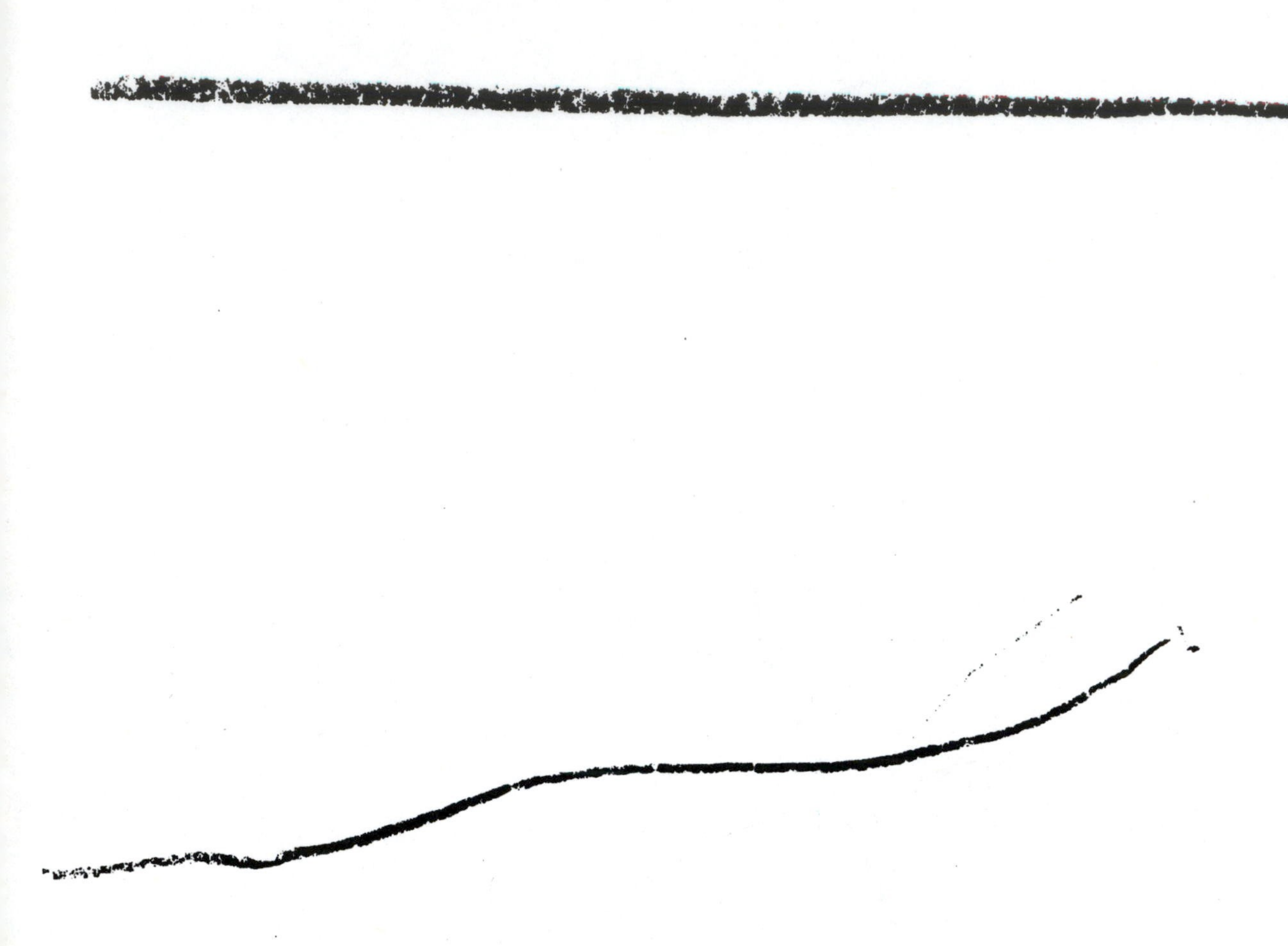

FIGURE 294

J. M. Dp. The Examiner now demonstrates a horizontal stroke. She imitates it.

FIGURE 295

J. M. Dp. But when the Examiner demonstrates a cross, she does not make an intersecting vertical and horizontal. She does not perceive the pattern of the new figure though she was able to imitate its component parts.

(Figures 296-299) No speech other than "mama" in a boy of three years 3 months. Dry labor after 8 months gestation. Birth weight 5 lbs 14 oz. Moderate spastic paraplegia. Upper extremities unimpaired. No involvement of mouth, tongue and lips. Selected items on Stanford-Binet, Leiter, and Cattell Scale indicate average intelligence. Gesell Developmental evaluation yields average values in all adaptive items with the exception of drawing tests. Fine motor activity well controlled. Matches geometric forms but is unable to reproduce them graphically when they form a pattern. He is unable to imitate a cross though he is quite capable of imitating its components: the vertical and horizontal strokes. This difficulty indicates perceptuo-motor impairment, commonly seen in organic cerebral dysfunction. This child has cerebral palsy. His communication disorder is probably of central origin. Audiometry yields equivocal, inconsistent results, with free-field responses at 55 db. This finding is questionable but even if correct it does not account for a total absence of speech and comprehension of speech. Impression: central language disorder in a child with clear evidence of brain damage (spastic paraplegia.).

FIGURE 296

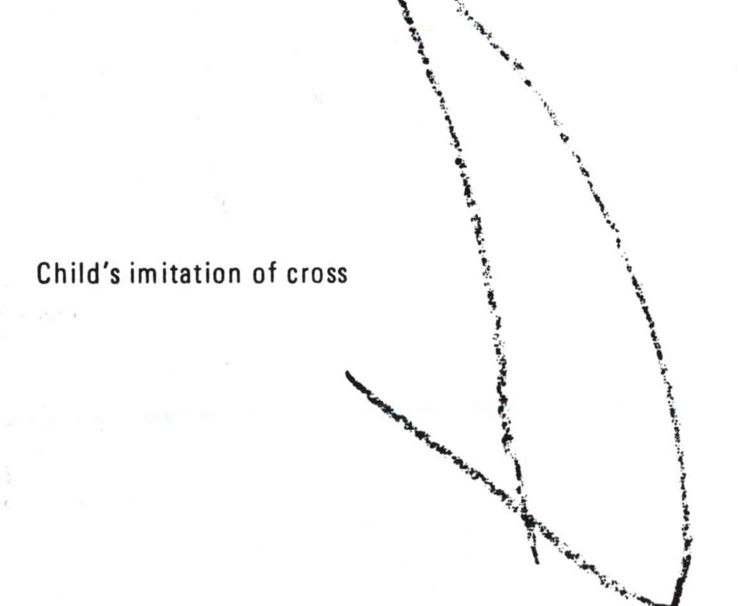

Child's imitation of cross

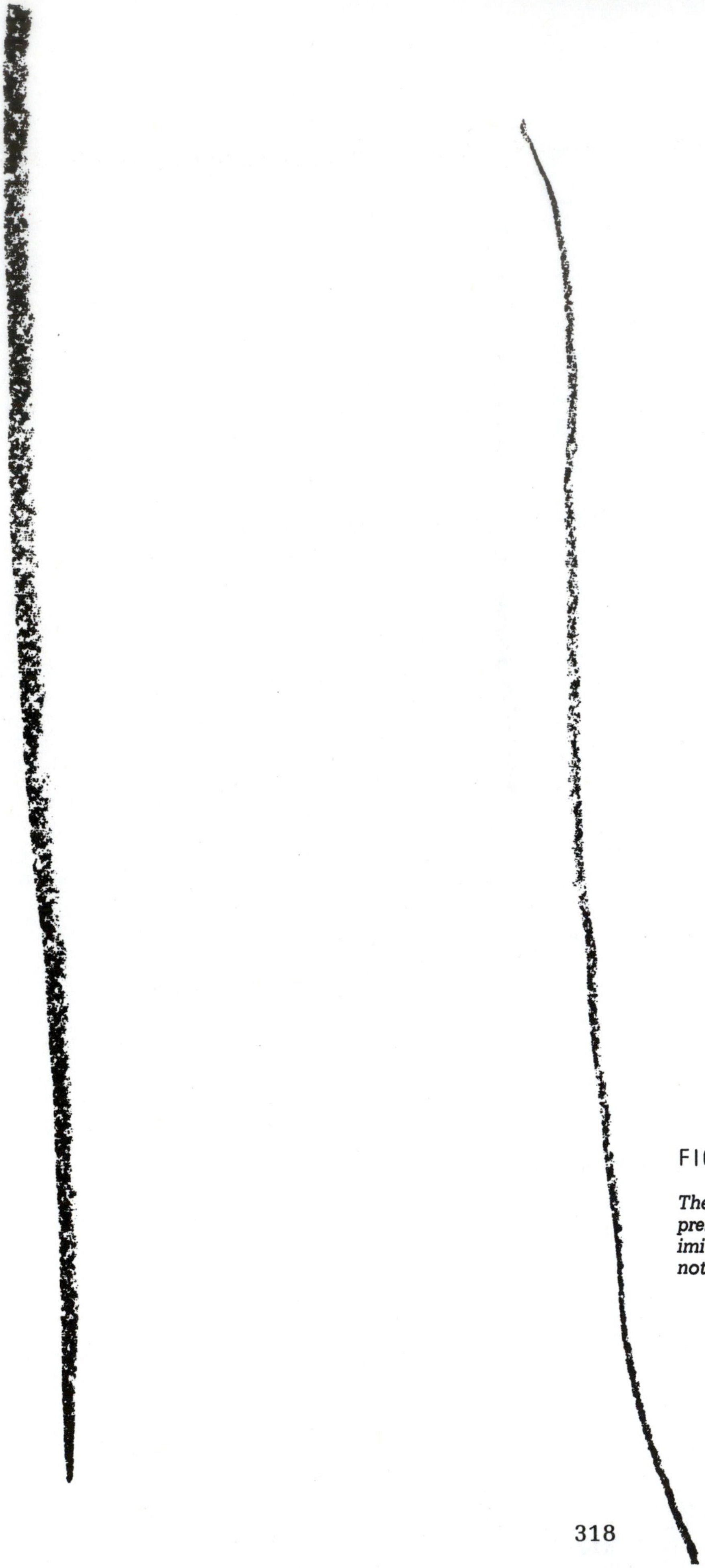

FIGURE 297

The elements that constitute the cross are presented separately. The child is able to imitate vertical and horizontal strokes but not the pattern of a cross.

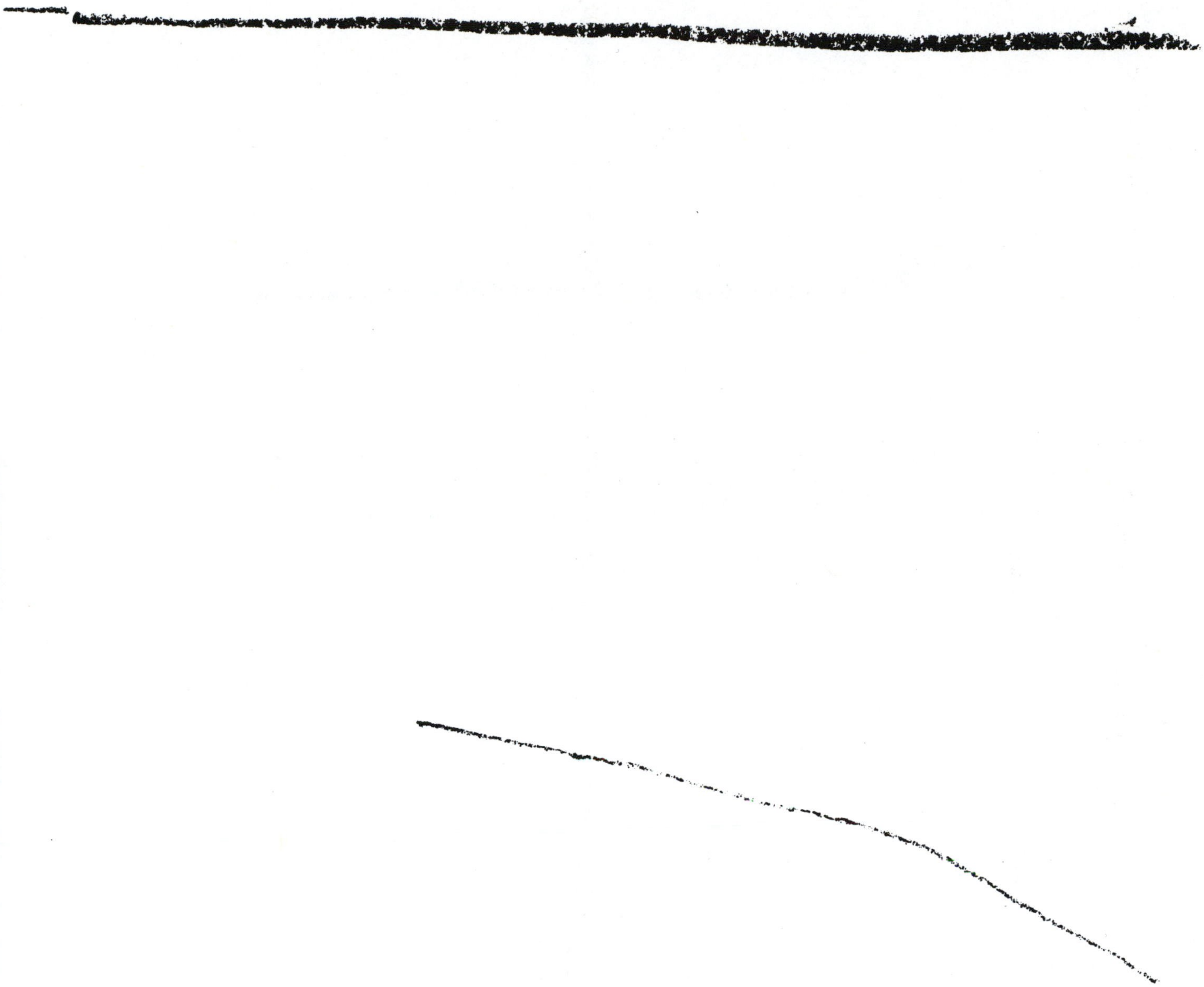

FIGURE 298

The cross is separated into its constituent elements.

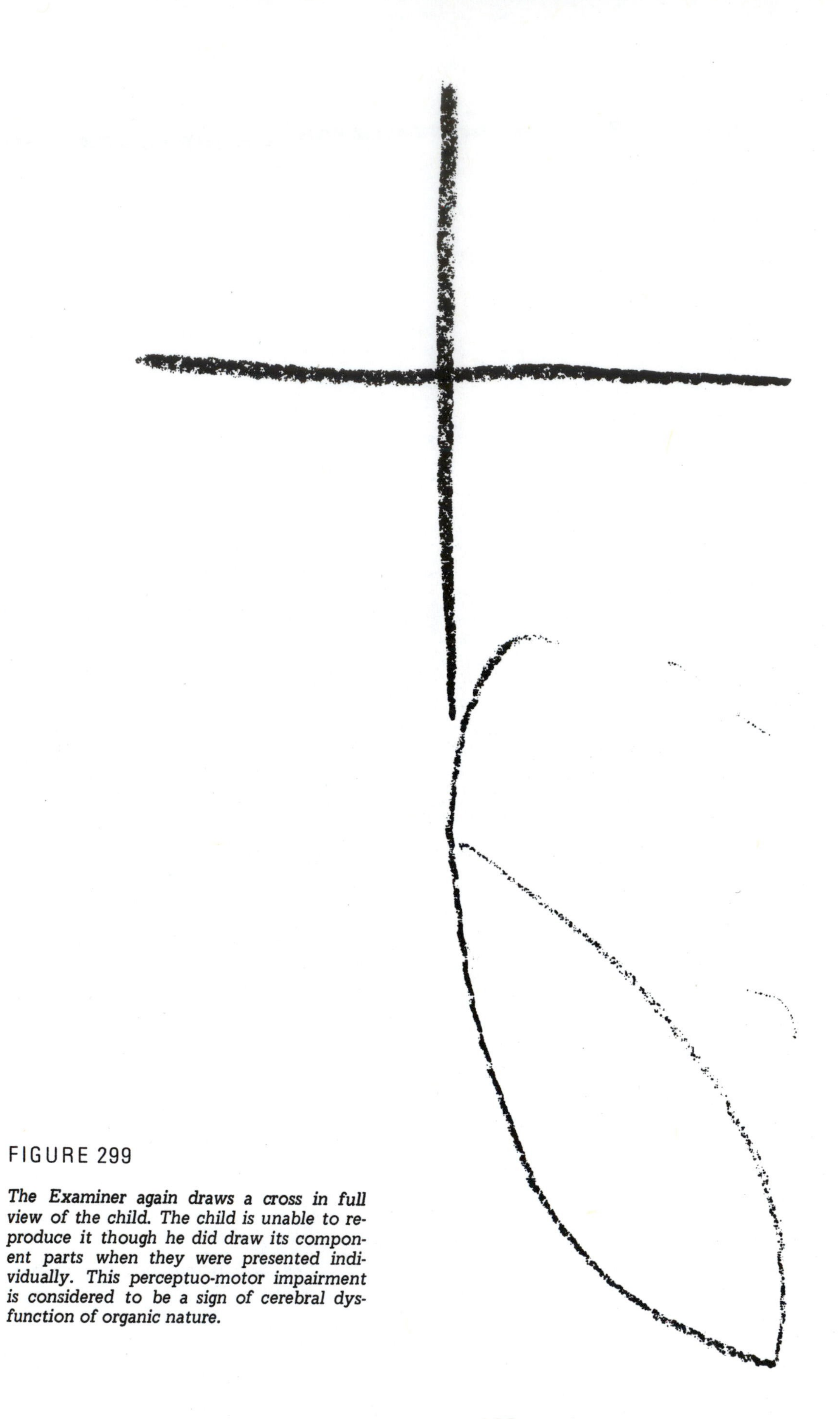

FIGURE 299

The Examiner again draws a cross in full view of the child. The child is unable to reproduce it though he did draw its component parts when they were presented individually. This perceptuo-motor impairment is considered to be a sign of cerebral dysfunction of organic nature.

COMMUNICATION DISORDERS
AS MANIFESTATIONS OF PERSONALITY DISORDERS

24

COMMUNICATION DISORDERS AS MANIFESTATIONS OF PERSONALITY DISORDERS

When the failure to speak is a manifestation of pathology involving the personality as a whole, as in psychological withdrawal, human figure drawings are bizarre, often unrecognizable, poorly integrated and scattered with no connection between parts of the body, these being distributed in a disorganized manner over the entire paper. In some children who are progressing favorably, the body parts come together in subsequent drawings made when, in response to therapy, the personality has become better organized. The communication disorder is one aspect of the child's withdrawal from social stimulation, though it is often the disorder that first brings the child to professional attention.

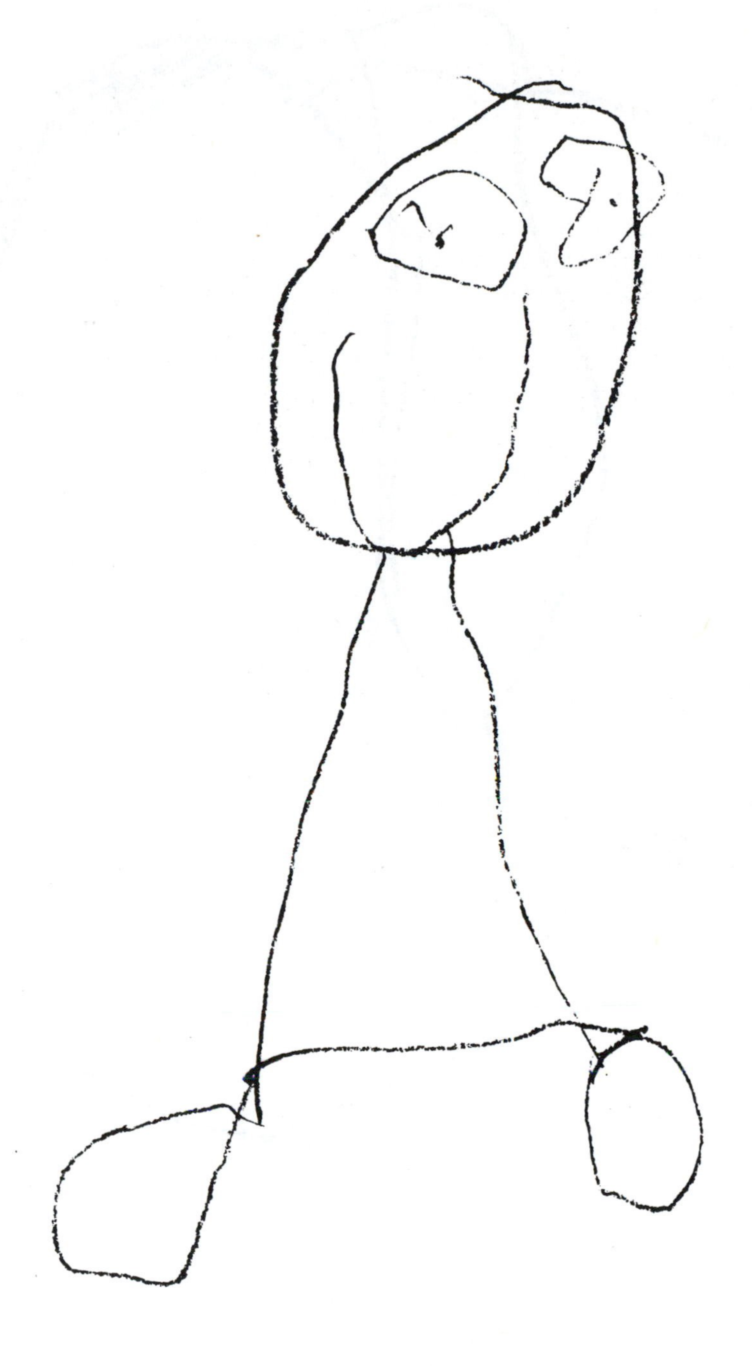

FIGURE 300

Pre-psychotic behavior. Boy. Chronological age six years 6 months. Average intelligence but immature, bizarre concept of body image expressed in human figure drawing. Delayed onset of speech. Heedless but not auditorily impaired. Whirls readily. Excited by anti-gravity play. Unable to relate effectively to children or adults. Resists change.

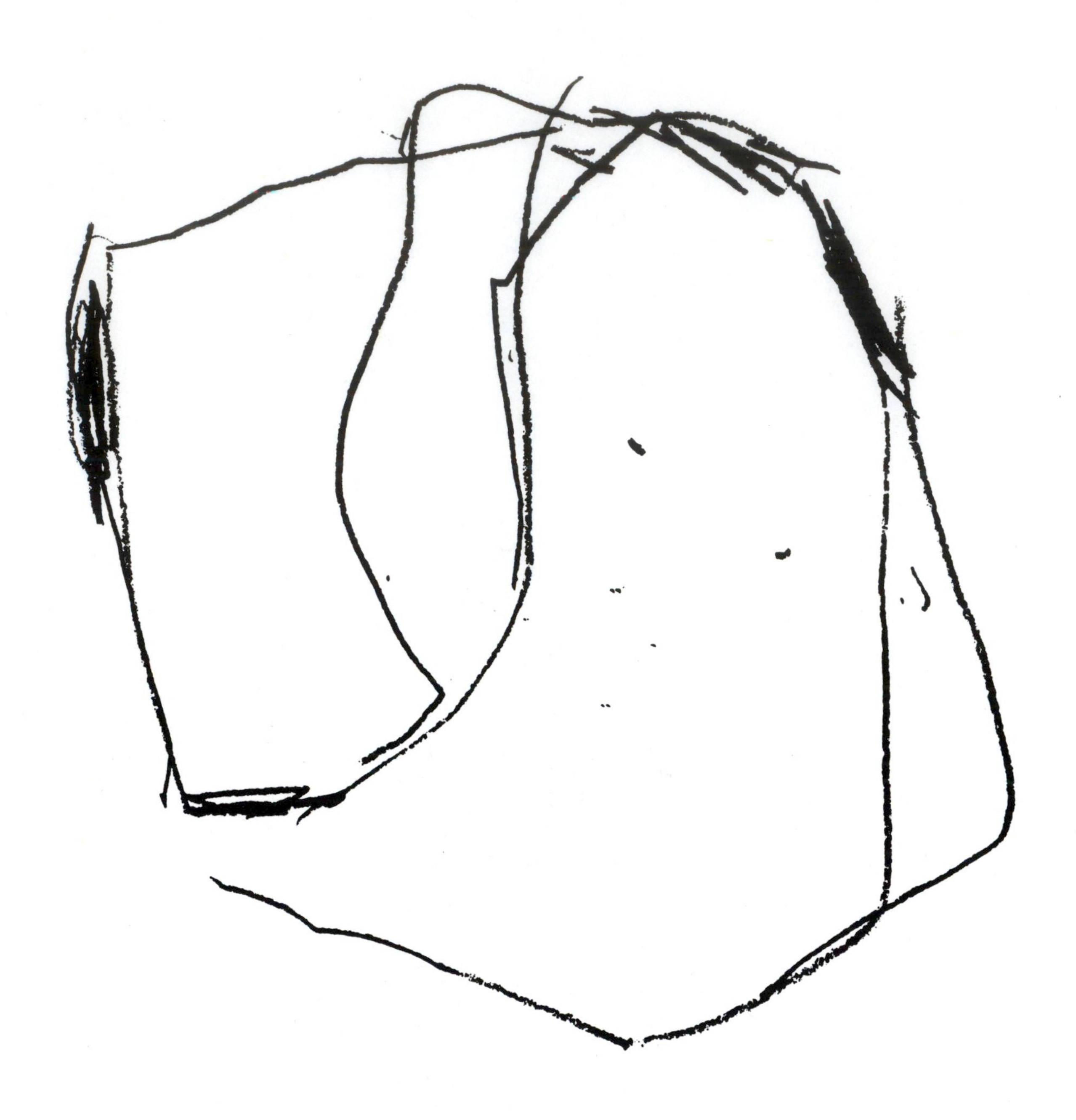

FIGURE 301

This drawing of a person (MOMMY) is not recognizable. S. S. age six years 6 months boy. Delayed speech development, vocabulary limited to about 5 words. Personality disorder. Hears and comprehends speech, but self-contained and generally heedless.

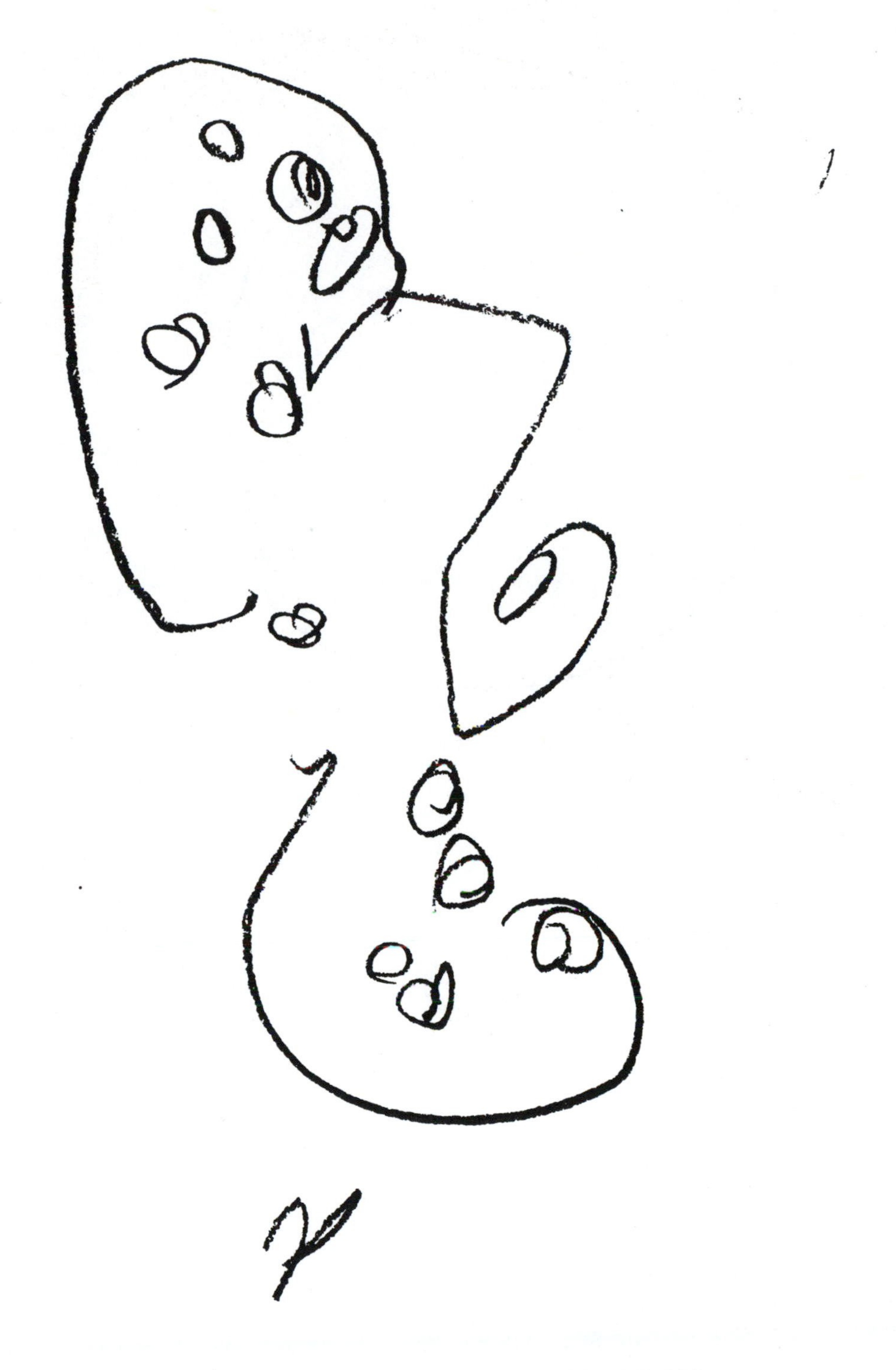

FIGURE 302

Bizarre drawing of DADDY by S. S. age six years 6 months. Communication disorder due to personality disorder. Hearing unimpaired; comprehends speech but tends to ignore it.

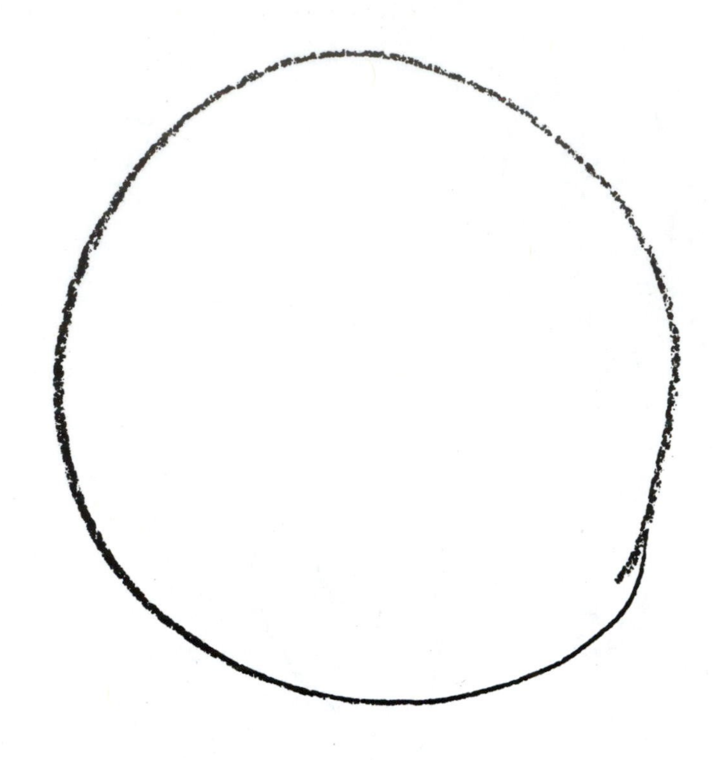

FIGURE 303

Note tiny imitation of Examiner's circle.

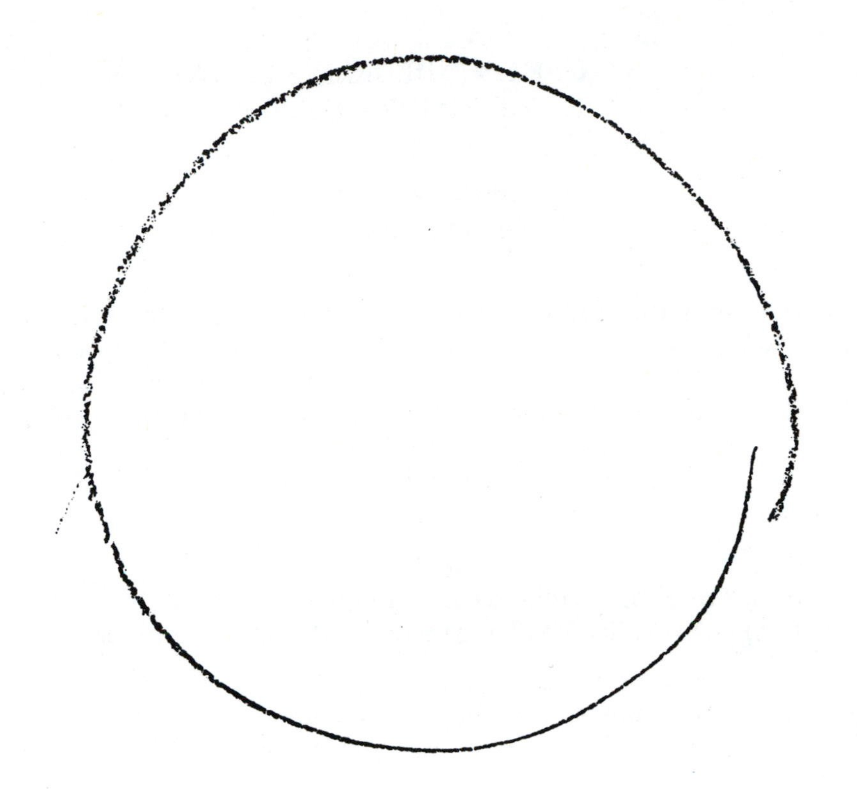

FIGURE 304

25

USE OF CHILDREN'S DRAWINGS IN THE STUDY OF PERSONALITY

Kinesthetic Drawings by Insecure Children: The Expression of Feelings

The drawings that follow were made by young children who were not being cared for by their natural parents. They had been institutionalized for varying periods and then placed into boarding homes. Developmental evaluation by the present writer revealed them to be of average capabilities but inhibited, excessively suspicious, and lacking the joie de vivre that characterizes the child who has developed a sense of trust and reaches out freely to exploit and enjoy the outside.

The attention of the reader is called to the following features: pressure and continuity of strokes, degree of expansion of the drawing, determination of strokes.

With these guideposts in mind, it will be noted that the drawings are lacking in symmetry, executed with light, wavering strokes, and restricted to a small area of the available space.

A significant positive correlation has been noted by several investigators between the above named factors and the clinically observed behavior of the child (W. Wolff, V. Lowenfeld, W. E. Martin, and D. E. Damrin).

FIGURE 305

Spontaneous scribble by timid, insecure boy of 27 months. He had been in a foster-home the past 7 months.

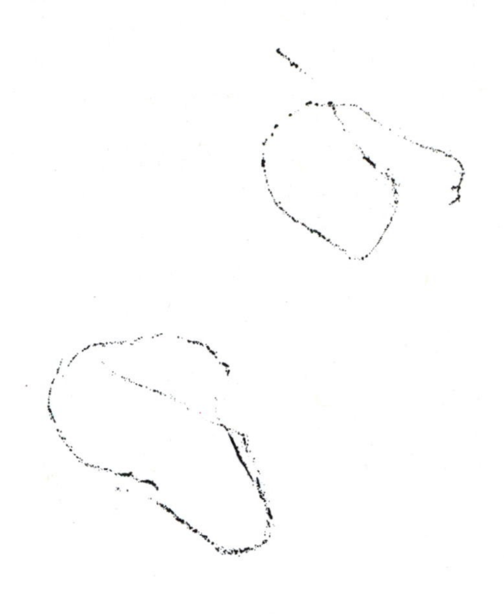

FIGURE 306

Spontaneous kinesthetic drawing by insecure foster child of three years 9 months. Behavioral development within average range.

FIGURE 307

Spontaneous kinesthetic drawing by 34 months male child of fully average mentation. Insecure.

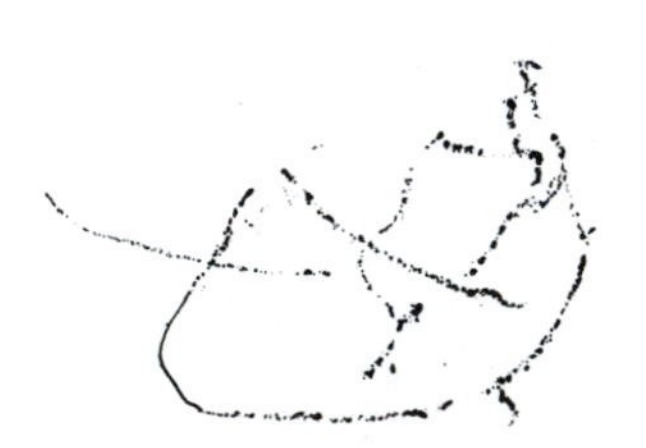

FIGURE 308

Spontaneous kinesthetic drawing by an insecure child, female, of two years 8 months. Living in foster home. Average mentation.

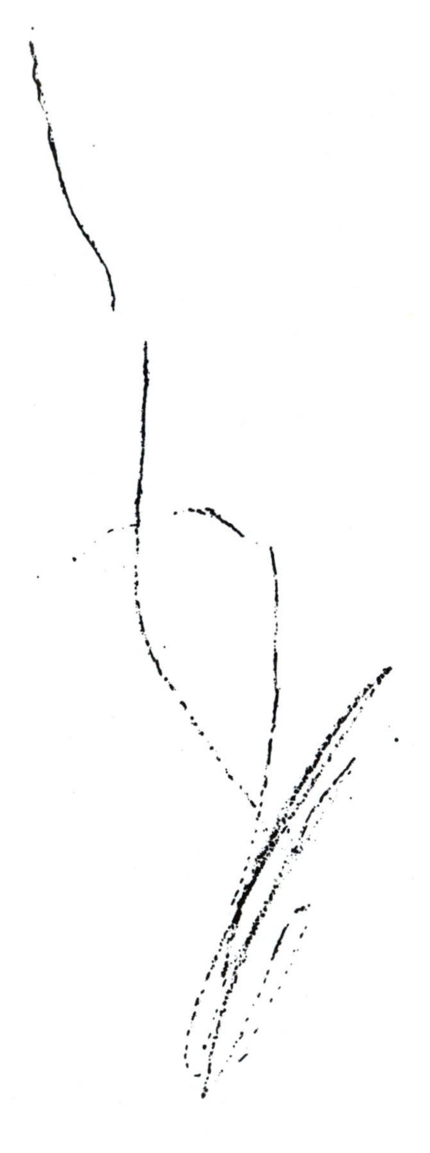

FIGURE 309

Insecure female child of 29 months. Living in a foster home. Spontaneous kinesthetic drawing.

FIGURE 310

Spontaneous drawing by insecure child of three years 3 months in a foster home.

Insecure child. The drawings on the following pages (Figures 311, 312) are by a girl of 37 months. The first is a spontaneous drawing; note the light pressure strokes, interrupted, staccato lines, and use of only a portion of the available space. The child's mother developed rubella during the first trimester of pregnancy. She sought an abortion and was refused. Feelings of rejection dominated her attitude both pre- and post-partum. The child attends special school because of sensori-neural hearing loss. Her need for approval is not satisfied in the home. She is excessively seeking from the teachers the approval that she is deprived of in her home. The second drawing is her imitation of the Examiner's circle. Note how small and hesitant are the circles drawn by the child.

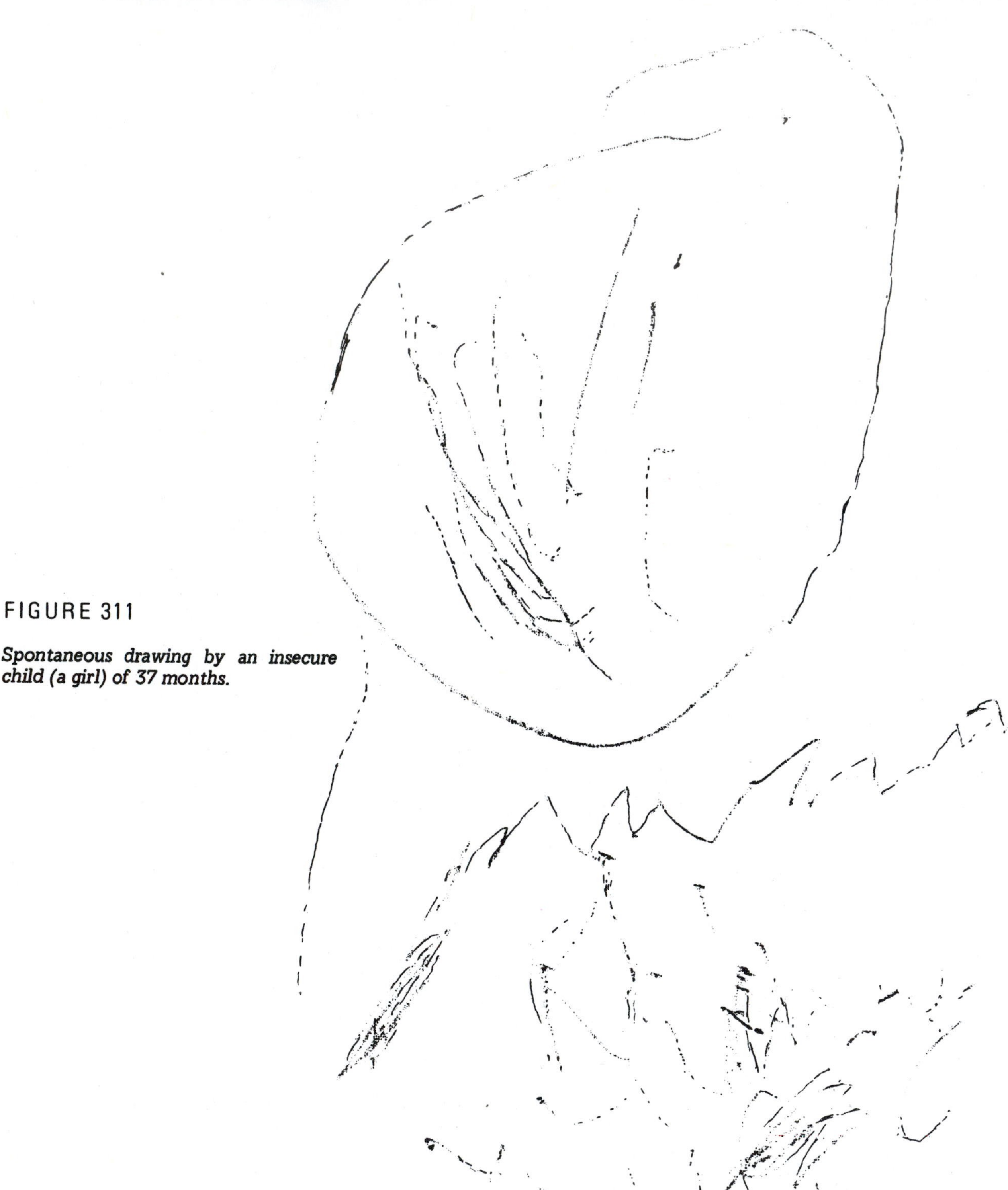

FIGURE 311

Spontaneous drawing by an insecure child (a girl) of 37 months.

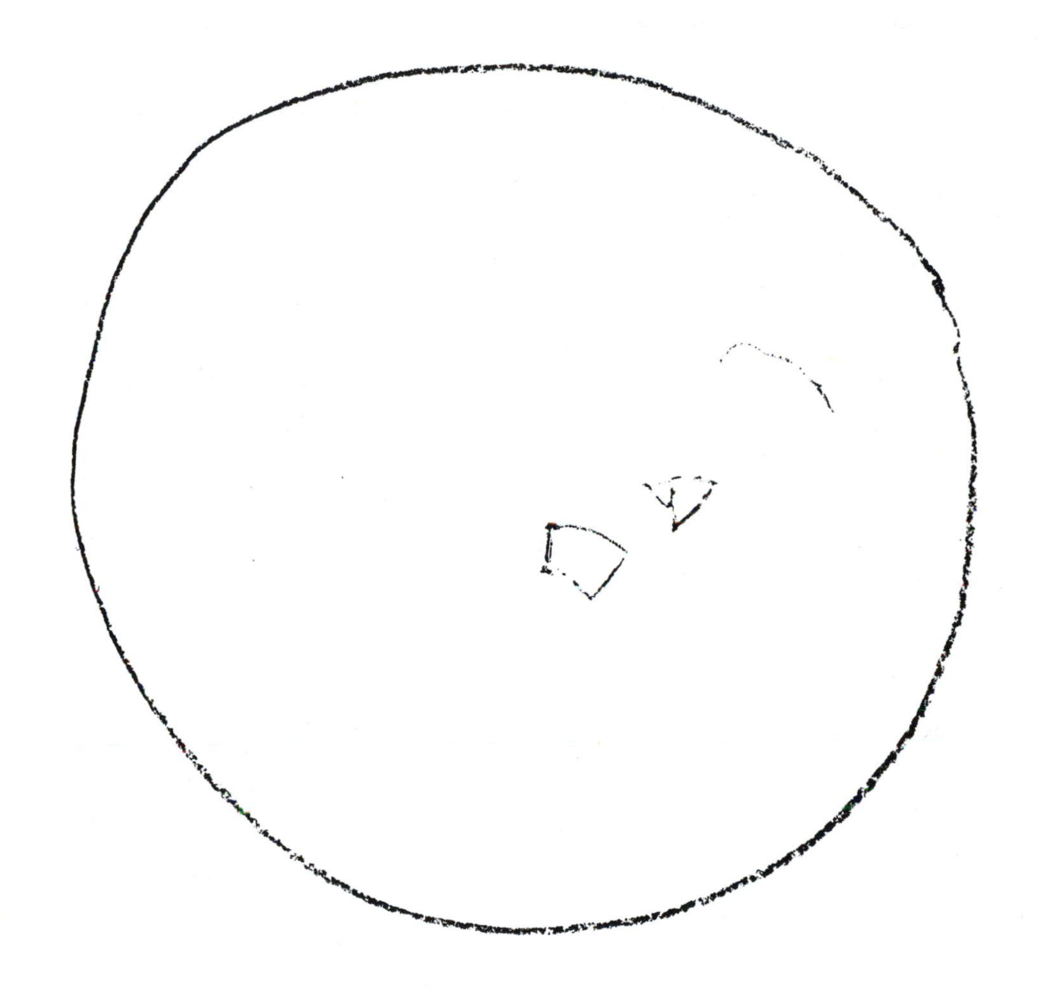

FIGURE 312

Copy of the Examiner's (large) circle by an insecure girl of 37 months.

Kinesthetic Drawings by Secure Children

In sharp contrast to the inhibited, wavering, indeterminate, restricted, barely visible markings and strokes of the insecure, socially displaced child are the determined, forceful, expansive configurations by the secure child, living with his own or with his adoptive parents.

These drawings express the freedom of movement and intellect that find joy and satisfaction in exploring and exploiting the world outside.

The crayon is applied with strong pressure, with dash and sweep so that the lines cover a large area of the paper with continuous, determined strokes.

FIGURE 313

Spontaneous drawing by timid boy of three years 4 months.

FIGURE 314

Uninhibited, strongly assertive, aggressive boy of three years 5 months

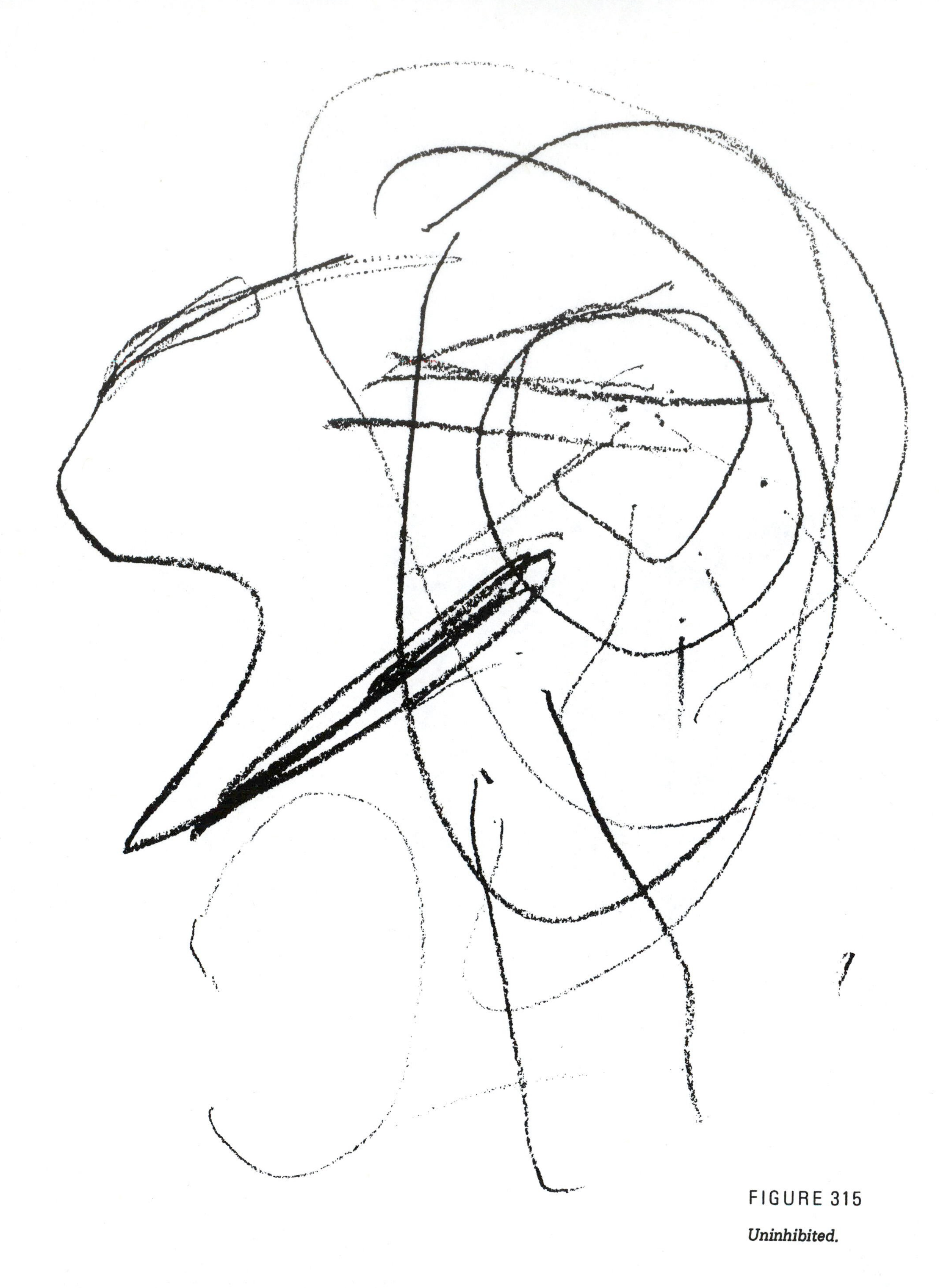

FIGURE 315

Uninhibited.

FIGURE 316

Drawing of a man by a boy of 4 years 4 months. Uninhibited. Tends to go out of bounds in his behavior as well as in his drawing.

FIGURE 317

Drawing of a man by a bright, exuberant, assertive boy of four years.

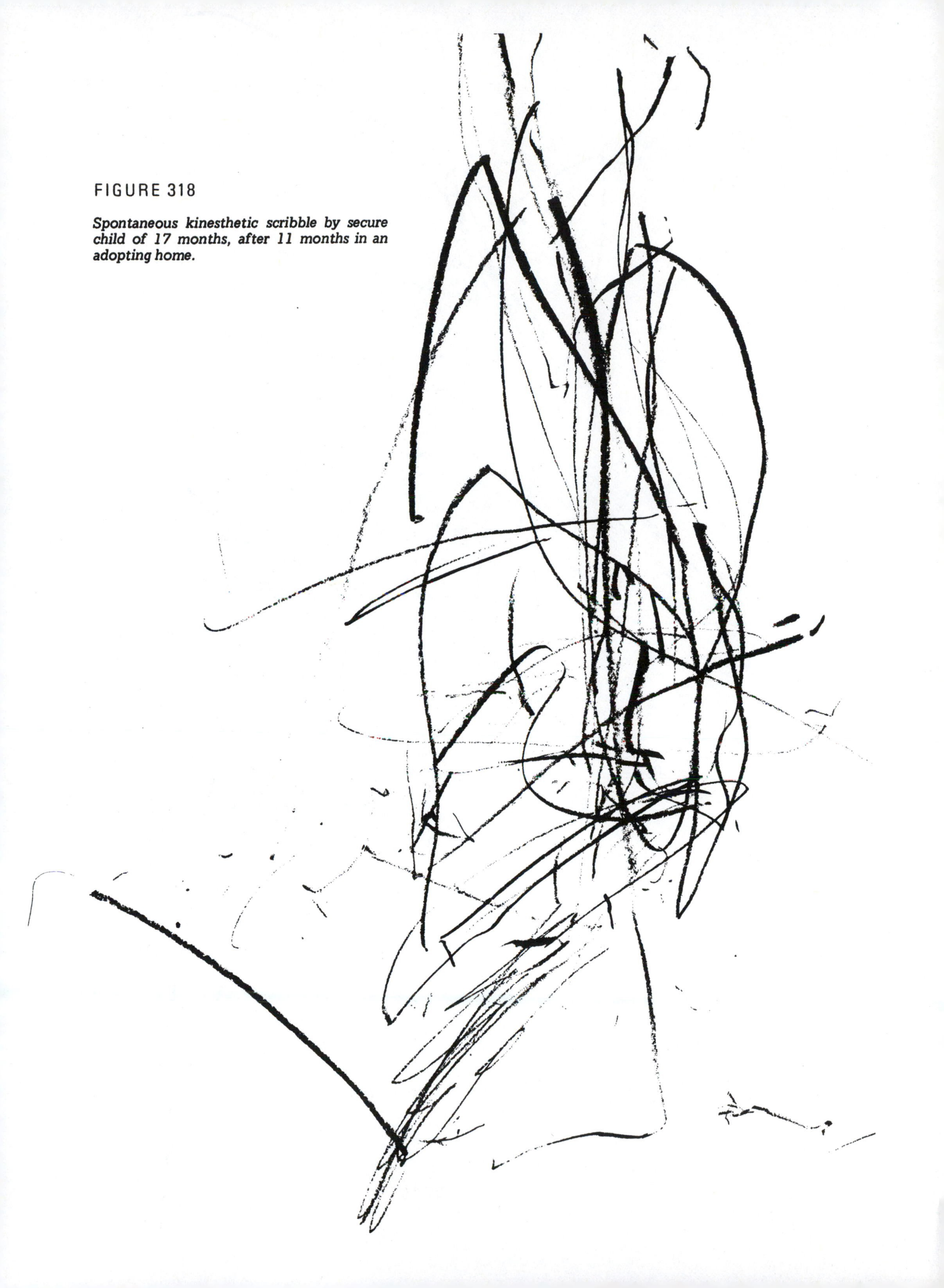

FIGURE 318

Spontaneous kinesthetic scribble by secure child of 17 months, after 11 months in an adopting home.

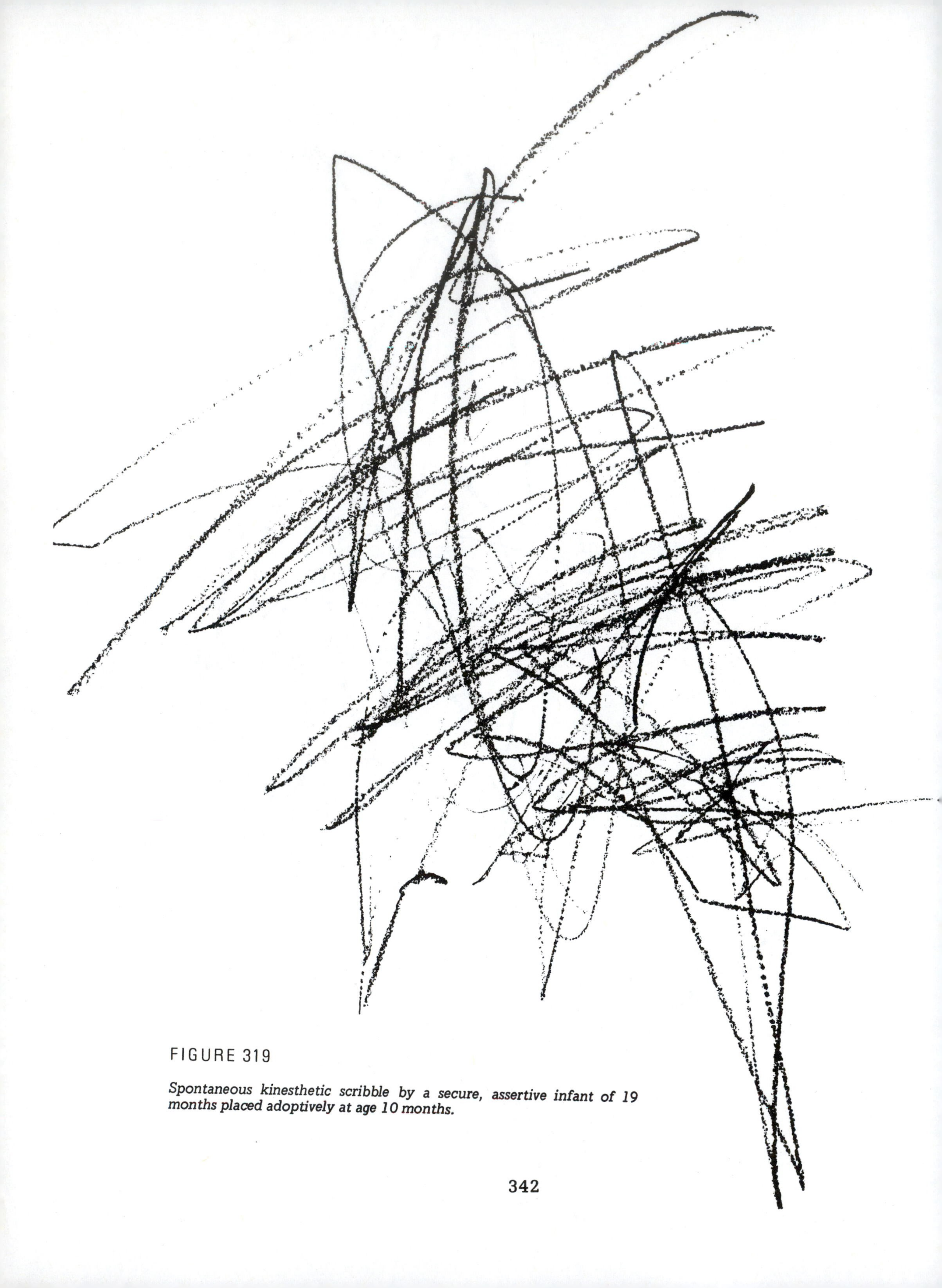

FIGURE 319

Spontaneous kinesthetic scribble by a secure, assertive infant of 19 months placed adoptively at age 10 months.

FIGURE 320

Kinesthetic scribble by a secure 36-month male living in his own home.

FIGURE 321

Spontaneous drawing by secure girl of 39 months living in her own home.

Some investigators, notably W. Wolff, have described sex differences in drawings during this early period that precedes representation. Wolff writes of a feminine preference for horizontals as against a male preference for verticals. And going further, he interprets a preference for horizontals with low pressure in boys as indicating feminine orientation, while a masculine note is indicated by verticals executed with high pressure by girls. The present writer has not been impressed by sex differences and does not feel himself in a position to confirm or deny their existence.

The horizontal position being that of rest and the vertical that of motion, preference for one or the other direction in drawing has been related to differences in energy level and mobility (W. Wolff). Here, the present writer feels that the developmental factor has been neglected. The early scribbling is poorly controlled and consequently without definite direction. As manipulation of the crayon comes under increasing cortical control, the child is able to make a vertical, a circular, and a horizontal stroke in that progressive order and at the average chronological ages of 18 months, two years, and two and a half years for the three strokes. This progression is maturational and is independent of sex or activity level.

There is danger of reading more than the scribbling conveys. To hold the imagination in check, one's attitude should lean towards conservatism. Between rejection of the scribblings as meaningless and the other extreme of expressionistic interpretation there is an area of objectivity that offers significant data regarding the relationship between graphic activity and personality. Correlating significantly with personality are pressure and determination of strokes, continuity of strokes, and extension or restriction of the drawing.

FIGURE 322

Weeping figure, probably herself. Drawing of person by five year 9 month girl, V. R. Body parts are not integrated though many parts are present (hair, eyes, eye brows, nose, head, legs). Note the tears, the child was in a boarding home at the time; her natural mother was in and out of the picture.

FIGURE 323

T. P. Age four and a half. The circles on the cheeks are tears.

FIGURE 324

J. W. age six, recently placed in an adopting home after having been in several foster homes is not aware that this time it is to be his permanent home. He has obviously drawn himself and there are tears streaming down his cheeks. Beside him is the home he is longing for.

26

PERSONALITY DISORDERS

Human figure drawings may shed light on a whole range of disorders of the personality. More revealing and more lasting than words, these drawings are of considerable diagnostic and prognostic value. As permanent documents, they may be compared with subsequent drawings as indicators of progress, halt, or regression. Their interpretation is difficult, but those who have studied them seriously find them indispensable. In many instances, the drawings are an eloquent expression of immaturity, hostility, depression, fear. In the more serious neurotic and psychotic disorders, the drawings, with their bizarre features, scatter of body parts, and disunity, reflect the disorganization of the personality, while favorable response to treatment may result in corresponding changes in the drawings, as the figures become more recognizable, more cohesive, less agitated and tormented.

Machover calls attention to the following features as expressive of the personality structure: size, placement, type of lines, stance, erasures, and shadings. The expression of emotion in the drawing, joy, sadness, belligerence, are undoubtedly expressions of the child's own feelings where it is clear that the child is drawing himself. In drawing the adult, the child is often expressing his concept of the parent. The dominant, aggressive figure is large regardless of actual size, and provided with the organs of aggression—accentuated arms and fingers. The unstable character has small feet. The tiny head seen in drawings by the disturbed and depressed contrasts strikingly with the pre-eminence accorded the head in drawings of normal children. Profusion of hair, weapons, and certain articles of clothing are sexual symbols by means of which the child unconsciously indicates the area of disturbance.

The drawing of a person, though following in the normal child a predictable sequence and biological time-table, is nevertheless, a personal document just as individual as the innumerable variations on the same theme of Virgin and Child, in which the individuality of each artist is inherent in his work.

FIGURE 325

Early infantile autism. Spontaneous drawing by a girl of four years 4 months.

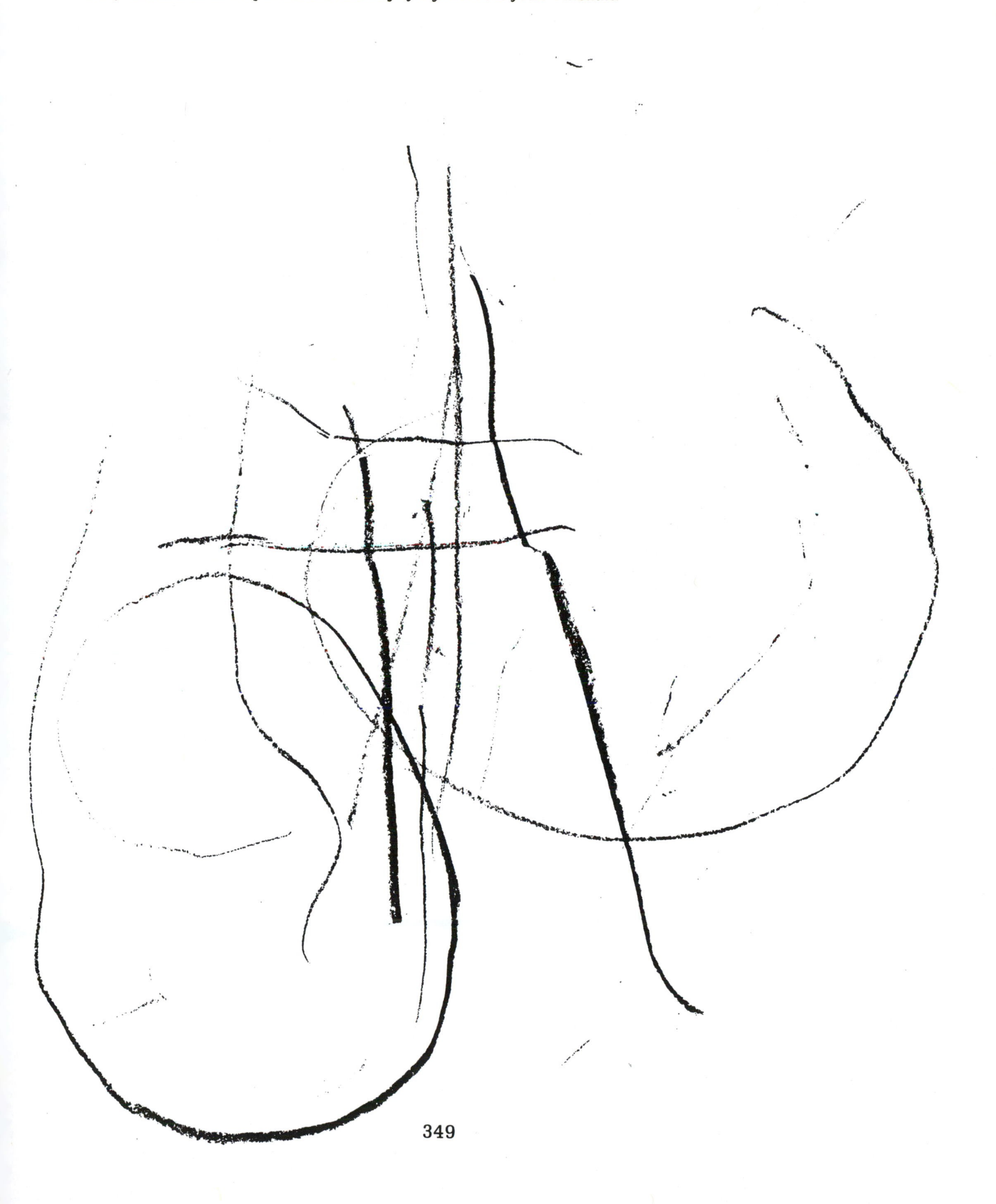

FIGURE 326

Poorly integrated personality. Many changes of boarding homes. Stutters. Chronological age: 4 years 8 months. Note lack of integration, fragmentation.

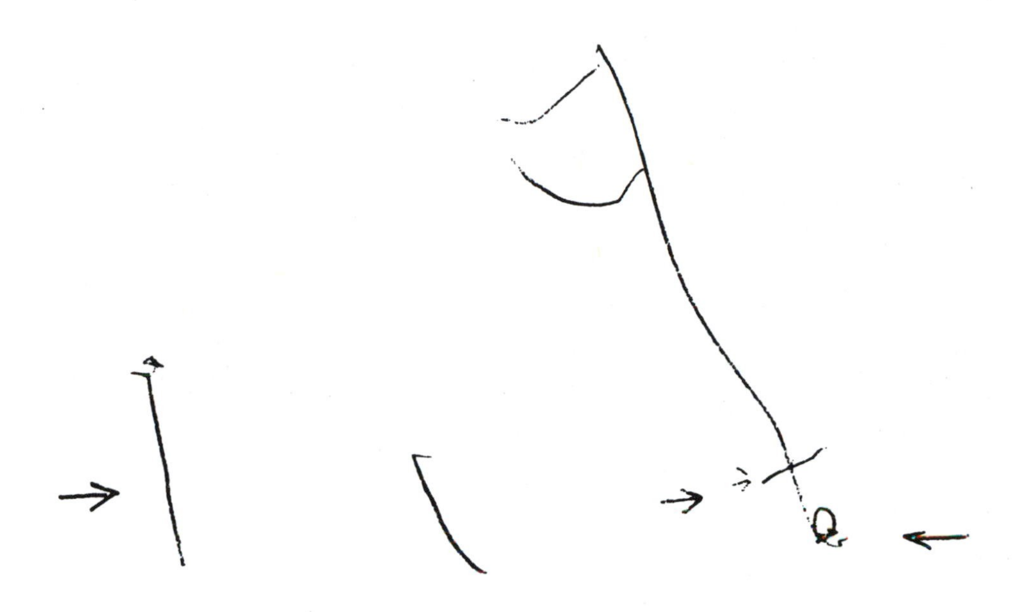

FIGURE 327

Drawing by a boy, age four years 10 months. Diagnosis: childhood schizophrenia. Had been on electroshock therapy with some improvement. This drawing of a man shows disorientation and disorganization. The figure is inverted, the head is very small.

FIGURE 328

Spontaneous drawing by the same mentally ill child.

FIGURE 329

Early infantile autism. Spontaneous drawing by a boy of six years 2 months.

FIGURE 330

V. C. age five years. Female. The child described this drawing as representing a man dressed in a lady's wig. Diagnosis by psychiatrist: schizophrenic reaction; catatonic type. Apart from its bizarre features, the drawing indicates a fully average intelligence (Goodenough score: 10).

FIGURE 331

V. C. drawing by a five-year-old girl. She has omitted her parents. Her sister Barbara is the family favorite and has been drawn twice. (Incidentally, this points out the lower level of the family figures as compared with the single figure on the preceding page).

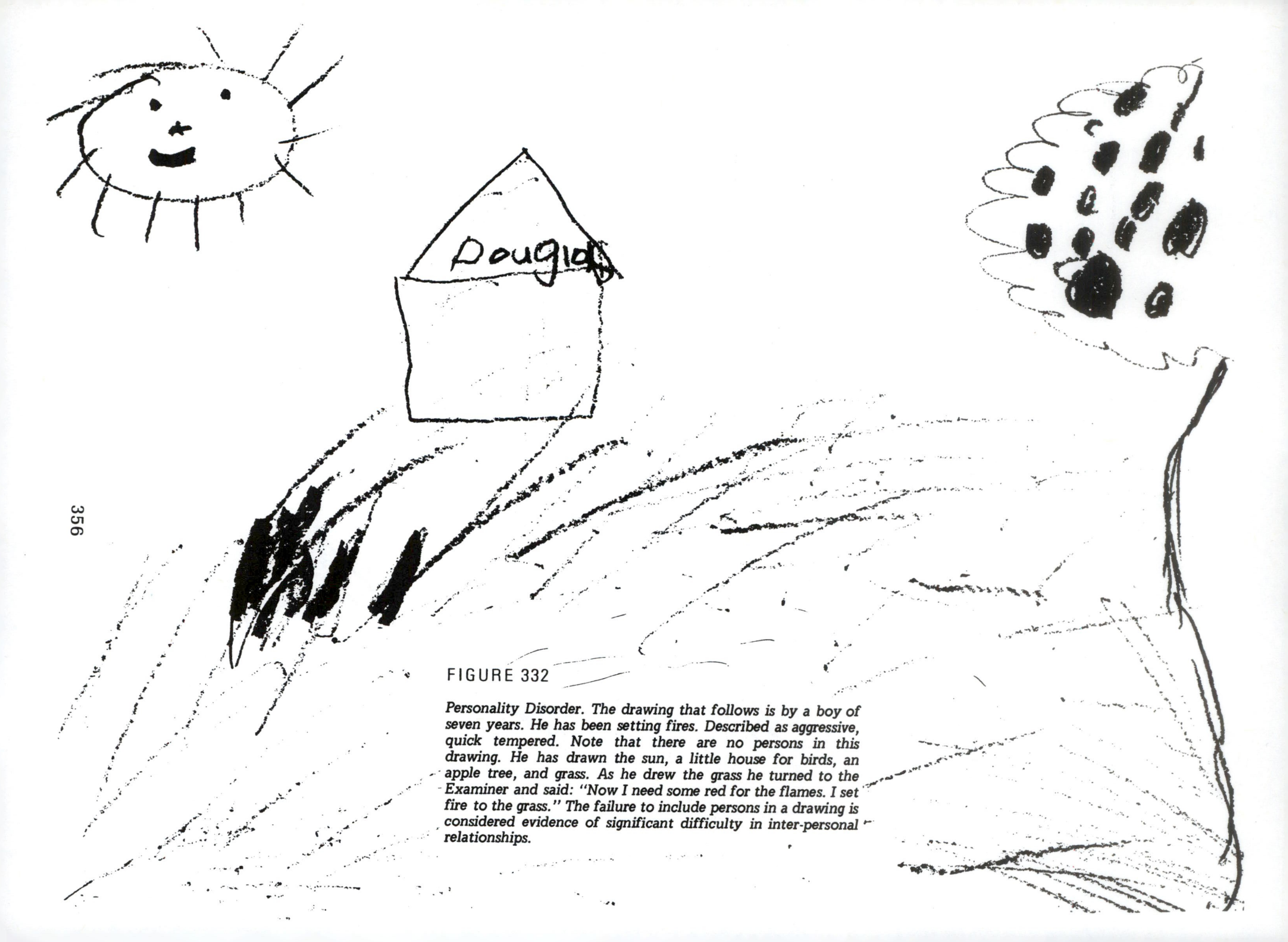

FIGURE 332

Personality Disorder. The drawing that follows is by a boy of seven years. He has been setting fires. Described as aggressive, quick tempered. Note that there are no persons in this drawing. He has drawn the sun, a little house for birds, an apple tree, and grass. As he drew the grass he turned to the Examiner and said: "Now I need some red for the flames. I set fire to the grass." The failure to include persons in a drawing is considered evidence of significant difficulty in inter-personal relationships.

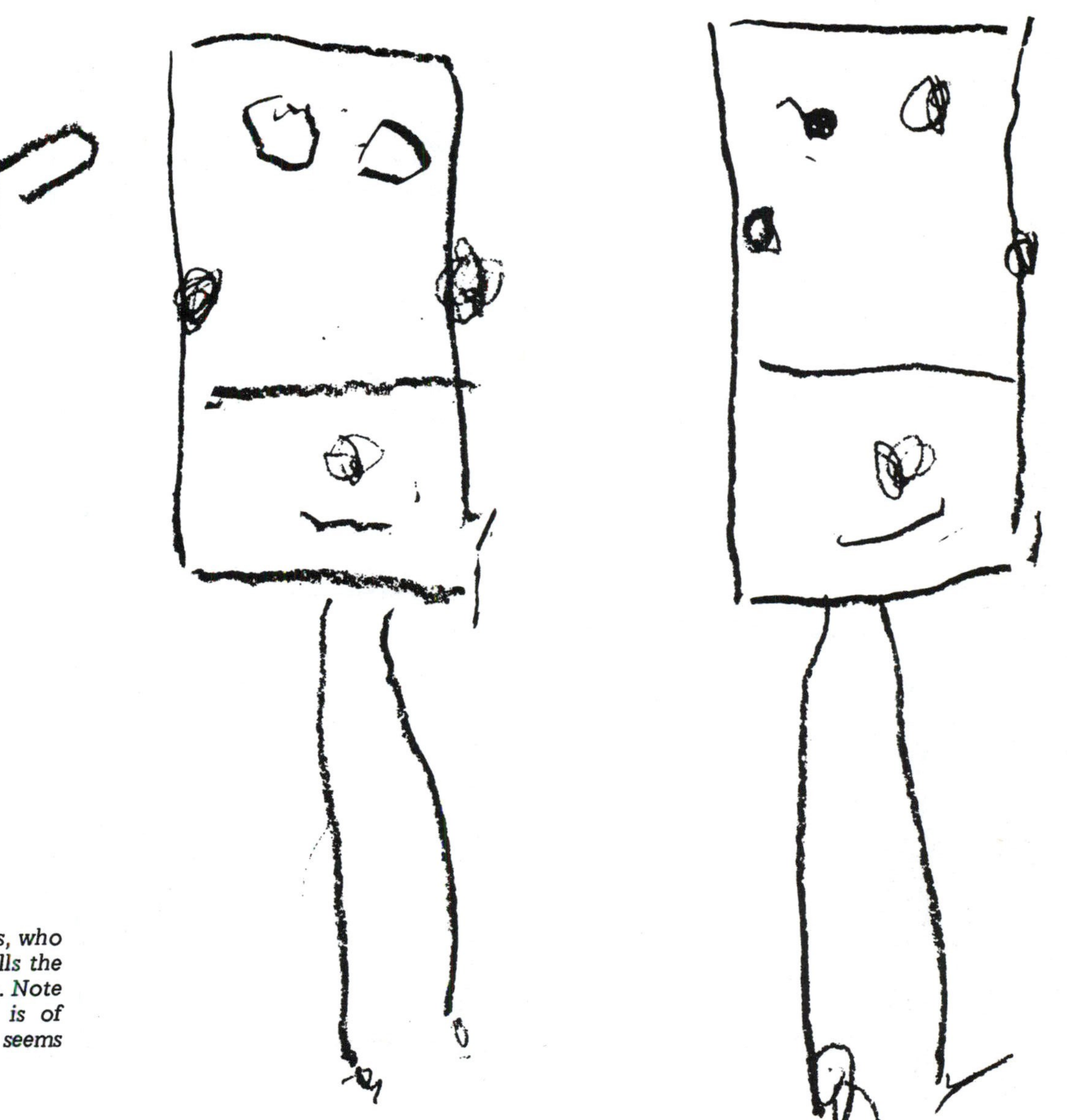

FIGURE 333

Spontaneous drawing by a girl age five years, who is in a foster home since age three. She calls the figure a glass window. It has human features. Note mechanization and symmetry. The child is of average intelligence. Sociable but affect seems bland.

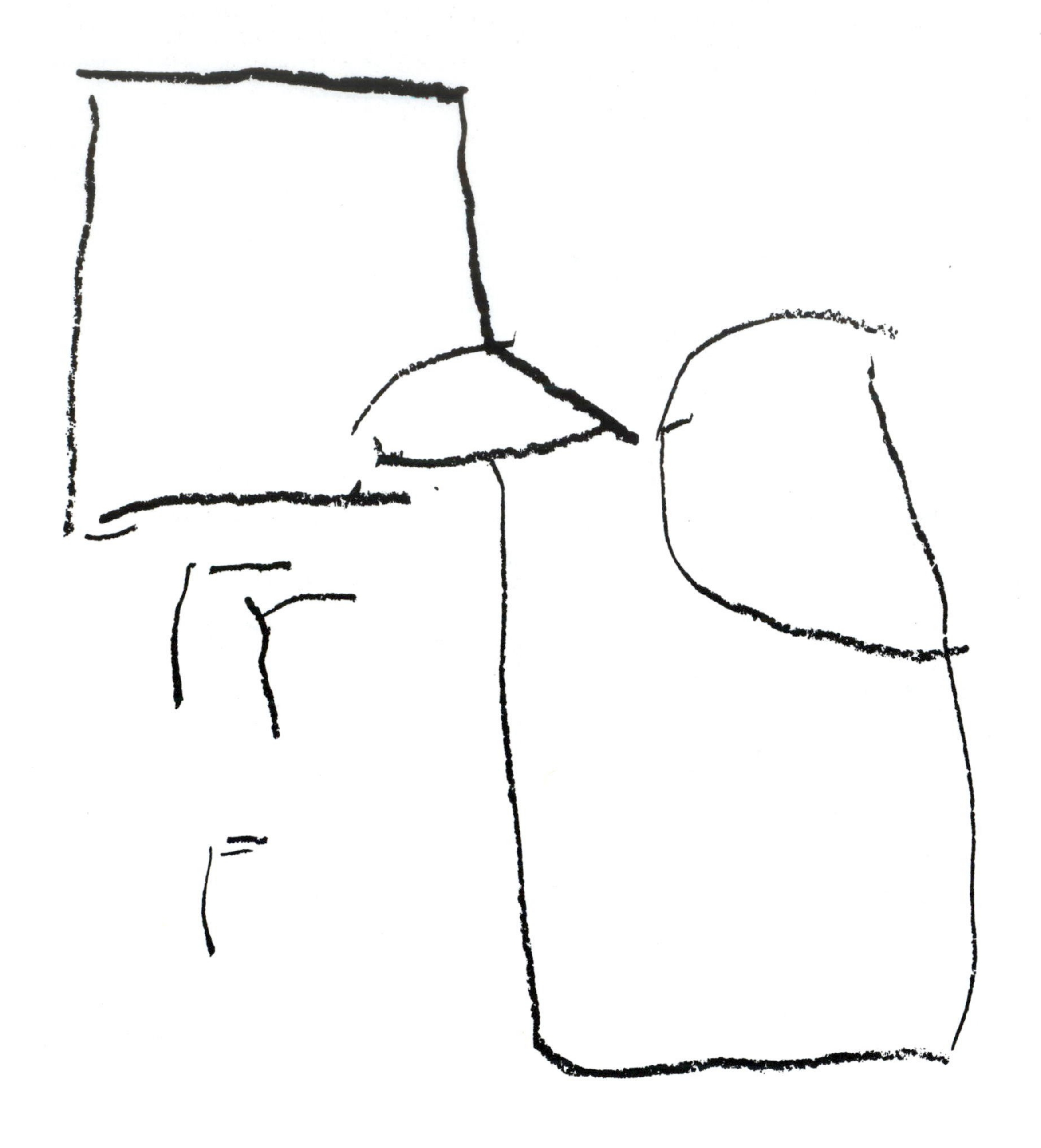

FIGURE 334

Spontaneous drawing by V. T. age five years. Boarding past 2 years. Female. Calls her drawing "a machine that you put something in".

The following series of drawings (Figures 335-337) is presented to show how they may document the change that has come about in a child. The first two drawn at age six years 4 months are strange and ghost-like and reflect the emotional disorder that afflicted the child at that time. The other drawings made when she was eight years 5 months of age express the improvement that was clinically evident. The later figures are realistic, attractive, and free from the bizarre features that characterized her earlier drawings.

FIGURE 335

FIGURE 336

FIGURE 337

Initially emotionally disturbed; subsequently improved.

The following series of 3 drawings (Figures 338-340) are by an emotionally disturbed boy of ten years. He is in and out of contact with his environment. His speech is distinct and organized into sentences but often echolalic. He is able to read fairly well. He is moody and unpredictable. The first drawing is spontaneous: a face can be identified among a disorganized variety of circles, lines, and many dots; these last were made vehemently. The second drawing is of a man. The figure is recognizable. The third drawing is of his family. Although he is an only child, he reveals his confusion of identity by drawing a series of seven figures. Note the immaturity of these figure drawings of the family as compared with his drawing of a single person. As has been stated previously, the single figure tends to evoke an intellectual response, while the family drawing mobilizes feelings rather than intellect. Certain features of his behavior and the birth history indicate the association of minimal cerebral dysfunction to complicate the clinical picture. Gross and fine motor coordination are fair.

FIGURE 338
Spontaneous drawing by R. L. age ten years. Emotionally disturbed.

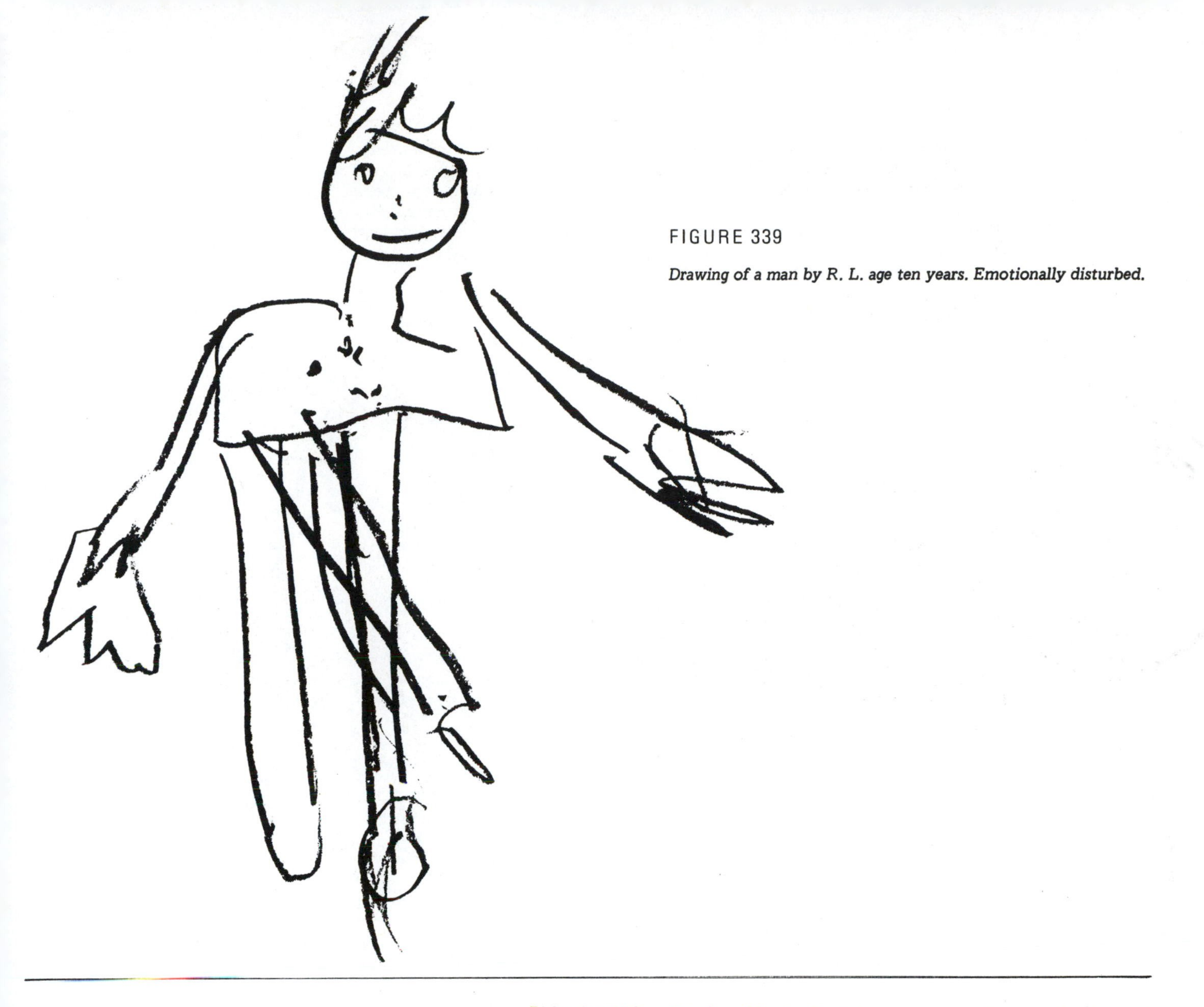

FIGURE 339

Drawing of a man by R. L. age ten years. Emotionally disturbed.

FIGURE 340 *Drawing of family. By R. L. age ten years. Emotionally disturbed.*

Personality Disorder: Shading of the figures as an expression of anxiety. The three drawings (Figures 341-343) that follow are by a boy of eleven years 6 months. He is an adopted child, who has been manifesting disturbing behavior. He has had to undergo major surgery for removal of objects from his stomach. There are many tiny marks on some of the faces. What do they mean? There is a great deal of shading of the human figures.

FIGURE 341

H. T. C. A.: 11 years 6 months.

FIGURE 342

Drawn by H. T. Boy. Chronological age: eleven years 6 months.

FIGURE 343

H. T. C. A: Eleven years 6 months.

FIGURE 344

R. X. Drawings (Figures 344-345) by a hetero-sexually active pubertal boy age 12 years 6 months. Three episodes of fire-setting. Enuresis. Nail-biting. Intelligent child. Unmotivated at school. Absent, ineffectual father. In the first drawing, he has made a bed in an interior. In the second drawing, the bed appears again but in an incongruous outdoor scene. These drawings were made when he was nine years of age.

FIGURE 345

27

CONCLUSION

An attempt has been made to show that even the earliest scribbles of infants just over a year have meaning and that the drawings of young children are self-projections, that they reveal the feelings as well as the mind and thought of the child. Meaning may not be apparent. To discover it one must turn back the clock and see the world again through the eyes of a child. This is not easy for the adult; it may not even be quite possible. Yet the attempt will have to be made, as it is the only way. The effort will be rewarding. As permanent records, the drawings may be studied at leisure and compared with earlier drawings by the same child as well as with those by his peers.

This book was really meant to be about young children. I believe that they have been well represented by their drawings.

At first glance the drawings appear defective. Only the recognition that there are two worlds—that of the child and that of the adult—will enable us to see these drawings as expression of a different vision, one that is fresh and clear, timeless, unobscured. Disregarding optical reality, the child will ignore perspective, see through walls, sides of ships, and bellies of horses, drawing what he knows to be there, what impresses him, what he desires, expressing his intellect, his age, and his feelings.

The drawings are less susceptible than speech to the influence of defenses. More than words can tell, they are valuable aids to understanding the child and his problems. They tell us more than we can decipher. The temptation to over-interpret must be resisted. Accordingly, I have limited my observations to what I believe to be clearly based upon the drawings, avoiding interpretations that would be mere speculation. The reader, however, may have good reason to elaborate on what I have written about specific drawings and about the young artists who created them.

This was not meant to be a scientific treatise. There are no statistics and no graphs. Just a journey through the fascinating world of childhood. Our guide has been a child. He seems to be striving to find his Self. Silently, yet eloquently through his drawings, he reveals his thought and his feelings. Usually happy—for that is the mood of childhood even in adversity—but sometimes lost and bewildered in a voiceless appeal for help, he may be trying to tell us where it hurts.

APPENDIX

NORMS FOR THE IMITATION AND COPYING OF GEOMETRIC FORMS

Definition of Terms

IMITATION. Having secured the child's attention, the Examiner draws the figure and then hands the crayon or pencil to the child. The child attempts to reproduce the figure having seen how it was made.

COPY. The Examiner shows the child a card on which a figure has been printed (or drawn), saying, "make one just like it on the paper."

In *imitating,* the child may simply be reproducing the movement. *Copying,* a basically different situation, calls upon a more complicated sequence of sensory, organizational, and motor functions. In imitation, the functions involved are visual and motor. In copying, perception must intervene, uniting and elevating the two. Unless the figure is perceived as a pattern, as more than just its component lines, the reproduction will not be satisfactory. Impairment in any one function, visual, perceptual, and fine motor will be reflected in the result. Isolation of the impaired function can be achieved by eliminating the other two. For example, when a child of five is unable to make a satisfactory copy of a square, is his difficulty visual, perceptual, or motor? The difficulty is most likely to be perceptual if vision is found to be normal and if tests of fine motor coordination reveal normal ability to control hands and fingers. Unfortunately, troubles do not generally come singly; differentiation may not be that simple.

NORMS

IMITATION. At two years imitates a vertical and a circular stroke. At 30 months imitates a horizontal stroke. At 36 months, imitates a cross.

COPYING. At 36 months copies a circle. At 48 months copies a cross. At 54 months copies a square. At 60 months copies a triangle. At 66 months copies a divided rectangle. At seven years copies a diamond.

The Bender Visual Motor Gestalt Test in which the child copies a variety of geometric patterns is of diagnostic value for determining the maturational level particularly between the ages of six and eleven years in normals and beyond that age in the mentally subnormal and in the neurologically impaired.

Ref: Gesell, A. and Amatruda, C. S.: Developmental Diagnosis; Terman L. M. and Merrill, M. A.: Measuring Intelligence; Bender, L.: A Visual Motor Gestalt Test and Its Clinical Use.

REFERENCES

Anastasia A. and Foley, J. P., Jr.,: An Analysis of Spontaneous Drawings by Children in Different Cultures. *J. Appl. Psychol.* 20:689–726. 1936.

Baker, H. and Kellog, R.: Children's Scribblings. *Pediatrics.* 40:382–390. Sept. 1967.

Bender, L.: A Visual Motor Gestalt Test and its Clinical Use. *Amer. Orthopsychiat. Assoc.* New York. 1938. 3–5, 11–19, 26, 35, 98, 135–149.

Bender, L.: The Drawing of a Man in Chronic Encephalitis in Children. *J. Nerv. & Mental Dis.* 41: 277–286. 1940.

Biber, B.: Children's Drawings: From Lines to Pictures. Bureau Educ. Experiments. New York. 1934. 23-29, 32-24, 43.

Biederman, C.: Art of the Evolution of Visual Knowledge. Red Wing, Minn. 1948. 31–38.

Bihalji-Merin: Modern Primitives. Harry N. Abrams, Inc. New York. 1959. 23–25.

Diringer, D.: The Alphabet: A Key to the History of Mankind. 2nd Ed. Philosophical Library, New York. 1953. 21–32.

Elkind, D. and Scott, L.: Studies in Perceptual Development: I. The Decentering of Perception. *Child Devel.* 33: 619–631. Sept. 1962.

Elkind, D., Koegler, R. R., and Go, E.: Studies in Perceptual Development: II. Part-Whole Perception. *Child Devel.* 35: 81–92. Mar. 1964.

Erben, W.: Marc Chagall. Frederick A. Praeger. New York. 1966. 14.15.24,29,M.

Gesell, A. and Ames, L. B.: The Development of Directionality in Drawing. *J. Genet. Psychol.* 68: 45–61. 1946.

Gesell, A. and others: The First Five Years of Life. Harpers. New York. 1940. 137–153, 157–170.

Gesell, A. and Amatruda, C. S.: Developmental Diagnosis. Paul B. Hoeber, Inc. New York. 1941. 346–348.

Gilson, E.: Forms and Substances in the Arts. Charles Scribner & Sons. New York. 1966. 20, 116.

Gombrich, E. H.: The Story of Art. Phaidon. New York. 1957. 78, 96, 115, 163–165, 386–388, 422–M3.

Goodenough, F. L.: Measurement of Intelligence by Drawings. World Book Co., New York, 1926. 20, 116.

Grözinger, W.: Scribbling, Drawing, Painting. Praeger. New York. 1955, 20–28.

Harris, D. B.: Children's Drawings as Measures of Intellectual Maturity. Harcourt, Brace & World, Inc. New York. 1963. 229.

Jianou, Ionel: Brancusi. Tudor Publishing Co. New York. 1963. 16.

Jourdain, F.: *L 'Art et* l'Enfant. Le Point, *Revue Artistique* et *Litteraire. Juillet.* Mulhouse, France. 1953. 9,15,18.

Kellog, R.: The Psychology of Children's Art. Random House. New York. 1967.

Kennedy, W. A. and Lindner, R. S.: A Normative Study of the Goodenough Draw-a-Man Test on Southeastern Negro Elementary School Children. *Child Devel.* 35: 33–63.

Kunstler, C.: *Gauguin-Peintre Maudit. Librairie Floury.* Pads. 1934. 88, 91, 154, 180, 181.

Lowenfeld, V. and Brittain, W. L.: Creative and Mental Growth. 4th ed. Macmillan Co. New York. 1964. 20–52.

Luquet, G. H.: *Les Dessins d'un Enfant; etude psychologique. Librairie Felix Alcan.* Paris. 1913. vu, 3–11, 119, 225–228.

Machover, K.: Personality Projection in the Drawinq of the Human Figure. Charles C. Thomas, Springfield, 111.1949. 4-10, 20–23, 36-41, 53, 60, 82–99, 118.

Machover, K.: Human Figure Drawings of Children. J. Proj. Tech. 17: 53–92, 1953.

Malraux, A.: The Voices of Silence. Doubleday & Co., Inc. Garden City. 1953. 285–287.

Martin, W. E. and Damrin, D. E.: An Analysis of the Reliability and Factorial Composition of Ratings of Children's Drawings. Child Devel. 22: 134–136, 143. June 1951.

Megroz R. L.: Profile Art through the Ages. Philosophical Library. New York. 1949. 4–13, 126.

Meier, N. C.: Art in Human Affairs. Whittlesey House. New York. 1942. 24, 35, 57.

Montessori, M.: La Scoperta del *Bambino. Garzanti.* Milan. 1953. 305–311.

Myklebust, H. R. and Brutten, M.: A Study of the Visual Perception of Deaf Children. *Acta Otolryng.* Stockholm. 1953. Suppl. 105: 9-18, 116–120.

Piaget,J.: The Language and Thought of the Child. Meridian Books. World Publ. Co. Cleveland, Ohio 1966. 189.

Prudhommeau, M.: *Le Dessin de l'Enfant. Presses Universitaires de France.* Paris. 1947. 10, 29–33, 38–53.

Read, H.: Art and Society. Schocken Books. New York. 1966. 13–15, 110–114.

Ricci, C.: L'Arte dei *Bambini. Zanichelli,* editore. Bologne. 1887. 3–73.

Schilder, P.: Contributions to Developmental Psychiatry. International Universities Press, Inc. New York. 1964. 49, 53–55, 116.

Spiegel, L. A.: The Child's Concept of Beauty: A Study in Concept Formation. *J. Genet. Psychol.* 77: 11–23. 1950.

Spitz, R. A.: The First Year of Life. International Universities Press, Inc. New York. 1965. 53–86.

Terman, L. M. and Merill, M. A.: Measuring Intelligence. Houghton Mifflin Co. Boston. 1937. 230.

Thomas, R. M.: Effects of Frustration on Children's Painting. *Child Devel.* 22: 131. June 1951.

Udry, J. R.: A Research Note on Children's Concept of Beauty. *Merrill-Palmer Quarterly.* 12: 165-172. Apr. 1966.

Wolff, W.: The Personality of the Preschool Child. Grune & Stratton. New York. 1946. 134-148, 205-264.

Zervos, C.: Constantin Brancusi. *Editions "Cahiers d'Art".* Paris. 1957. 103.

INDEX OF NAMES

INDEX OF SUBJECTS